LINGUISTICS AND PHONETICS

LINGUISTICS AND PHONETICS

[For B.A./M.A. (English) Courses of All Universities]

By
B.D. SHARMA

ANMOL PUBLICATIONS PVT. LTD.
NEW DELHI - 110 002 (INDIA)

ANMOL PUBLICATIONS PVT. LTD.
4374/4B, Ansari Road, Daryaganj
New Delhi - 110 002
Ph.: 23261597, 23278000
Visit us at: www.anmolpublications.com

Linguistics and Phonetics

First Published, 2005

ISBN 81-261-2120-3

PRINTED IN INDIA

Published by J.L. Kumar for Anmol Publications Pvt. Ltd., New Delhi - 110 002 and Printed at Mehra Offset Press, Delhi.

Contents

Preface

Lingustics and Phonetics as a paper is being taught at the graduate and post graduate level in M.A. (English) syllabus in almost all the Indian Universities. This book is a simple and easy introduction to a very difficult and complex discipline known as linguistic science. All the fundamentals of language change, phonetics, morphology, classification of sounds and different forms of language have been presented in a simple manner. Thus the matter presented here would be of interest as well as great use to the students of graduate and post graduate level.

The major topics dealt in this book are—Linguistics; Classification of Sounds; Indian Worlds in English; Language Change; Phonetics and Phonology; Phonetics Alphabet; Morpheme and Morphology.

B.D. Sharma

1

Linguistics

The word 'Linguistics' has been derived from Latin lingua (tongue) and istics (knowledge or science). Etymologically, therefore, linguistics is the scientific study of language. But it is the study not of one particular language but of human language in general. It studies language as a universal and recognizable part of human behaviour. It attempts to describe and analyze language. The field of linguistics comprises under-standing of the place of language in human life, the ways in which it is organized to fulfil the needs it serves, and the functions it performs.

So linguistics is that science which studies the origin, organisation, nature and development of language descriptively, historically, comparatively and explicitly, and formulates the general rules related to language. Diachronic (historical) linguistics studies the development of language through history, through time, for example, the way in which French and Italian have evolved from Latin. Synchronic linguistics investigates how the people speak and use language in a given speech community at a given time. In Comparative linguistics one is concerned with comparing two or more different languages.

Linguistics, therefore, is the science that describes and classifies languages. The linguist identifies and describes the units and patterns of the sound system, the words and morphemes, and the pharases and sentences, that is the structure of language, as completely, accurately, and economically as possible.

LINGUISTIC LEVELS

By 'linguistic levels' is meant the levels of language structure. There is a considerable difference among the linguisticians about the number and terminology of linguistic levels. Robert Hall (1969 : 32) recommends three levels-**phonology** (phonemics-phoentics), **morphology** and **syntax.** R.H. Robins (1971 : 11) mentions **phonology, grammar** and **semantics**. Hockett (1973 : 137-138) advocates the following five levels which he calls 'subsystems:

(i) **The Grammatical System:** a stock of morphomes, and the arrangements in which they occur;

(ii) **The Phonological System:** a stock of phonemes, and the assignments in which they occur;

(iii) **The Morphophonemic System:** the code which ties together the grammatical and the phonological system;

(iv) **The Phonemic System:** the ways in which sequences of phonemes are converted into sound waves by the articulation of a speaker, and are decoded from the speech signal by a hearer;

(v) **The Semantic System:** which associates various morphemes, and arrangements in which morphemes can be put, with things and situations, or kinds of things and situations.

Hockett calls the first three of the above "central" subsystems, and the last two "peripheral" subsystems.

Such a labelling of names, however, should not lead one to confusion. There are no basic differences about the structure of language. Such a classification is done by the linguist for the sake of convenience in the study of the subject-matter, *i.e.* lanuage which is a complex phenomenon. All these levels are **inter-related aspects** of his subject-matter, quite often over-lapping. Any separation or classification should not be treated as rigid or opaque. A linguist has to describe human language, and human beings do not use just one level of it at a time.

There are three aspects of language activity, or three types of pattern in language, the material, the structural and the environmental leading to three separate linguistic levels-SUBSTANCE, FORM AND CONTEXT. "The substance is the raw material of language; auditory (PHONIC substance) or visual (GRAPHIC substance). The form is the organization, the internal structure, it is grammer + lexis. The context is the relationship between form and situation, which we call meaning (Semantics). The linguistic science has to explain language at all these levels. These levels are explained below:

(i) Phonetics. Phonetics is the study of speech processes including the anatomy, neurology and pathology of speech, the articulation, classification and perception of speech sounds. Phonetics is a pure science and need not be studied in relation to a particular language, but it has many practical applications, *e.g.* in phonetic transcription, language teaching, speech therapy, communications engineering. Some phoneticians consider phonetics to be outside the central core of linguistics proper, but most would include it under the heading 'linguistic science'. The linguistic aspects of phonetics, *i.e.*, the study of sound systems of particular languages is part of phonology.

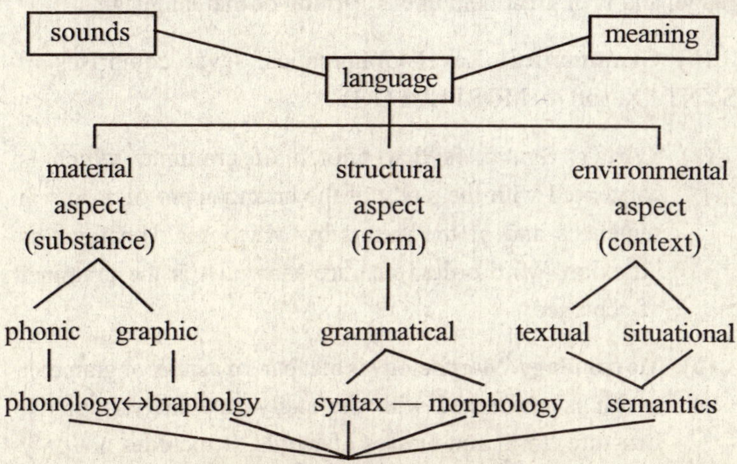

(Levels of Linguistic Analysis)

The study of phonetics can be divided into three main branches, ARTICULARTORY PHONETICS, the study of the movement of the speech organs in the articulation of speech, ACOUSTIC PHONETICS, the study of the physical properties of speech sounds such as frequency and amplitude in their transmission, and AUDITORY PHONETICS, the study of hearing and the perception of speech sounds.

Laboratory Phonetics. Experimental phonetics or instrumental phonetics are general terms for phonetic studies which involve the use of mechanical and electronic apparatus. Several sophisticated insturments are used in modern times for this purpose.

Phonetics Substance. Phonetic substance, as opposed to the visual or graphic material of writtten language, refers to the auditory aspects or sound features of spoken language, as studied by articulatory, acoustic and auditory phonetics.

Phonology. Phonology is the study of speech sounds of a given language and their function within the sound system of that language. It covers both **phonemics** (synchronic phonology) and **diachronic phonology** (sound changes in the history of a given language). So phonology is the functional phonetics of a particular language, and is of great help in the learning of that language.

(ii) Grammatical Level–Grammatical level comprises of *(a)* SYNTAX, and *(b)* MORPHOLOGY.

(a) Syntax. Syntax is that branch of grammar which is concerned with the study of the arrangement of words in sentences and of the means by which such relations as inflexion, word order, etc., are shown. It is the grammer of sentence.

(b) Morphology. Morphology is that part of syntax or grammer which is concerned with the study and analysis of the structure, form and classes of words. It includes not only synchronic studies (morphemics), but also the history and development of word-forms (diachronic morphology). Morphology is the grammer of word.

(iii) Semantics. Semantics is the study of meaning and its manifestation in language. Formerly meaning was studied under philosophy and logic. But now it has become a part of the linguistic study. Its smallest unit is "sememe", the minimum functional unit of meaning. But sememe cannot be established with the same type of precision as phonemes, morphemes, and syntactic units.

IS LINGUSTICS A SCIENCE?

Linguistics is the sientific study of language. Like all other sciences linguistics has a well-defined subject matter. viz, natural languages, living or dead; it employs careful methods to observe, record and analyse the various phenomena related to its subject matter and hopes to present unprejudiced, objective and verifiable descriptions. The approach and methodology of linguistics is scientific. It is as inductive as a science could be, and is based on observations, formation of hypothesis, testing, verification, tentativeness and predictiveness. Like a scientist a linguist observes his data. Some of his methods of observation include simple listening, phonetic transcription, and the use of various instrument, such as oscillograph, soundspectograph, kymograph, chromograph mingograph, laryngoscope, endoscope, sonograph, autophonoscope, breathing flask, strobolaryngoscope, electric vocal tract, pitchmeter intesitymeter, speechstretcher, formant graphing machine, etc. Records and cassettes made in these ways help in various kinds of objective description. A linguist has his language laboratory too.

Again, like a scientist a linguist develops hypotheses, makes generalized statements and tests them against the fact of languages. When a linguist or a phoneticial makes a statement about languages, he makes it on the basis of observation. First he observes linguistic events. He finds some similarities and contrasts on the basis of which he makes sound generalizations. On the basis of these generalizations hypotheses are for-mulated to account for the events. These are tested by further observations, and out of them is constructed a theory of how language works. From the theory are derived methods for making statements about linguistic events. The statements link the theory to the events it is set up to account for, and they can now be evaluated by reference both to the theory and to the events; the best statements are those which make maximum use of the theory to account most fully for the facts.

The linguist also hopes to be in position to make prediction about unobserved linguistic data on the basis of those observed, and build a general theory which would explain and relate all the facts to be found in individual languages. Predictions about grammars and dictionaries can be made by him. And finally like a true scientist, he is constantly engaged in discovering more about languages in refining his methods of investigation, and in constructing better theories. He also tries to find out linguistic universals.

Like any scientific discipline, linguistics too is not static. Viewpoints and theoretical methods in the field, change even in fundamental ways from time to time, and different aspects come to receive primary focus at different times. Linguistics has more than its share of unresolved controversies and unsolved questions, which is a part of its fascination and challenge.

Finally, the closeness of Linguistics with other natural sciences like mathematics, physics, physiology, biology, zoology, etc., is another proof of its scientific nature. 'It touches on physics through acoustics, on physiology through the structure of the human vocal organs, on zoology through the comparative study of the communicative systems of living beings.' A glance on any book on transformational-generative grammar would convince any objective onlooker how linguistics is becoming more and more scientific. Furthermore, as mentioned by R.H. Robins, linguistics in its operations and statements is guided by three canons of science: *(1)* exhaustiveness, the adequate treatment of all the relevent material *(2)* consistency, the absence of contradiction between different parts of the total statement. and within the limits imposed by the two preceding principles; and *(3)* economy, whereby, other things being equal, a shorter statement or analysis employing fewer terms is to be preferred to one that is longer or more involved. Consequently, linguistics is getting more and more technical and sophisticated every day. Yet it is not a pure science. Its position, says R.A. Hall, is between the natural and social sciences, like that of geology. To Robins it is an 'empirical science', and within the empirical sciences it is one of the social sciences', because its subject matter concerns human beings and is very much different from that of natural sciences.

Nevertheless, linguistics is the scientific study of language. It may be inductive or deductive; it is, however, objective, precise, tentative and systematic; it is concerned with reportable facts, methods, and principles; it works by means of observations, hypotheses, experiments and tests, postulates, and inferences; it makes generalization and predictions; it formulates theories; its products are descriptive, verbal or algebraic statements about language.

ASPECTS OF LINGUISTICS

The structure of language is very complex. Language has an internal structure consisting of two sub-structures–sound and meaning, also known as expression and content. It is the network of association between expression and content that structures language. Neither sound nor ideas alone are language. **Expression** is the system of sounds, words, phrases, sentences as spoken, heard, felt, or imagined independently of their particular meanings. The expression system is most completely observable in spoken language. **Content** is the system of classified units of cultural meaning and their combinations and relations in language, or ideas, social situations, meanings the facts of fantasies about mans's existence, and the things man reacts to and tries to convey to his fellows.

The smallest unit of full expression is the sentence which may consist of a single utterance or more than one utterance arranged according to the system of the language. Sentences are made up of parts such as words and phrases and clauses. Words having meanings, such as quality, thing, process, or they have a structural functions to organize other words in a meaningful sentence. Words are made up of parts of words such as suffixes, prefixes, and stems. These smallest parts of expression associated with some meaning are called **Morphemes.** Morphemes are made up of phonemes. The smallest segment of sound that can change one word into another–for example, /k/,/p/,/b/ and /h/ in the words kill, pill, bill, hill, is called the **phoneme.**

LINGUISTICS AND RELATED FIELDS OF STUDY

(1) Linguistics and Anthropology. Broadly speaking, anthropology is the study of mankind and of culture. Its main subdivisions are physical anthropology and cultural anthropology. Linguistics is a branch of cultrual anthropology. The chief contribution of cultural anthropology, as a whole, to the study of language has been the broadening of linguists' outlooks so that their horizons include, not only languages, but culture of many diffetent types. It has helped in removing the misconception that one language is superior to the other, in accepting a generalization that all languages are complex and are adequate to the needs of the respective communities, and in establishing certain linguistics universals. It has also made clear to the linguist the fact that languages are not 'primitive, although cultures may be primitive. Furthermore, a language is a language even if it has no writing system.

Modern linguistcs, particularly in its early phases in the United States, received a great impetus from the attempts of anthropologists who studied the culture of "primitive" peoples. Linguists had to devise new ways and techniques of linguistic analysis to study the languages of these primitive races and tribes. As a result their methodologies and theories were enriched. They also stood benefited by the similarities and contrasts between those hitherto unknown languages and the known European languages. Another positive contribution of cultural anthropology to linguistics lies in the furnishing of data for the interpretation of meanings, on both the grammatical and the lexical levels.

On another level, linguistics has made a very valuable contribution to the methodology of social sciences, through the concept of the functional unit and the distinctive feature of behaviour, etc. Anthropology has benefited from linguistics in the field of individual and social group, learning process, correlation between heredity and linguistic struture, etc. The fact that man's dialect is the mirror of his culture, has also been beneficial to anthropologists and sociologists.

Now-a-days, the relationship between linguistics and anthroplogy is less close. But at the same time a new discipline called sociolingustics is expanding rapidly, meaning thereby that sociology and linguistcs are getting closer.

(2) Linguistics and Philosophy. The association between philosophy and language and linguistics has indeed been historically very long. In fact, it were the philosophers who first of all speculated on language., Plato's Dialogues have explicit reference to language, and so have the Vedas and the Upanishadas of the ancient Indians. In the field of semantics, philosophy has provided tremendous insight to the linguists. The structural linguistics ignored meaning because they thought it to be a subject of philosophy.

One of the major concerns of Greek and Roman philosophers was to determine the nature of being and the categories into which it fell. Aristotle established three main "categories of predication," things or "substances", qualities, and actions. And the traditional concepts of parts of speech to have originated from there.

On the other level, metaphysical systems can only be communicated to others by the use of words in sentences constructed in language known to the philosopher and his readers or listeners. Philosophers had to coin numerous terms to communicate their matephysical and mystical experience. Sanskrit philosophers went to the extent of equating the word with 'Brahma' (God). Some of the major features of systems of logic and metaphysics are partly determined by certain predominant features of the structure of the language used in the philosopher's community.

Yet there are deep-rooted difference between philosophy and linguistics. The philosopher's concern is with 'the uses of language for certain purposes that are common to many communities; he is not interested in the detailed differences between languages. The linguist's concern is with 'the details of each language for its own sake', and he evolves and evaluates theories primarily to deal with particular languages. The linguist is particularly interested in the formal structuring of the sentences of a language; the philosopher is interested in the logical structure and the inferential possibilities of the propositions they express irrespective of the grammar of any particular language. Hence both these disciplines are getting remote from each other these days.

(3) Linguistics and Psychology. Linguistics studies human language. Whether language is behaviour or a cognitive process or both, is still a controversial issue; yet it is well accepted that psychology is the study of human behaviour and human mind. Hence both linguistics and psychology are closely related.

Investigations and attempts to find out answers to certain fundamental questions like the following ones are likely to provide invaluable clues to the linguist: What is the principle of learning ? How is language learned by a child ? Does the learning of the mother or native tongue involve the same processes as the learning of a second or a foreign language ? Is language-learning a result of stimulus-response, imitation, repetition and reinforcement, or of exposure ? Can a child whose brain is injured in an accident, relearn a language ? Does the loss of linguistic skills affect his other skills ? What roles do memory, motivation, age and aptitude play in language learning ? Surely the answers to such questions would help both the linguist and the scientist.

(4) Linguistics and Geography–Linguistics and geography are also inter-related disciplines. The growth of a new discipline or branch called 'linguistic geography' stands as a valid evidence to prove our proposition. Geographical conditions, trees, plants, birds, animals, planes, mountains, rivers, deserts, etc. have a bearing on language. The language of the people of a thick forest with a rich store of animals may be richer in the names of trees and animals than the language of the people living in the desert. If there is little interaction between one community and another community, for example in the hilly areas, because of the obstacles created by hills and rivers, the cases of language change would be less frequent. Oceans and seas also bring a sea-change in language. The languages of India are different from the languages across the Atlantics; and so are the languages of other countries isolated by the oceans. The languages across the Himalayas are different from those below the Himalayas. Languages of North India have few similarities with those of South India.

The study of the names of persons, places, temples, rivers, mountains, etc. has helped the comparative linguists in the 19th century in establishing the family-history of languages. Languages also have affected geography. Most of the states in India are framed on linguistic basis. Secession of Bangla Desh from Pakistan took place partly because of the linguistic differences. Thus, geography has been changing because of languages. All such facts are of great importance for the linguist. They help him in supporting or rejecting his hunches and in describing languages in a better way.

(5) Linguistics and Literature. The relationship between linguistics and literature is like that of the hammer nd the anvil. If a linguist wants to study a language like Sanskrit, he has no other source of his data but the literature of the Sanskrit language. Literary criticism and literary scholorship, together with philosophical studies, constituted a part of linguistics of Western Europe. Grammatical rules and systems of grammar were drawn up on the basis of literary works and the types of sentence structures and word forms found therein. The linguist has taken over the concepts of metres, rhymes, rhythms, stresses and intonations from literature.

As linguistics progresses in the analysis of features like stress and length, and many concomitant characteristics of utterances as yet not fully investigated or understood, in the comparison from different points of the syllable structure of language and of their words structures, and in the statement of their grammatical and colloquial patterns, linguists may expect to be able to penetrate more deeply and more delicately in making explicit the many components of language that great authors and generations of composers of oral literature have unconciuosly seized on and moulded into works of literary art.

Linguists are concerned with literature becuase it is their business to discover wherein literary discourse differs from everyday non-literary discourse and to investigate the role of the functors in determining the effect of literary style. A language like Sanskrit, which does not have any system of articles , is of course incapable of the particular literary effects made possible in English by the presence of the article: on the other hand, its special structural characteristics make possible its own peculiar literary effects which, say, English cannot attain. The recurrence and frequency of nasal and glottal sounds in the end positions of words in Sanskrit gives it a musical effect which is different from that of English.

The nature of language is of vital concern to the students of literature, because language is the medium in which literature is written. A creative writer is never wholly free from linguistic and cultural considerations or limitations howsoever unconscious of these he may be literally. He has to choose his structures and sounds according to the kinds of aesthetic effect he wants to create. His creation is determined by the structure of the language. The structure determines what can and cannot be said in the language, just as his cultural background determines the semantic content of his work. All linguistic levels exert an influence on his creativity and on what he creates. All these factors influence his style. Word-formation can often be used as a source of particular literary effects.

(6) Linguistics and the Natural Sciences. Linguistics touches the natural sciences such as physics, physiology and zoology. Acoustics brings linguistics near physics, the structure of the human vocal organs near physiology, and the communicative systems of living beings and their comparison near zoology. A fairly detailed knowledge offered by these sciences about how soundwaves are framed, transmitted and received, what are the organs and articulatory processes involved in the production of speech, are of immense help to the linguist. On the basis of such information he classifies sounds, and determines their characteristics. Physiology provides him knowledge about brain and the central nervous system.

A general connection between biology and zoology and liguistics lies in the relation of human language to the communicative systems of animals. Such comparative studies have helped linguists in finding out the history of human language. Is man an ape that can do a little better ? Is there any difference between human communication system and animal communication? If there is any difference, what is the nature of this difference ? Do animals have brain ? Answer to questions like these can be found out through collaboration between the biologist and the linguist.

Language is speech uttered out of mouth. Hence the answers to questions like–how are sounds produced ? How does the wind come out of the lungs through the windpipe to the vocal cords to pass through the mouth or nasal passage ? How do various speech organs such as vocal cords, soft palate, tongue, teeth, lips, etc. affect the sound ?– are of primary interest and investigation for the linguist. He can find out answers to such questions from the biologist.

Science has contributed a great deal to the methodology of linguistics. It has formalized it; it has made it much more rigorous, objective and scientific. It has helped the linguist to describe language too. Yet in its methodology, linguistics is 'intermediate' between the natural and social sciences. This is because of the subject matter of linguistics which is complicated and full of many variables. Predictions of the linguist are not exactly like those of the natural scientist. Linguistics may, therefore, be compared with geology rather than with chemistry or physics in matter of approach and methodology.

(7) Linguistics and Logic and Mathematics. Like philosophers, mathematicians and logicians are also interested in finding out what the fundamental entities of language are, what operations are performed, what relations exist between such entities in a proposition, what the rules of formation and transformation of these propositions are and how universal the validity of these proposition is. Answers to such questions and the logical structure of the sentences of a language have also been a matter of interest and investigation for linguists. Transformational-Generative Grammar of Chomsky is a chemcial mixture of linguistics, logic, mathematics and psychology.

Whereas logic is mainly interpretative and explanatory, linguistics is mainly descriptive. Yet mere descriptions do not help the linguist; he needs explanatory adequacy too. This he can get from logic. Similarly logic is also indebted to linguistics. It is carried on with the help of language, hence it has to keep a sharp scientific eye on the use of words and sentences.

(8) Linguistics and Communications Engineering. Communications Engineering is concerned with the transmission of speech as such by wire and radio waves, and conversion of linguistic signals into written message. Linguistics can help the communications engineer in understanding the linguistic nature of his material to be transmitted. The linguist can also help us to estimate the value of the different phonetic components in the sound wave which result from successive speech articulations, and their localization into different band of frequencies.

Mechanical analysis of speech by instruments such as spectograph, taperecorder, gramophone, radio, television, telephone may help a linguist a great deal. For example, Charles Fries studied American living usage by bugging telephones. All these are the gifts of communications engineering.

Invention of 'machine translation' is the work of the linguist-engineer. Further linguistic analysis, semantic, collocational, and grammatical that is involved in the process of translation, may make this machine more useful and applicable than it is in its present form.

TYPES OF LINGUISTICS

Keeping in view the interdisciplinary relationship between Linguistics and other branches of knowledge with which it is associated.David Crystal has explained various types of linguistics, each type named after the branch of knowldege with which it is connected or on whose method and concepts it bases its conclusions. These types, as enumerated by Crystal are as follows:

(i) **Apthropological Linguistics.** The study of language variation and use in relation to the cultural patterns and beliefs of the human race, as investigated using the theories and methods of anthropology.

(ii) **Applied Linguistics.** The application of linguistic theories, methods, and findings to the elucidation of language problems that have arisen in other domains. The term is especially used with reference to the field of foreign language learning and teaching, but it applies equally to several other fields, such as stylistics, lexicography, translation, and language planning, as well as to the clinical and educational fields below.

(iii) **Biological Linguistics.** The study of the biological conditions for language development and use in human beings, with reference both to the history of language in the human race and to child development.

(iv) **Computational Linguistics.** The study of language using the techniques and concepts of computer science, especially with reference to the problems posed by the fields of machine translation, information retrieval, and artificial intelligence.

(v) **Educational Linguistics.** The application of linguistic theories and methods to the study of the teaching and learning of a language (especially a first language) in schools and other educational settings.

(vi) **Clinical Linguistics.** The application of linguistic theories and methods to the analysis of disorders of spoken, written, or signed language.

(vii) **Ethnolinguistics.** The study of language in relation to ethnic types and behaviours, especially with reference to the way social interaction proceeds.

(viii) **Geographical Linguistics.** The study of the regional distribution of languages and dialects, seen in relation to geographical factors in the environment.

(ix) **Mathematical Linguistics.** The study of the mathematical properties of language, using concepts from such fields as algebra, computer science, and statistics.

(x) **Neurolinguistics.** The study of the neurological basis of language development and use human beings, especially of the brain's control over the processes of speech and understanding.

(xi) **Philosophical Linguistics.** The study of the role of language in the elucidation of philosophical concepts, and of the philosophical status of linguistic theories, methods, and observations.

(xii) **Psycholinguistics.** The study of the relationship between linguistics behaviour and the psychological processes (*e.g.* memory, attention) thought to underline it.

(xiii) **Sociolinguistics.** The study of the interaction between language and the structure and functioning of society.

(xiv) **Statistical Linguistics.** The study of the statistical or quantitative properties of language.

(xv) **Theolinguistics.** The study of the languages used by biblical scholars, theologians, and others involved in the theory and practice of religious belief.

DESCRIPTIVE, HISTORICAL AND COMPARATIVE LINGUISTICS

General linguistics includes a number of related subjects involved in the study of language as understood in the preceding paragraphs. General linguistics can broadly be divided into three sub-divisions–descriptive linguistics, historical linguistics and comparative linguistics.

1. Descriptive Linguistics is concerned with the description and analysis of the ways in which a language operates and is used by a given set of speakers at a given time. The time may be present. The time may equally well be the past, where adequate written records are available. Nor is the descriptive study of a particular language concerned with the description of other languages at the same time. Descriptive linguistics is often regarded as the major part of general linguistics, and certainly the fundamental aspect of the study of language.

2. Historical Linguistics is the study of developments in languages in the course of time. It is the diachronic study of the language. It studies language change, and the causes and results of such changes as have occurred from time to time.

3. Comparative Linguistics is concerned with comparing from one or more points of view two or more different languages. Comparative linguistics traces the evolution of language and, by comparing one with another, establishes the relationships between them. This comparison is generally done between the languages which are genetically related, that is, those that have developed from some common source.

Comparative and historical linguistics may be said to have begun in 1786, the date when Sir William Jones made the famous statement pointing out that Greek, Latin, Sanskrit,Celtic and Germanic appeared to have sprung from a common source. The old name for the subject was Comparative Philology.

❐

2

Classification of Sounds

An ideal description of speech sounds should include information concerning the production, transmission, and reception stages of sounds, *i.e.*, it should describe a sound in terms of the movements of the organs of speech, the nature of the sound which is produced and the features perceived by a listener. But such a description would be lengthy, complex and cumbersome, and may provide information much of which may be irrelevant to particular purpose. Whereas sounds known as 'consonants' are described mainly in terms of their articulation but in the description of 'vowel' sounds the auditory impressions will dominate. Furthermore, in our phonetic analysis the syllable has been considered the basic unit, the theory being that each movement of the respiratory muscles, called a chest-pulse, produces a syllable, and "nothing less than a syllable can be produced."

1. **Syllable, Vowel and Consonant.** The units or sections into which words are divided while pronouncing them, are called syllables. The *Syllable* is a unit of pronunciation consisting of a vowel alone or of a vowel with one or more consonants. A vowel is the *nucleus* and consonant a *marginal element* in the syllable, that is, a consonant either at the beginning or at the end of a syllable. A consonant at the end of a syllable is called an arresting consonant, and at the beginning of a syllable is called *releasing consonant*. The marginal elements are not obligatory. These may occur either before the nucleus or after the nucleus, or some before and after the nucleus. The word pick consists of one syllable which consists of two marginal elements /p/ a releasing consonant and /k/ an arresting consonant

and of a nucleus /i/, which is a vowel. It is also possible to have a cluster of two or three consonants before and / or after the nucleus. For example, in school/ sku: 1/, we have the cluster of two consonants /s/ and /k/ which is the first marginal element. Some syllables are made up of the nucleus alone *e.g.* 'eye' or I /ai/. Usually it is a vowel, for example /i:/ in seat/si:t/, which forms a nucleus in a syllable; but in words of more than one syllable in English the nucleus can also be a consonant, *e.g.*/n/ and /l/ in the second syllable of *button* and *apple*.

It is also possible to explain the syllable in terms of the pulmonic air stream mechanism. In the production of speech, the air from the lungs does not come out in a continuous stream at a constant pressure. The muscles of the chest push the air out in small puffs at the rate of approximately five times a second, and each puff of air produces a syllable. Each movement of the muscles of the chest is known as a chest-pulse. In order to produce a stressed syllable a re-inforced chest-pulse is used. The English word president has three syllables /prez-i-dent/, and the first syllable is stressed. And it is on the arrangement of stressed and unstressed syllables and the way they follow one another that the rhythm of a language depends.

The structure of a syllable can be represented by the formula CVC, C standing for consonant and V for vowel. Examples of some common structures of syllables used in English are cited below:

The Structure of the Syllable	*The Examplification of the Structure*	*The Nucleus*
(1)	*(2)*	*(3)*
V	I or eye /ai/	/ai/
CVC	pack, back, lack, sack that	/æ/

Contd.

(1)	(2)	(3)
CV	die/dye/dai/	/ai/
	in/in	/i/
VC	eat/i:t/	/i:/
	add/aed	/æ/
VCC	ink / ink/	/i/
	eagle/i : gl/	/i:/
CVCC	fox foks/	/ɔ/
CCVC	school/sku : 1/	/u:/
CCCVC	street/stri : t/	i/
	straight/streti/	/ei/
CCVCC	crisp/krisp/	/i/
CVCCC	masks/ma:sks/	/a:/

It is on the basis of the number of syllables that the words are classified into monosyllabic, disyllabic and polysyllabic words. We have also seen that English permit initial consonant clusters of more than one C element in words such as sky/skai/ (CCV), and of three consonants in words such as script/skript (CCCVCC). English also permits consonant clusters in the final position. Looks/luks/CVCC) has a cluster of two consonants; sixth/siks/ θs/ (CVCCC) has a consonant cluster of three consonants, and sixths/ siks θs (CVCCCC) has a cluster of four consonants in the final position. In the monosyllabic word comb– koum/, the structure of the syllable is CVC, because the final /b/ is silent and therefore it does not exist in the structure of the syllable. Sometimes two syllables in a word may be fused into one by supressing a vowel sound in pronunciation, *e.g.* wa–t (e) ry, lit (e) ral. This process is known as *Elison* or *Slurring*.

2. **Consonants.** The word consonant has been derived from the Greek word **consonautem** which means the sound produced with the help of some other sound (vowel). Both the ancient Greeks and Indians defined the consonant as a sound produced with the help of a vowel. But such a definition is faulty and incomplete. First there are sibilant consonants such as /s, f, z, dz/ and some laterals & nasals which can be pronounced without the help of any vowel. Secondly, there are some languages which have words without any vowel. For example, an African language Ibo has words as /n/ and /gn/. Similarly, strc prst skrz krk ('Don't put a finger in your mouth') is a sentence in the Czech language which has no vowel at all. Hence a consonant has been defined by most modern phoneticians and linguists as a sound which is produced by a stoppage or partial stoppage of the breath, that is to say, in the production of a consonant the movement of air from the lungs is partially or fully obstructed as a result of narrowing or a complete closure of the air passage.

3. **Contoids and Vocoids.** The classification of sounds into vowels and consonants is customary irrespective of phonetic, phonological, or orthographic references. The current classification following Pike divides the sounds into **vocoids** (vowel sounds), **contoids** (consonant sounds), and **semi-vocoids** or **semi contoids** (for example /w/ and /j/ in English). The terms contoids and vocoids refer to **phonetic** form only, without any reference to phonological function. **A vocoid,** according to Pike, is a segment formed with an open approximation of the articulators, with or without a velic closure, and with central passage or air stream. All other segments are contoids. The terms **vowel** and **consonant** are then reserved for phonological function. /w/ and /j/ are vocoids phonetically, that is, they are

produced as the vocoids (vowel sounds) are produced, but they do not form the nucleus of a syllable in English; hence their function is like that of other consonants. In other words, these are the sounds which in form are like vowels but in their function they are like consonants. Hence these are called **nonsyllabic vocoids.** /n/ nd /l/ are phonetically contoids (since in the production of /n/ there is a structure of complete oral closure and in the production of /l/ there is a structure of complete closure in the centre and the air passes through the sides only), but when they form syllabic nuclei, they are called **syllabic contoids e.g., in bottle** and **button.**

Two Kinds of Contoids and Vocoids

In English, there can be syllabic vocoids, non-syllabic vocoids, syllabic contoids and non-syllabic contoids. Syllabic vocoids are all vowel sounds; they function as syllable nuclei. Phonetically the vocoids are vowels and their phonological function is that of a syllabic vocoid. The first-segment in the word inn/in/is a syllabic vocoid. Non-syllabic vocoids are the sounds which are phonetically vocoids (are produced like vowels), but phonologically are contoids (function like ordinary contoids and do not form a nucleus in a syllable, and represent the C element in the syllable.) The first segment in wet/wet,/ is a non-syllabic vocoids. So is the first segment in /yet/jet/ a non-syllabic vocoid. Syllabic contoids are the sounds which are phonetically contoids (are produced like consonants) but their phonological function is that of syllabic nucleus, that is they represent the V element in the structure of a syllable. /l/ in apple and battle and /n/ in button are syllabic contoids. Non-syllabic contoids (also called consonants) are the sounds that phonetically are contiods and phonologically represent the C (marginal) element in the structure of a syllable.

4. Description of Consonants. The description of a consonant will include five kinds of information:

(A) ***The Nature of the Air-stream Mechanism.*** Most speech sounds and all normal English sounds are made with an ingressive pulmonic air-stream, *e.g.*, the air pushed out of the lungs.

(B) ***The State of Glottis.*** A consonant may be voiced or voiceless, depending upon whether the vocal cords remain wide apart (voiceless) or in a state of vibration (voiced).

(C) ***The Position of the Soft Palate.*** While describing consonants we have to mention whether they are oral sounds (produced with soft palate raised, thus blocking the nasal passage of air) or nasal sounds (produced with the soft palate lowered).

(D) ***The Articulators Involved.*** In the description of consonants, we have also to discuss the various articulators involved. The articulators are active (the lower lip and the tongue) and passive (the upper lip, the upper teeth, the roof of the mouth divided into the teeth-ridge, the hard palate, and the soft palate, and the back wall of the throat pharynx). In the production of a consonant the active articulator is moved towards the passive articulator. The chief points of articulation are bilabial, labiodental, dental, alveolar, post-alveolar, palato-alveolar, retroflex, palatal, velar, uvular, and glottal. In the case of some consonantal sounds, there can be a secondary place of articulation in addition to the primary. Thus, in the so-called dark /l/ , in addition to the partial alveolar contact, there is an essential raising of the back of the tongue towards the velum (velarization); or again some post-alveolar articulator of 'r' (r) as in red are accompanied by

slight lip-rounding (labialization). We can classify consonants according to the place of articulation.

(E) ***The Nature of Stricture.*** By the nature of stricture we mean the manner of articulation. This stricture of obstruction made by the organs may be total, intermittent, partial, or may merely constitute a narrowing sufficient to cause friction.

When the stricture is that of a complete closure, the active and passive articulators make a firm contact with each other, and prevent the passage of air between them. For instance in the production of /p/ as in **pin** and /b/ as in bin, the lips make a total closure.

The stricture may be such that air passes between the active and passive articulators intermittently. Such a stricture is called intermittent closure, and involves the vibration of the active articulator against the passive. The Scottish /r/ as in **rat** is an example. The intermittent closure may be of such a short duration that the active articulator strikes against the passive articulator once only. The English /r/ in the word **very** is an example; the tip of the tongue (active articulator) makes one tap against the teeth-ridge (passive articulator).

In the partial stricture, the air passes between the active and passive articulators continuously, but with some difficulty. The sounds thus produced are clear /l/ and dark /l/ in late and hill, the clear and the dark 'l' respectively.

And lastly, the stricture may be such that the air, while passing between the active and passive articulators, produces audible friction. /f, v, θ, o, s, z, f, z, h/ in English are examples of this kind of stricture. Or the air may pass without friction. Examples are /w/ in wet, /j/in yes and flap /r/ as in **butter.** A stricture which involves audible friction, can be called a stricture of close approximation, whereas one which involves no such friction can be called a stricture of open approximation.

If we are to describe some of the consonant sounds in terms of the **point**s discussed in the preceding paragraph, we shall do that in the following manner (we shall not make any reference to the air-stream mechanism since we have already mentioned that all English sounds are made with a pulmonic ingressive air-stream):

1. /p/ in the English word pack.

    (i) The vocal cords are held apart and the sound is voiceless.

    (ii) The soft palate is raised and the nasal passage is closed.

    (iii) The active articulator is the lower lip.

    (iv) The passive articulator is the upper lip.

    (v) There is a stricture of complete closure.

2. /b/ in the English word back.

    (i) The vocal cords vibrate, and the sound produced is voiced.

    (ii) The soft palate is raised and the nasal passage is closed.

    (iii) The active articulator is the lower lip.

    (iv) The passive articulator is the upper lip.

    (v) There is a stricture of complete closure.

3. /g/ in the English word **god.**

    (i) The vocal cords vibrate, and the sound produced is voiced.

(ii) The soft palate is raised and the nasal passage is closed.

(iii) The active articulator is the back of the tongue.

(iv) The passive articulator is the soft palate.

(v) There is a stricture of complete closure; the back of the tongue makes a complete closure with the soft palate.

4. /t/ in the Englsih word cat.

(i) The vocal cords are wide apart, and the sound is voiceless.

(ii) The soft palate is raised and the nasal passage is closed.

(iii) The active articulator is the tip of the tongue.

(iv) The passive articulator is the teeth ridge.

(v) There is a stricture of complete closure. The tip of the tongue makes a firm contact with the teeth ridge.

5. /m/ in the English word **man.**

(i) The vocal cords vibrate and the sound is voiced.

(ii) The soft palate is lowered and the air passes through the nose.

(iii) The active articulator is the lower lip.

(iv) The passive articulator is the upper lip.

(v) There is a stricture of complete oral closure.

6. /v/ in the English word **van.**

(i) The vocal cords vibrate and the sound is voiced.

(ii) The soft palate is raised and the nasal passage is closed.

(iii) The active articulator is the lower lip.

(iv) The passive articulators are the upper front teeth.

(v) The stricture is one of close approximation.

(The lower lip is brought very near the upper front teeth. The air passes between them with audible friction.)

7. /y/ in the English word **yet.**

(i) The vocal cords vibrate and the sound is voiced.

(ii) The soft palate is raised.

(iii) The active articulator is the front of the tongue.

(iv) The passive articulator is the hard palate.

(v) There is a stricutre of open approximation. The front of the tongue is brought near the hard palate but the space between them is sufficient for the air to pass without any audible friction.

CLASSIFICATION OF SOUNDS

The sounds which the organs of speech produce are mainly of two kinds:—*(A)* Vowels and *(B)* Consonants.

Vowels are the voiced sounds that are produced without any obstruction or friction. They are purely musical sounds. All other articulated sounds are consonants are both breathed and voiced sounds. Some are produced as a result of obstruction in the mouth while some are produced on account of some friction in the mouth caused by the articulators (active and passive) while still others are nasal. *i.e.* produced when the breath passing through the nose.

Since consonants contribute more towards making an utterance distinctive than vowels do let us begin with the consonants first. But before dealing with the consonants and vowels in detail, let us have a glance over the phonetic letters representing both consonants and vowels vis-a-vis symbols of general Indian English.

Consonants

1.	|p|	as in	paper	| PeIp∂ |	Same as in R.P. (British)
2.	|b|	as in	bag	| b æ p |	"
3.	|t|	as in	tale	| teIl |	"
4.	|d|	as in	dust	| d^st |	"
5.	|k|	as in	cap	| k æ p |	"
6.	|g|	as in	go	| g∂∪ |	"
7.	|tʃ|	as in	chair	| tʃe∂ |	"
8.	|d_3|	as in	joy	| d_3 ⊃I |	"
9.	|f|	as in	fear	| fI∂ |	"
10.	|v|	as in	very	| veri |	same as in R.P.
11.	|θ|	as in	month	| mauθ |	$\theta = t^h$
12.	|ð|	as in	there	| be∂ |	same as in R.P.
13.	|S|	as in	Sea	| Si: |	"
14.	|z|	as in	zone	| z∂un |	"
15.	|ʃ|	as in	Shine	| ʃ2In |	"
16.	|3|	as in	leisure	| le3∂ |	"
17.	|h|	as in	house	| h2∪s |	"
18.	|m|	as in	mother	| m^ð∂ |	"
19.	|n|	as in	nine	| n2In |	"
20.	|η|	as in	King	| κm |	"
21.	|l|	as in	Lame	| leim |	"
22.	|r|	as in	rain	| rein |	"
23.	|j|	as in	yes	| j es |	"
24.	|W|	as in	Wool	| W∪l |	—

The Vowels

1.	| i: |	as in	see	| Si: |	same as in R.P.
2.	| I |	as in	sit	| sIt |	"
					General Indian English
3.	| e |	as in	pen	| Pen |	| e | = | ε |
4.	| æ |	as in	man	| m æ n |	same as in R.P.
5.	| a: |	as in	ask	| a:sk |	"
6.	| ¬D |	as in	hot	| h¬Dt |	"
7.	| ⊃: |	as in	ball	| b⊃:l |	| ⊃: | = | D: |
8.	| ∪ |	as in	Cook	| k∪k |	same as in R. P.
9.	| u: |	as in	room	| ru:m |	"
10.	| ^ |	as in	Cup	| k^p |	| ^ | = | ∂ |
11.	| 3: |	as in	bird	| b3:d |	| 3: | = | θ: |
12.	| ∂ |	as in	about	| ∂b2∪t |	—
13.	| eI |	as in	pay	| pei |	| eI | = | θ: |
14.	| 2I |	as in	right	| r2it |	same as in R.P.
15.	| ⊃I |	as in	boy	| b⊃I |	"
16.	| ∂∪ |	as in	go	| g∂∪ |	| ∂∪ | = | ð: |
17.	| 2∪ |	as in	now	| n2∪ |	| 2∪ | = | a∪ |
18.	| I∂ |	as in	here	| hI∂ |	same as in R.P.
19.	| e∂ |	as in	there	| ðe∂ |	"
20.	| ∪∂ |	as in	poor	| pu∂ |	"

CLASSIFICATION OF CONSONANTS

Consonantal sounds are classified on the basis of *(i)* voicing, *(ii)* place of articulation, and *(iii)* manner of articulation.

(i) **Voicing.** On the basis of voicing, sound can be classified into voiced and voiceless sounds. The voiced sounds in English are /b, d, g, v, ð, z dʒ, m, n, ŋ, I, r, w, j/. The voiced sounds in Hindi are/ ग, घ, ज, झ, ड, ढ, द, ध, ब, भ, य, र, ल, व, म, न, and other nasalized consonants and all vowels.

All the vocoids and semi-vowels are voiced sounds, whereas among the consonants some are voiceless. If the vocal cords vibrate when a sound is produced, it is said to be voiceless.

(ii) **The Place of Articulation.** Consonants are divided as given in following table on the basis of the articulatory points at which the articulators actually touch, or are at their closest.

The Classification of English Consonants According to the Place of Articulation

Classification	*Articulators*	*Examples from English*
Bilabial	Upper lip and lower lip	/p b m w/
Dental	Teeth and tip of tongue	/ θ ð/
Labio-dental	Lower lip and upper teeth	/f v/
Alveolar	Alveolar (teeth) ridge and tip and blade of tongue	/t d s z r l n/
Post-alveolar	Hard palate and tip of tongue	/r/
Palato-aveloar	Hard palate-aveolar and tip, blade and front of tongue	/ʃ/ʒ/ ʃ /dʒ/
Palatal	Hard palate and front of tongue	/j/
Velar	Soft palate and back of tongue	/k g ŋ/
Glottal	Glottis (vocal cords)	/h/

This table includes the classification of all the consonants of English. To exemplify the classification of the consonants in Hindi we can present this table in the following way:

The Classification of Hindi Consonants According to the Place of Articulation

Classification	*Articulators*	*Examples from Hindi*
Velar	Soft palate and back to tongue	(क ख ग घ ङ)
Palatal	Hard palate and tip and front of tongue	(च छ ज झ ञ अ य श)
Retroflex (Cerebral or cacuminal)	Hard palate and tip of tongue curled back	(ट ठ ड ढ ण र)
Dental	Teeth and tip of tongue	(त थ द ध न)
Labio-dental	Lower lip and upper teeth	(व)
Bilabial	Two lips	(प फ ब भ म)
Alveolar	Alveolar ridge and lip and blade of tongue	(र ल स)
Glottal (laryngeal)	Glottis (vocal cords)	(ह)
Uvular	Uvula and root of tongue	(क ख ग)

(iii) The Manner of Articulation. According to the manner of articulation, which describes the type of obstruction caused by the narrowing or closure of the articulators, the consonants can be divided into stops, affricates, fricatives, nasals, rolls, laterals, and semi-vowels or frictionless continuants. We shall discuss these one by one.

(1) **Stop.** In the production of a stop, the oral and nasal passages are closed simultaneouly. The active and passive articulators come in contact with each other forming a stricture of complete closure and preventing the air from escaping through the mouth. The soft palate is raised and thus the nasal passage is also blocked. (This is also known as velic closure). The air behind the oral closure is compressed, and when the active articulator is removed from contact with passive one, the air escapes with an explosion. Stops are also known as mutes, explosives, plosives or occlusives. /p/ in **pat** and /b/ in bat are the example of stops.

(2) **Affricate.** If the stop is not held for any appreciable time and released slowly, we get an affricate rather than a plosive, *e.g.* /tʃ/ in chair and /ds/ in **jail.**

(3) **Nasal.** In a nasal contoid, the breath stream is interrupted at some points in the oral cavity or at the lips, while being allowed to enter the nose and create resonance there. Thus a nasal is produced by a stricture of complete oral closure. The soft palate is lowered and the air passes through the nose. All nasal sounds are voiced. Examples /m,nv/ in English.

(4) **Trill (or Rolled Consonants).** In the production of a trill, the active articulator taps several times against the passive articulator. The stricture involved can be called a stricture of intermittent closure. Scottish /r/, for example in **red,** in which the tip of the tongue strikes against the teeth ridge a number of times, is called a trilled consonant. In Hindi words like **Ram**/ ra : m/ and rath /r θ/ we have this variety of /r/.

(5) **Flap.** For a flap the active articulator strikes the passive articulation once only. For example the /r/ in the English word **very**, in which the tip of the tongue strikes against teeth ridge only once.

(6) **Lateral.** Laterals are produced by a stricture of complete closure in the centre of the vocal tract, but the air passes out every one or both side of the tongue. For example, /l/ in **late.**

(7) **Fricative.** In the production of a fricative consonant the stricutre is one of close approximation. The active articulator and the passive articulator are so close to each other that passage between them is very narrow and the air passes through it with audible friction. Example are /f/ in face, /v/ in vain /θ/ in think, /ð/ in them, /ʃ / in sail, /ʒ/ in zero, /f/ in ship, /z/ in measure, /h/ in hat.

(8) **Frictionless Continuant.** In the production of a frictionless continuant the stricture is that of open approximation. For example in the production of /r/ in **red, read, real, ready,** the active articulator (tip of the tongue) is brought just behind the passive articulator (alveolar ridge) so that there is plenty of space between the two articulators, and the air passes between them without friction; and hence the term "frictionless continuant." Hindi "v" as in **vah** is a frictionless continuant. Gimson includes the English /r/ in words like **red** and **read** among the frictionless continuants, but the English (r) also occurs as a fricative as in **try, cry, pray grow, very, sorry.** Jones includes it in the list of fricatives and Gimson in the list of frictionless continuants.

(9) **Semi-vowel.** A semi-vowel is a vowel glide functioning as a consonant *i.e.*, as the C element in syllable structure. In terms of articulation semi-vowels are like vowels, but they dont't behave like vowels. Semi-vowels are never stable; they can never be pronounced by themselves. They are sounds in transition. Examples are /j/ in jet and /w/ in **wet.** These are also called semiconsonants too.

(10) **Fortis and Lenis.** When we have voiceless/voiced pair, the two sounds are also distinguished by the degree of

breath force and muscular effort invovled in the articulations *e.g.*s is comparatively strong or **fortis,** and z is comparatively weaker lenis.

We summarize the classification of the consonants in English on the basis of the manner of articulation in the following table.

Name of the class	*Structure Involved*	*Examples*
Stop	Complete closure	/p b t d k g/
Affricate	Closure, then slow separation	/tʃ dz/
Fricative	Narrowing, resulting audible friction	/f v θ δ s z /ʃ 3/
Nasal	Complete closure in mouth, air escapes through nose	/m n B/
Rolled	Rapid intermittent closure	/r/
Lateral	Closure in the centre of mouth, air escapes over the sides of tongue	/l/
Frictionless Continuant	Slight narrowing, not enough to cause friction	/r/
Semi-vowels/ Semi-consonants	Slight narrowing, not enough to cause friction.	/wj/

IDENTIFICATION OF CONSONANTS

We can describe and identify a consonant briefly by using a three-term label, indicating *(i)* whether the sound is voiceless or voiced, *(ii)* the place of articulation; and *(iii)* the manner of articulation. For example, /p/ in **pant** can be described as a voiceless, bilabial stop (or plosive), /b/ in bet as a voiced, bilabial stop, /m/ in **mango** as voiced bilabial nasal, /ŋ / in **hand** as a voiced velar nasal, /z/ in **zoo** as a voiced alveolar fricative, /tʃ / in chair as a voiceless palato-alveolar affricate; /f/ in fan as a voiceless labio-dental fricative, and so on so forth. We should have described the consonants of English in these terms while dealing with the phonology of English, but we list them below to facilitate study:

Consonants are represented on a two-dimensional grid. The grid takes account of three features of each sound; *(i)* whether the sound is **voiced** or **voiceless;** *(ii)* **the point of articulation;** *(iii)* **the manner of articulation.** In the grid of points of articulation are set out horizontally and the types of manner of articulation are arranged vertically. If we classify consonants according to the organs which articulate them, we find seven main classes of consonants. They are labial consonants and are also called lip-consonants .

Indian students can easily pronounce, with intelligibility, consonants like p, t, k, b, d, g, m, n, h, j. But they need some effort to familiarize themselves with the rest of the consonents and to use them intelligibly in their own speech.' It is hoped that the followed description of each of the difficult consonants will be of some help to our students:

> I as in song, ink. This is called voiced velear nasal. In making this sound the soft palate is lowered so as to touch the back of the tongue and close the mouth-passage. The air is thus forced to pass out through the nasal cavity. The place of articulation is generally at the velum, though there may be a degree of variation as to which part of the velum is used. This sound occurs sometimes in the company of I sound as in finger, anger, youngest and so on.

> F as in foot, safe and offer. This is a voiceless labio-dental fricative. In producing this sound the lower lip is brought against the upper teeth. The air passage is thus restricted and a slight friction is caused, Some Indian students find it difficult to distinguish between p and f. In making the sound p, both lips touch each other and the air passage is completely blocked. But in the formation of f sound the

upper lip is almost idle. The lower lip and upper teeth join to produce this sound by narrowing the air passage.

V as in van, move and so on. This s a voiced counterpart of f. Like f, it is a labio-dental fricative. The mechanism of producing this sound is the same as that of f. The difference is simply that f is voiceless and V is voiced. In rapid speech V of and have are dropped before another consonant, especially when they are followed by the word the.

O is the voiceless dental fricative. This is one of the difficult sounds for Indian students. In pronouncing this the tip of the tongue is set against the upper teeth. The tongue-tip tends to touch the upper teeth, but does not actually touch them. If the tongue is made to touch the upper teeth, it blocks the air passage resulting in production of a plosive consonant which exists in many Indian languages.

Ô as in 'tham' and this. This is voiced counterpart of Q. The tongue position and the manner of production are the same as for Q. But this is a voiced sound, while Q is a voiceless consonant. Sometimes Q and Ô are interchangeable in English. For examples, in compounds, words like 'with-draw, with-hold, the medical sound is pronounced Q by some people and Ô by others.

Z as in zeal and choose. This is a voiced alveolar fricative. The manner and place of production of this sounds are the same as those of S. The difference is that this is voiced.

S as in see (si :) acid (asid). This is a voiceless alveolar fricative. This is generally articulated with the tip of the tongue tending to touch the teeth ridge. The resulting restriction of the air-passage causes friction which produces, hissing sounds. Some however pronounce the sound with the blade of the tongue raised towards the teeth ridge, while keeping the tip of the tongue down near the lower teeth. The resulting sound is not very much exactly S.

ʃ as is ship (Sip) notiọn. This is called voiceless palato-alveolar fricative. This is one of the frequently mispronounced sounds. Some of us cannot distinguish between S and S. It should be noted that S is a hissing sound and S is a sort of whistling sound. Try to whistle without pictruding your lips, that is keeping them in ventral position and you get the S sound. This is produced by the combined activity of the blade of the tongue and the front part of the hard palate.

j as in yard, young, issue. This is one of the two semi-vowels; the other is W. j is a voiced palatal consonant. It is called as semivowel because sometimes it is difficult to notice where precisely the vowel i: ends and the consonants j begins. i: is the vowel sound nearest to j i: is pronounced by raising the front part (just behind the blade) of the tongue towards the hard palate. If slightly frontier part of the tongue is raised, the result as j sound, a consonant.

W as in win, wait, walk. This is a voiced bi-labial consonants, but, paradoxically called semi-vowel. The vowel sound interest to this is u :. The affinity between the vowel u: sounds and the consonant w is due to the lip position in their pronunciation. In both cases the lips are brought into activity they are rounded.

It has been said that I is not a difficult sound for our students. But there are two chief varieties of this sound in Received Pronunciation. Both of them have the same Primary articulation of the tip of the tongue against the teeth ridge. When v or ve takes the final position in a word or when r is followed by a consonant. Similarly in words ending with r or re, it is generally silent as for example in poor, fire, pure.

Where r is pronounced three chief varities of it are distinguished. They are as follows:

(a) Fricative r—This is the usual sound given to the written r when it is followed by a vowel in a word. Examples, red, arrive and so on. This is not a difficult sound to pronounce. But it should be borne in mind that r is always pronounced when it is followed by a vowel, unless it is followed by e in final position.

(b) Intrusive r—This is a r sound which does not exist in spelling, but intrudes when the word is pronounced in the company of certain other words. This r is generally inserted when words spelt with final-a are followed by words beginning with a vowel. Some regard this sort of intrusive r as bad pronunciation on the ground that it does not correspond to spelling. In Modern times there has been a tendency to avoid it.

(c) Linking r—When a word ending with written r is followed in the sentence or phrase by a word beginning with a vowel, usually r has a consonantal value. But where such words are pronounced by themselves r sound is silent. There are some words ending with r uttered in isolation and in the company of words beginning with vowel sounds.

CLASSIFICATION OF VOWELS

Vowels are the voiced sounds. In classifying vowels four important points have to be considered. The first is the height of the tongue while producing a vowel sound and according to this, we have high, low and mid vowels. The tongue can be raised or lowered in the mouth and these movements of the tongue naturally correspond with the movements of the jaw, when the tongue is raised high in the mouth, the vowel formed is called a high one and when the tongue occupies the middle of the mouth, a mid vowel is formed. This low position of the tongue involve a still greater lowering of the lower jaw and opening of the mouth more widely. Examples of high, mid and low vowels are heard in bit, bet and bat respectively. The second basis for the classification of vowels is the activity of the lips which may or may not assume a rounded shape while vowels are produced. When the lips are rounded, we have rounded vowels and when the lips remain passive or unrounded we have unrounded vowels. In pronouncing a vowel the tongue may be remaining embraced and hard or soft and slack. The first condition results in the production of slack vowels. The fourth classification of vowels depends on whether the tongue is drawn back in the mouth so as to allow the back part to come into play or advanced so as to make the front part to come into play. When the back part of the tongue comes into play we say back vowels are formed and when the front part comes into play we say front. At the same time if the tongue lies flat in the mouth so that its whole upper surface is used in articulation, we say that flat vowels are produced. The main difference between consonants and vowels is, that in consonants the air stream is either altogether trapped for an instant or, so far narrowed that a certain amount of friction is caused, but in vowels the mouth passage is not sufficiently closed to produce friction.

Infact the distinction between consonants and vowels depends upon the degree of narrowing of the mouth passage through which the air has to escape. A sound in which there is either an audible friction or a short but complete stoppage of the air, is called as consonant sound in which there is an uniterrupted flow of the air-stream are called vowels, it should be borne in mind that among consonants some are voiced and some are voiceless or breathed, but all vowels are voiced sound.

The following conventionalised diagram shows the first two aspects of vowel classification looking at this diagram, one can easily understand the quality of vowels whether they are open or close and whether they are front, back or central.

Vowels represented by the vertical lines are all back-vowels. There is no difference in the degree of their backness. But as we proceed upward along the line we come progressively towards close vowels. It can also be noticed that as we proceed along the line pronouncing those vowels, we progressively round our lips, Thus a : is a full open vowel and u : at the other end is close vowel. It can also be noticed that as we proceed along the line pronouncing those vowels, we progressively round our lips. Other vowels on the line are intermediate between these two.

Vowels along the slant line on the left are front vowels because they are produced by raising the front part of the tongue. On the top of this line is i : which is the miximum close-vowel and as we come down pronouncing these vowels, the mouth progressively opens. Thus oe is the most open vowel among front vowels. Other vowels on the line are intermediate between i : and oe. It should also be noted that as we come down the line pronouncing the vowels. We progressively coming towards back vowels and hence the slantness in the line.

It is difficult to describe vowel sounds, because people's vowels vary greatly and there may not be any correspondence between the vowels of the writer on phonetics and those of his reader. To overcome this difficulty, writers on phonetics have established a set of "specially selected vowel sounds which can conveniently be used as points of reference from which other vowels can be measured". Such selected vowel sounds are called cardinal vowels.

Let us study each vowel in detail:

Vowel No. 1—i :, as air sea (si :), meet (mi : t). The diagram shows that this is a close, front, unrounded vowel. In final position, some people use the diphthongal variety of this sound. The diphthong may be phonetically represented by ij.

Vowel No 2—i, as in words like sit, city. This is a front, unrounded vowel between half close and half open positions,

Vowel No 3—e, as in words like ten, men, bread. This is a front, unrounded vowel between half close and half open positions.

Vowel No 4—oe, as in word, like man, sat, that. This is a front unrounded vowel which, is phonetically represented by the symbol x. Different people use different shades of this vowel. If the vowel is given slightly frontier articulation it ceases to be a vowel and becomes the consonant 'ja'.

Vowel No 5—a :, as in words like calm, father and farther. This is an open back unrounded vowel. This should not be confused with No. 4. In pronouncing this sound some people open the mouth widely as if they were jawing.

Vowel No 6—o, as in words like not, doll, hop. This is a back vowel produced with the mouth almost open and the lips slighly rounded.

Vowel No 7—o:, as in words like or (o:) saw, thought. This is a back vowel with the mouth position more or less as that in the case of No. 6.

Vowel No 8—u, as in words like push, could, look. This is a back vowel with the mouth almost closed and the lips slightly rounded.

Vowel No 9—u, as in words like moon, rude. This is a back, rounded, nearly close vowel. This can be said to be lengthened variety of No. 8. Different shades of this vowel are found among different people.

Vowel No 10—n, as in words like dull, fun, done, blood. This is a half open central unrounded vowel. In rapid speech some people exchange this sounds with a: or ∂. Care must be taken to avoid this.

Vowel No 11—∂: as in words like fur, search, word. This is a half close and half open variety of central unround vowel. Various shades of this sound are heard among the speakers of received pronunciation.

Vowel No 12—∂, as in words like age, children nature, china, suppose. This is a very close sound and therefore it is difficult to describe it with precision. This is called a neutral vowel and it never occurs in accented syllables. It takes the place of most other vowels when we utter them in rapid speech, without stress. It is a central, unrounded vowel pronounced with the mouth held between half close and half open position and the lips taking netural position.

WRITTEN FORMS AND BASIC FUNCTIONS OF LANGUAGE

The spoken form of any given language is liable to undergo change and development in the course of its history. The development undrgone by the English language in the last one thousand years can be understood by comparing a passage of old writing English with a passage from Modern English. Written language always come later than the spoken form and spoken form of any word is a symbol of the thing referred to by that word. The written form is the symbol of that symbol; and so it is twice removed from the referred thing. The primitive form of writing meant carving, painting or drawing of the symbolic elements or the visible features of an experience. When the association between the written symbol and the spoken word becomes fixed, the symbol may come to lose original pictorial value and to deviate from its older form. At this stage the association has come to be one of written symbol and spoken sound regardless of the meaning borne by the sound. Later the symbol are only used in phonetics and the number of symbols are reduced. The alphabets of many Indian languages as well as the national alphabets of Japanese consists of such syllabaries. Syllabaries is a further simplification of writing when these characters are used to represent not whole syllables but single sounds of the language as in Greek, Latin and derived alphabets, including in English. Writing is an outgrowth of drawing. Probably all peoples make pictures by painting drawing scratching or carving. These pictures aside from other uses sometimes serve as messages or reminders that is they modify the conduct of the beholder and they may be persistently used in this way. The Indians of North America are skilful draftmen and in older times made extensive practical use of pictures.

The records and messages, like writing, have the advantage of being permanent and transportable, but they fall short of writing in accuracy since they bear no fixed relation of linguistic forms and accordingly do not share in the delicate adjustment of the latter. In the use of pictures we can often see the beginnings of the transition, and traces of it remain in the actual systems of writing.

Real writing uses a limited number of conventional symbols we must therefore suppose that in the transition the pictures become conventionalized. The way of outlining each animals for instance, becomes so fixed that even a very imperfect sketch leaves us doubt as to the species of animal. To some degree it is true of the pictures of **American Indians**. In actual system of writing we often find symbols which still betray this origin. When the picture has become rigidly conventionalised we may call it a character. A character is a uniform mark or set of marks which people produce under certain conditions and to which accordingly, they respond in a certain way. Once this habit is established, the resemblance of the character to any particular object is of secondary importance, and may be obliterated by changes in the convention of forming the character. The other more important place of the transition from the use of picture to real writing is the association of the characters with linguistic froms. Most situations contain features that do not lead themselves to picturing; the picture-user resorts to all sorts of devices that will elicit the proper response.Thus we saw the Indian drawing twenty nine strokes above his beaver to represent the number of beaver-pelts. Instead of depicting the process of exchange by a series of pictures, he represented it by two crossed lines with the sets of traded objects at either side.

When a picture user was confronted by a problem of this kind, we may suppose that he actually spoke to himself and tried out various wordings of the troublesome message. Language, after all is our one way of communicating the kind of things that do not lend themselves to drawing. If we make this supposition we can understand that the picture-users might in time arrange the characters in the order of the spoken words of their language, and that they might develop a convention of represening every part say every word, of the spoken utterance by some character.

In real writing some characters have a twofold value. For which they represent both a picturable object and a phonetic or linguistic form; other characters having lost their pictorial value, represent only phonetic or linguistic form, purely pictoral characters that are not associated with speech-forms sink into subsidary use. The linguistic value predominates more and more especially as the characters because conventionalized in shape, losing their resemblance to pictured objects. The characters become symbol that is marks or groups of marks that conventionally represent some linguistic form and respond to the symbol as they respond to the hearing of the linguistic form. Actually the writer utters the speech from before or during the act of writing and the hearer utters it in the act of reading, only after considerable practise. Do we succeed in making these speech-movements inaudible and inconspicuous? It is different that languages is used to serve a multiplicity of purposes. In accordance with the different purposes to be served, language is used in different ways and we respond differently to each particular use of language. For example, there is the language of science, journalism, advertising, political oratory, political effusion and prayer and worship. In these instances language is used as if it were a multipurpose tool which could be put to a variety of uses as and when required. Many people fail to understand the subtle and complicated nature of language.

One of the basic functions of languages is to communicate information of some kind or another. Information here can include propaganda of all kinds. All informative discourse is used to describe the world around us and to reason about it.

Besides informative there are two other basic functions of language. There are the expressive and the directive functions. Science provides us with instances of the best informative discourse. Poetry gives us the finest examples of the expressive function of language. The poetry cannot be communicated whereas in information it needs expression of language. All poets attempt to communicate their own feelings and attitude. When the poet Robert Burns compares his love to a red rose, which is newly sprung in June, or to melody that is sweetly played in tune, he is trying to express the emotion which he feels keenly and trying to arouse similar feelings in the readers. Not only poets but other people also use expressive language to express their tender feelings. The lover uses the expressive language to convey his passions and tenderness to his beloved. While dealing with expressive language we are not to apply the common standard of truth or falsehood, correctness or incorrectness. We must bear in mind the fact that the purpose of the poet in writing his poetry is not to convey information but to express emotion and to arouse it in the reader. There is no doubt that some poems have informative contents which cannot be denied while dealing their total effect.

The third basic function of language is to cause some overt action. The common examples of directive function of language are commands and requests. Commands are distinguished from request in a very subtle way and any command can be turned into a request by adding "please" at the beginning or by a suitable change in the tone of the voice or in the expression of the face. As directive discourse has no truth, value, it cannot be described as true or false.

The examples of informative, expressive and directive language have been compared by giving M. Copi to chemically pure specimens. This three fold division cannot be applied to all languages mechanically because very often we find in the most ordinary use of language, a combination of all three functions. For example a poem may be both informative and directive. A sermon at the same time is both directive and expressive. The serman preached may also contain some facts which are conveyed through the informative use of language. A treatise on science, though primarily informative can also convey to the reader something of the writers enthusiasm and thus serve the expressive function of language. In addition to this, it may also be directive in function in as much as it bids the reader to check for himself whether the conclusions arrived at by the author are correct. Thus we find that most ordinary uses of language involve all the three basic functions of conveying information, evincing emotion and inducing action.

The scholars stated that the grammatical features of language in philosoplical terms took no account of the structural difference between languages, but obscured it by forcing their descriptions into the scheme of Latin Grammar. They had not observed the sounds of speech and confused them with the written symbols of the alphabets. This fails to distinguish between actual speech and the use of writing distorted also their motions about the history of language. They saw that in medieval and wisdom times highly cultivated persons wrote and also spoke good Latin, while less educated or carden scribes made many mistakes; failing to see that this Latin-writing was an artificial and academic exercise, they concluded that languages are preserved by the usage of educated and careful people and changed by the corruptions of the vulgar. In the case of the modern languages like English they believed, accordingly that the speech forms of books and of upperclass conversation represented an older and purer level from which the vulgarism of the common people had braunched off as "corruptions" by a process of **"linguistic decay"**. The Grammarions felt free, therefore to prescribe fanciful rules which they derived from consideration of logic.

Outside the tradition of Europe, several nations had developed linguistic doctrines chiefly on an antiquarian basis. The Arabs had worked out a grammar of the classical form of their languages, as it appears in the Koran, on the model of this the Jews in **Mohammedan** countries constructed a **Hebrew grammar.** At the Renaissance, European scholars became acquainted with the tradition, the term root, for the central part of a word comes from Hebrew grammer. In the far East, the Chinies had gained a great deal of antiquarian linguistic knowledge, especially in the way of lexicography.

It was in India, however, that there arose a body of knowledge which was destined to revolutionize European ideas about language. The Brahmin religion guarded as sacred tests some very ancient collections of hymns, the oldest of these collections, the Rig-Veda, dates in parts at a conservative estimate from about 1200 B.C. As the languages of these text grew antiquated, the proper way of pronouncing them, and their correct interpretation became the task of a special class of learned men. The **antiquarian** interest in language which arose in this way, was carried over into a more practical sphere. Among the Hindus, as among us, different classes of society differed in speech. Apparently these were forces at work which led upper-class speakers to adopt lower class forms of speech. We find the Hindu grammarians extending their interest from the scriptures to the upper-caste language and making rules and lists of forms descriptive of the correct type of speech, which they called **Sanskrit**. In time they worked out a systematic arrangement of grammar and lexicon. Generations of such labours must have preceded the writing of the oldest treatise that has come down to us, the grammar of "Panini". This grammar, which dates from somewhere round 350 to 250 B.C. is one of the greatest movements of human intelligence. It describes with the minutest detail, every inflection, derivation, and composition and every syntactic usage of its author's speech. No other language to this day has been so perfectly described. It may have been due in part, to this excellent codification that Sanskrit became, in time, the official and literary language of all of Brahmin India. Long after it had ceased to be spoken as anyone's native language it remained the artificial medium for all writing on learned or religious topics. Some knowledge of Sanskrit and of the Hindu Grammar had reached Europe, through missionaries.

MOMENTOUS CHANGES IN THE ENGLISH LANGUAGE

Professor Scherillo, in his history of the origins of Italian literature, commenting upon the statement frequently made that Dante created the Italian language, reminds his readers that this is claiming for the Italian poet a function like that of Adam in Eden, when he gave names to all the beasts of the field and the fowls of the air! A similar reminder might appropriately have been addressed to those writers who have called Chaucer the creator of English. Such a statement of course totally misrepresents the development of the language. Chaucer employed the London speech of his time, and a minute comparison of his usage with that of the contemporary London archives. At least Mr. Henry Bradley, in the light of his experience in editing the New English Dictionary, was very cautious about attributing such contributions to the poet. It is even doubtful if Chaucer had any important part in making the East Midland the dominant dialect. The speech of the capital would have become standard English if he had never written a line. But he did add greatly to its prestige and distinction. The very fact that he wrote in English instead of French was significant. He developed the resources of the language for literary use, and set an example which was followed by a long line of poets.

Chaucer's language, then, is late Middle English of the South East Midland type. As compared with Anglo-Saxon or some of the other dialects of Middle English, its inflections are simple and offer little difficulty to the reader to today. But many words retained a syllabic *-e,* either final or in the ending *-es* or *en,* which afterwards ceased to be pronounced, and the vowels had in general their present continental rather than their English sound. For metrical purposes, consequently, Chaucer's language was very different from ours, and it is impossible to read his verse properly—to say nothing of appreciation it—without having some knowledge of the older pronunciation and grammatical forms. It is because this knowledge was lost from the fifteenth century down to the middle of the nineteenth that many of Chaucer's most enthusiastic admirers among English poets and critics has regarded his meter as irregular and rough.

The brief grammatical outline that follows is intended to supply the reader or student with such knowledge of Chaucer's sounds and inflections as is necessary for the intelligent reading of the verse. To save space, certain inflectional forms, such as the principal parts of strong verbs, which are registered in the Glossary, are not repeated here. The Glossary also records exceptional forms, like the contracted third singular present indicative of verbs or "petrified" datives of nouns, and it shows the nominative forms of nouns and adjectives when they are likely to gave any trouble because of their unlikeness of modern English.

PRONUNCIATION

Vowels and Diphthongs. There is considerable inconsistency in the spelling of the vowels and diphthongs. Vowels are commonly, but not regularly, doubled to indicate length—not only *e*, as in modern English *e.g.* "deed" but also *a* and *o,* and rarely *i.*

Sound	*Pronunciation*	*Spelling*	*Examples*
ā	like *a* in "father"	a, aa	names, caas.
ă	like *a* in Ger. "Mann"		acan, that,
ā (close)	like *a* in "fate"	e, ee	sweete.
ē (open)	like *e* in "there"	e, ee	heeth.
ĕ	like *e* in "set"	e	tendre.
e (the neutral vowel	like *a* in "about"	e	yonge, sonne.
Ī	like *i* in "machine"	i, y	ryden, shires.
Ĭ	like *i* in "sit"	i, y	this, thyng.
ō (close)	like *o* in "note"	o, oo	good, bote.
ō (open)	like *oa* in "broad"	o, oo	holy, rood (vb.)
ŏ	like *o* in "hot"	o	oft, lot.
ū	like *oo* in "bloot"	ou, ow, ogh	fowles, droghte.
ŭ	like *u* in "full"	u, o	but, yong, songen pt. pl.).
iū	like *u* in "mute"	u, eu, ew	Pruce, vertu, salewe.
ēi	like ē in + *i*	ai, ay, ei, ey	sayle, day, wey.

Contd.

Sound	*Pronunciation*	*Spelling*	*Examples*
ē̇u	like *ou* in "house"	au, aw	cause, draughte.
ēu	like ē + *u*	eu, ew	knew.
ēu	like ē + *u*	eu, ew	lewed.
oi	like *oy* in "boy"	oi, oy	coy, joye.
ōu	like ō + *u*	ou, ow	growen.
ōu	like õ + *u*	ou, ow	knowen, sowle.
ou	like À + *u*	o (u), before gh	fo (u) ghte, tho (u) ght.

Some of the pronunications indicated in the accompanying table are only approximate, and others are doubtful. Chaucer's close ē and ō did not quite correspond to the vowels now heard in "name" and "note", which are really diphthongal (ē + a transitional i, ō + u). It is hard to judge in how many cases Chaucer's ã preserved the sound of a in German "Mann", and when it had the sound of æ, as in modern English "that" (and AS. "pæt"). The combinations eu, ew, represented not only the descending diphthong ē*u, ew* (as in knew, from AS. cnéow; lewed, As. læwed), but also the ascending diphthong iu (as probably in salewen, Fr. "saluer"). The first sound ultimately developed into the second (as in modern English "knew", "lewd"), and it is uncertain just what Chaucer's pronunciation was in individual cases. Similarly, in the combinations ou, ow, the original distinction between ōu (with close ō) and ōu (with open ō) was apparently breaking down, and the two classes of words are not kept apart in rime. But the diphthong ou (or various origins) before gh had a different sound, which developed into the modern long vowel in "thought" and "fought". The pronunciation of the diphthongs variously spelled ai, ay, ei, ey is a matter of disagreement. The sounds concerned are of different origins, some coming, from e + i or e + g (as in selyen, we, counseil), others from ee + g (as in day, fayn), and others from a + i (as in batayle, fayle). They had all fallen together so as to rime acceptably one with another. It is doubtful whether the pronunciation was āi (as in "aisle") or æi (approaching the modern pronunciation of "way", "day"). But a sound intermediate between the two seems probable.

The distinction between open and close ē and ō does not appear in Chaucer's spelling, and no simple rule can be given which will guide the reader in all cases. The modern spellings ea and oa ("heath", "boat") usually point to the broad pronunciation in Middle English, but there are many exceptions. The modern pronunciation—ō for Chaucer's ō (as in "rode") and oo (*i.e.*, long u) for his ō (as in "noon")—is a better test in the case of ō, but it fails with ē, where the two classes of sounds have fallen together (as in "seek" and "heath"). Even the evidence of etymology is not always decisive, for special conditions sometimes affected the development of words. But as a general rule ē (close) corresponds to AS. (or Old Mercian) ē,ēo, ON. ē and o, OF. (and Anglo-Norman) ē (close) ē (open), to AS. æe, ēa, and ĕ (when lengthened in Middle English), ON æe, and OF. (or Anglo-Norman) ē; ō (close), to AS. ō or ō lengthened before consonantal combinations, ON. ō, and OF. (or Anglo-Norman) ō (close); ō (open), to AS. or ON. ā and ŏ (when lengthened before a nasal or in open syllables and OF. ŏ (when lengthened in open syllables). For the assistance of readers who find it difficulty to apply these tests, cases of open ē and ō have been marked (ē and ō) in the Glossary of the present edition. Full treatment of the history of the sounds will of course be found in the Middle English grammars listed in the Bibliography, especially those of Luick and Jordan.

Consonants. Chaucer's consonants are pronounced for the most part as in Modern Enlgish. But there were no silent consonants, except h in French words like honour and g in French gn, which had the sound of single n (as in resigne, riming with medicyne). Ordinarily in the combinations gn (in native English words), kn (or cn), and wr, g, k and w were pronounced, and l was pronounced before f, k and m (as in half, folk, palmer). The sound of ng is held to have been regularly that of ng in "finger". Double g had sometimes the sound of dg (as in juggen), sometimes that of gg in "bigger" (as in frogges). The modern pronunciation is a safe guide. ch had the English sound (as in "church"), not the French ("as in "machine"). The spirant gh, which became silent in later English, had the sound of the German ch in "Ech" and "doch" (palatal after a front vowel, and guttural after a back vowel). R was trilled. S and th ought regularly to have been unvoiced (*i.e.*, with the sound of s in "sit" and th in "thin"), except when between vowels. Between vowels they were voiced (sounded as in Mod. Eng. "those"). But the distinction may not have been observed consistently, and the later voicing in many words (th in "these", "those", and s in "is", "was") may have begun in Chaucer's period. The suffix-cion (Mod. Eng. tion) had two syllables, and could rime with words in -on or in -oun. The spellings of the ending in the MSS are very inconsistent.

INFLECTIONS

The inflectional endings in Chaucer's language which differ from those in modern English can be briefly indicated for the various parts of speech. In many cases they consist simply of a final-e which in later English ceased to be pronounced.

Nouns. Many nouns have in the nominative case a final -e which is lost in modern English. It is not strictly an inflectional ending, but usually represents a final vowel in the language from which the word descends or is derived. Examples: ende, from AS. "ende"; name, from AS. "nama"; sone, from AS. "sunu"; entente, from OF. "entente." When the -e does not have a corresponding vowel in the source (as in carte, from AS. "cræy"), it is called unhistoric or inorganic. In a number of nouns Chaucer had two forms, one with the one without final –e. Such words are entered in the Glossary with an -e in parenthesis—as, for example, bliss (e).

The regular inflectional endings in the great majority of Chaucerian nouns are the same as in the Modern English—s or es in the genitive (or possessive) singular and in the plural. But there are a few exceptional forms to be noted, all of them obvious survivals of older inflections. Of course some of them, like the um-, lauting plurals, are familiar in modern English.

Gen. sg. without ending: a) in nouns of the AS. n-declension (chirche, lady, herte); b) in nouns of the AS. r-declension (fader, brother); c) in nouns with final s (Venus sone).

Dat. sg. This is normally without ending in Chaucer (in the hous, in my lyf). But in certain stereotyped phrases the old dative ending survived. Examples: on lyse, a-lyse, Mod. Eng. "alive"; on fyre, "afire"; to bedde, to shippe, with childe. Many of the phrases in which 'this so-called "petrified" dative survives are recorded in the Glossary.

Plural without ending: a) in AS. neuter nouns, and others, which had no ending in the nom. acc. pl. (yeer, but also yeres, deer, sheep, freend), b) nouns in -s (caas, pass); c) in umlauting nouns, which still form their plural by a change of vowel (men, gees, feet).

Plural in en: now rare, but common in AS. and represented by a number of cases in Chaucer (asshen, eyen or yen, hosen, fon, pesen, been). Parallel forms in -es usually also occurred.

Adjectives. The adjective, like the noun, sometimes has a final -e in the nominative case (swete, grene, drave). Such forms are recorded in the Glossary.

The English of Chaucer's period still preserved the old Germanic distinction, since lost, between the strong and the weak declensions. The latter occurs: a) when the adjective follows the article, a demonstrative or possessive pronoun, or a noun in the genitive (the yonge sonne, his halve course, Epicurus owne sone); b) when it is used with a noun in the vocative (O stronge God); c) often when it is used with proper names (faire Venus); d) perhaps in a few other cases when the adjective is used substantially, though other explanations of the ending can usually be found (the beste, where the article precedes; by weste, perhaps a dative). The ending of the weak adjectives is -e, which is also the regular ending of the strong plural. The following paradigm represents Chaucer's regular usage:

	Strong	Weak	Strong	Weak
Singular	yong	yonge	swete	swete
Plural	yonge	yonge	swete	swete

The inflectional -e, whether of the weak from or the plural, is usually not found in predicate adjectives, which are underlined. It is also rarely pronounced, though often written, in adjectives of two syllables, where it does not fall in with the rhythm of the verse (or, probably, of prose speech). In trisyllabic adjectives, however, where it makes a fourth syllable, it is often preserved. Compare the holy blissful martir with the semelieste man, O wommanliche wyf.

In addition to the regular weak and plural endings, Chaucer's adjectives show some exceptional forms. The old strong ending of the genitive signular -es is preserved in alleskinnes, "of every kind", noskinnes, "of no kind." There appear to be a very few datives in -e, survivals of the old strong dative inflection, though in most of the cases concerned other explanations of the ending as possible. Examples: of olde tyme, with harde grace, of purpos grete, in salte see, by weste—some of which may be explained as extensions of the use of the weak inflection. An old accusative ending is preserved in the combination halvendel (AS. "halfne dæl"). The AS. strong genitive plural survives in one word aller (also aller, alder, in composition), from "ealra". There are a few examples of plural adjectives with the French ending -es (places delitables, houres inequales). These occur chiefly in the works translated from the French.

The regular suffixes for the comparison of adjectives are the same as in modern English, -er and -est. In Anglo-Saxon both the comparative and the superlative took the weak inflection, and the corresponding forms are often spelled with a final e (-ere, -este) in Chaucer. But the ending is seldom pronounced in the verse except where it constitutes a second or a fourth syllable (The semelieste man). A few forms show the umlaut of the root vowel, as in Anglo-Saxon (lenger, strenger, elder, etc.), or the doubling of a final consonant (gretter, sonner). A number of adjectives are irregularly compared: good, bettre, beste; bad, badder, or werse (worse), werste (worste); muche (1), more or mo, moste (meste); lytel, lasse (lesse), leeste; etc. Such exceptional forms are registered in the Glossary.

Adverbs. The regular endings of Chaucer's adverbs are -e and ly or liche (the last two coming from the adjectival ending lich with the adverbial ending). Examples: brighte, smerte, royalliche or royally. There are a few adverbs in -es or -en, which correspond to AS. ending in -es or wan. Examples: ones, tyes, hennes aboven, abuten. With the forms in -es, properly genitives in origin, may be compared the adverbial phrase his thanks, "willingly". The exceptional form whilom appears to correspond to the AS. dat. pl. hwflum, but is probably to be explained as a late modification of Middle English whilen, into which the AS. from normally developed.

Pronouns. The pronouns are mostly like those in modern English. Exceptional forms, which might give the reader trouble, are resistered in the Glossary. The following special cases may be noted here.

In the first person, ich (Northern Ik) occurs beside I. The possessive adjectives myn and thyn take the regular -e in the plural. In the third person singular, the neuter genitive is the same as the masculine—his (not "its"). The spelling hise ("his", "its") is often found, in the manuscripts, with plural nouns, but the -e appears not to have been pronounced and has been struck off in the present text. The plural forms of the personal pronoun in the third person were: nom. they, gen. hire, dat., acc. hem, (the forms "their" and "them" not having yet come into London English). In the plural possessives oure, youre, hire, the -e seems to have been regularly unpronounced.

In the demonstrative thise (these) the final -e was almost invariably silent, and usually in the plural forms some, swiche, and whiche, when used pronominally. When used adjectivally these words are more likely to show an inflectional -e.

Verbs. Chaucer's verbs show the characteristic Germanic distinction between the weak and the strong conjugations. Strong verbs, often called irregular, make their preterite tense by the change of the root vowel (ablaut), and weak verbs, by the addition of an ending (de to te). The principal parts of the strong verbs, which for

Present tense (strong and weak alike)

Indicative		Subjective	
Singular	1. singe	Singular	singe
	2. singest	Plural	singe (n)
	3. singeth		
Plural	singe (n)		

the most part resemble those in modern English so closely as to be easily recognizable, are fully registered in the Glossary, as are also the forms of weak verbs that present any peculiarities. The inflectional endings are shown in the followings tables. Parentheses are used to indicate alternative forms. Thus n may always be dropped in the verbal ending en, the prefix y- may or may not be used with participles.

A number of verbs have contracted forms in the second and the third singular: lixt (liest), bit biddeth), fint (findeth), set (setteth), stont (stondeth), worth (wortheth). Such forms, when not easily recognizable, are recorded in the Glossary.

Preterite Indicative

Strong

Singular	1. song, sang
	2. song (e)
	3. song, sang
Plural	songe (n)

Weak

Singular	1. wende	lovede
	2. wendest	lovedest
	3. wende	lovede
Plural	wende (n)	lovede (n)

The preterite subjunctive, like the present has -e in the singular and -e (n) in plural

Imperative

Strong

Singular	2. sing
Plural	2. singeth, -e

Weak

Singular	2. loke	her
Plural	2. loketh, -e	hereth, -e

Strong verbs and long-stemmed weak verbs of the first class in Anglo-Saxon have regularly no -e in the second singular; other weak verbs have -e. But -e is often written in the manuscripts, and sometimes pronounced in the verse, in forms not historically entitled to it. Example: As sende love and pees bitwixe hem two. Such forms, which appears in longstemmed weak verbs in late Anglo-Saxon, are perhaps sometimes to be regarded as jussive subjunctives.

Infinitive. The ending is -en or -e in strong and weak verbs alike: singe (n), wene (n). In a very few verbs there is preserved an old gerundive or inflected infinitive with a dative -e: to done, to sene, to seyne.

Participles. The present active participle of all verbs, weak and strong, ends in -ing or -inge: singing (e), loving (e). The preterite passive participle of strong verbs ends in -e(n), of weak verbs, in -d or -t. Examples (y) sunge (n), (y) loved, (y-) taught. The prefix y- (from AS. ge-) is frequent with both strong and weak verbs. The preterite participle is ordinarily uninflected, but in a few cases has the adjectival plural ending in -e. Examples: Sing they ben tolde; with eres spraddle.

Preterite-present (or strong weak) verbs. These is a small class of verbs in the Germanic languages in which, an old strong preterite came to be used as a present tense, and a new weak preterite was formed to express past time. For example:

Present			Preterite		
Singular	1.	shal	Singular	1.	shodle
	2.	shalt		2.	sholdest
	3.	shal		3.	sholde
Plural		shull (en), shal	Plural		sholde (n).

The other preterite-present verbs are can (pret, kouthe, koude); dar (pret. dorste); may (pret. mighte); most (pret, moste); owe (pret. oughte), thar (pret. thurfte, but confused with dorste); and woot (pret. wiste). The peculiar forms of all these verbs are entered in the Glossary.

Anomalous verbs. The following four verbs show exceptional irregularities.

Goon, pret. yede and wente.

Doon, pret. dide.

Wil (e), wol (e), 2 sg. wilt, wolt, 3 sg. wil (e), wol (e), pl., willen, wil, wollen, wol; pret wolde. The -e of the 1 and 3 sg. present indicative, though apparently always silent, is often found in the manuscripts, and is historically justified (AS. wile, originally subjective).

Been. Pres. ind. sg. am, art, is; pl. been, be, rarely are (n). Pres. sbj. sg. be; pl. been, be. Pret. ind. sg. was, were, was; pl. were (n). Pret. sbj. sg. were; pl. were (n). Imperative sg. be; pl. beeth.

VERSIFICATION

The various verse-forms used by Chaucer are discussed in the introductions and notes to the separate works. But a few general directions may be given here for the reading of his lines.

The most important difference between Chaucer's English and modern English, for the purpose of versification, lies in the numerous final -e's and other light inflectional endings described in the preceding pages. These endings are ordinarily pronounced in the verse, and indeed are essential to the rhythm. They are also pronounced in rime, and Chaucer with almost complete consistency avoided riming words in -e with words not etymologically or grammatically entitled to that ending. But within the verse final -e is regularly elided before an initial vowel or before an h which is either silent (as in honour) of slightly pronounced (as in he, his, her, him, hem, hadde, and a few other words). Before initial consonants -e is ordinarily sounded, though there are cases or almost every page where it must have been either slurred or entirely apocopated. These statements apply, of course, only to the light, unstressed final -e, and not the long e (often spelled ee) in words like majestee or charitee.

Most of Chaucer's lines, if read naturally and with a proper regard to grammatical endings, have an obvious rhythm. But there are many cases, apart from doubful textual readings, where there is uncertainty as to elision or apocopation, or even a responable choice between two ways of rendering a line. Probably no rules can ever be laid down to settle all such questions. Certain characteristics of Chaucer's versification may, however, be borne in mind. His lines—as contrasted, for example, with those of Gower—have great freedom and variety of movement. He constantly shifts the position of the caesural pause. He often reverses the rhythm of a foot, substituting a trochaic for an iambic movement. Like most English poets, he not infrequently has an extra light syllable in a line (a trisyllabic foot in place of the regular iambus), though in such cases it is often impossible to determine whether to resort to apocopation. The extra syllable seems to have been most frequent in the caesural pause. One other irregularity, which some critics have condemned and the scribes themselves sometimes tried to correct by emendation, Chaucer certainly allowed himself. He not infrequently omitted the unaccented syllable at the beginning of a line. These headless, or ninesyllable, lines—seven-syllable in the case of the octosyllabic meter—are by no means objectionable when the initial stress falls upon an important word. When a preposition or conjunction gets this initial accent, there is perhaps more reason for the objections of the critics, but the evidence of the manuscripts makes it necessary to admit many such lines to the text.

In the following short passage from the General Prologue, which will serve as a specimen of scansion, the metrical stresses are marked with an accent ('), syllabic lighte's have a diaeresis ("), and elided or apocopated e's are underdotted. It will be understood, of course, that the metrical accents varied in strength, unimportant words receiving only a secondary stress.

A CLÉRK ther wás of Óxenfórd alsó,

That únto lógyk háddë lónge yg.

As léenë wás his hórs as ís a rákë,

And hé was nát right fát, I úndertákë,

But lóoked hólwë, and thérto sóbrely'.

Ful thrédbare wás his óvereste coúrtepy';

For hé hadde géten hym yét no bénefieë,

Ne wás so wórldly fór to háve offieë.

For hy'm was bévere háve at his béddes héed

Twénty bóokës, clád in blák or réed,

Of Áristótle and his philósophíë,

Than róbes r'iche, fíthele, or gáy sautríë.
But ál be thát he wás a phílosóphrë,
Yet háddë hé but lítel góold in eófrë;
But ál that hé my'ght of his fréendës héntë,
On bóokës ánd on lérnynge hé it spéntë,
And bísily' gán for the sóulës préyë
Of hém that yáf hym whérewith tó scoléyë.
Of stúdie tóok he móost eure and móost héedë.
Noght ó word spák he móorë thán was néedë,
And thát was séyd in fórme and réveréncë,
And shórt and quy'k and fúl of hy' senténcë;
Sównynge in móral vértu wás his spéchë,
And gládly wódle he lérne and gládly téchë,

THE TEXT

As already explained in the Preface to the present revised edition, and for the reasons there given, the following general introduction on the text has been reprinted here in substantially its original form. It sets forth the principles followed by the editor in the construction of his text, and the same principles hold for the second edition. In most of the works, too, very few textual changes have been made in revision. But in the case of the Canterbury Tales the Manly-Rieckert edition, referred to expectantly in the original Preface and in the following pages, appeared in 1940. Since it was based upon all known manuscripts, over eighty in number, the classification of authorities there given completely supersedes the tentative one in this work, which is here reprinted simply to show the basis of the editor's decision. The variants recorded in the Textual Notes are reprinted for the same reason, and for fuller information on both matters the reader should consult the Manly-Rickert edition. But a considerable number of readings have been altered in the text in the light of the new evidence in Manly's apparatus, and a list of these will be found on pages 883-885 at the beginning of the Textual Notes.

In the Textual Notes on the separate works will be found lists of the manuscripts and other authorities for the text, together with references to previous studies in their classification. Special problems, also, are discussed in the notes on the works in connection with which they arise. But here, in the introduction, may properly be given some account of the general method of the present edition.

The entire text has been made afresh by the editor. It is based upon his examination of all the published manuscript materials and photographs or collations of some of the more important unpublished sources. Account has been taken of the numerous studies that hae been made of the character and relations of the manuscripts, and it has been the editor's intention to pay due regard to critical principles. In fact the text may be called a critical edition, with one reservation. In the case of some of the more important works, including the Canterbury Tales, the manuscript materials accessible to the editor have not been exhaustive. But the best copies of all the works have been available for use as the basis of the edition, and enough others have been compared to make possible, in the editor's belief, the establishment of trustworthy texts.

The Canterbury Tales, for example, are preserved in some ninety manuscripts and early prints, complete or fragmentary. Photographs of all these copies have recently been brought together at the University of Chicago by Professor Manly and his associates, who are preparing a great critical edition. Their work, which is eagerly awaited by all Chaucerians, will shed new light on doubtful readings, and will probably make it possible for the first time to reconstruct the successive stages in the compositions of the Canterbury Tales. But it does not appear likely that a text based upon the complete collation would be materially different from one that can be constructed from the eight published manuscripts, which include the best copy, the Ellesmere MS., and are so distributed as to represent all the important groups of authorities. For the Pardoner's Prologue and Tale, of course, the editor has used the specimens published by the Chaucer Society, representing in all over fifty copies, upon which Zupitza and Koch based their classification of the authorities; and for the Clerk's Tale he has had the published specimens from eight additional manucripts. He has been further aided by the numerous citations of the readings of special passages printed in such textual studies as Professor Tatlock's paper on the Harleian Manuscript and the late Professor Brusendorff's Chaucer Tradition. In addition to all this printed material, the editor has collated the Cardigan MS., a superior copy which was not represented among the specimens printed by the Chaucer Society, and the Morgan MS., which is classified with those of less authority.

In textual method the present editor does not belong to the severest critical school. When the readings of the "critical text" or of a superior archetype appeared unsatisfactory or manifestly inferior, he has accepted help from other authorities more often than the strict constructionists might approve. He has seen no way of avoiding the exercise of personal judgment. But he has not practiced mere eclecticism, and in making his decisions he has endeavored to give constant attention to the relation of the manuscripts and to all relevant consideration of language, meter, and usage. Some of the problems that have arisen and they vary considerably in the diffeent works of Chaucer—may be briefly described.

In the Canterbury Tales, for example, as is fully set forth in the Textual Notes below, the A Type of manuscripts, represnted by Ellesmere, Hengwrt, Cambridge Dd, and Cambridge Gg—whether or not they all go back to a single archetype below the original—is generally accepted as of superior authority to the B type, which includes Harleian 7334. Corpus, Petworth, and Lansdowne. They are the basis of the present text, as of all recent editions. In the Pardoner's Tale, for which nearly all the authorities have been printed and compared, there seems to be no case where the reading of the more numerous manuscripts of type B is preferable. But elsewhere in the tales there are a few passages where the B readings seem to the editor superior to the A readings, and he has not hesitated to adopt them.

thus in the General Prologue, I, 510 (where, of course, only the eight published manuscripts and the Cardigan and Morgan copies were considered) chaunterie (B) clearly afford at better and more Chaucerian rhythm than chauntrye (A), which Professor Liddell, in his critical edition, retained in strict adherence to his archetype. Other examples of B readings acepted in the present text are ben (A leyn), PrT, VII, 676, Odenake (A Onedake). MkT, VII, 2072; out of the yerd (A into this yerd), NPT, VII, 3422; gilteless (A giltless), FrankIT, V, 1318; fayerye (A fairye), MerchT, IV 1743.

Although some editors would follow their archetype more strictly, the readings mentioned are of course entirely defensible from the point of view of critical method, since the original of the A manuscripts need not have been at all points superior to that of type B. More serious difficulties in adhering to critical procedure arise in connection with the baffling MS. Harl. 1334, the peculiar relations of which are said to have deterred Mr. Henry Bradshaw from editing the Conterbury Tales. Classified somewhat doubtfully by the textual critics among the manuscripts of type B, the Harleian copy shows evidence of contamination with the superior type A, and has many unique readings of great interest. Some editors, among them Professors Skeat and Mr. Pollard, have held it to contain Chaucerian revisions, and they have consequently felt free to draw upon any of its readings that seem intrinsically attractive. Other scholars have doubted the special authority of the manuscript, and, in the opinion of the present editor, it has been virtually disproved by Professor Tatlock in his study on the subject. Taking the more important passages where the Harleian readings are unique among the eight published manuscripts, Mr. Tatlock collated them with some thirty five other copies to discover how much support they might have, and then examined the readings themselves to determine their character and value. He showed that many which has been adopted by the editors were clearly scribal emendations, and in some cases very poor ones. The officious and entirely unnecessary substitution of cloysterlees for reccheless in the familiar passage of the General Prologue (I, 179) is typical of the procedure of this anonymous editor. Again, in KnT, I 1906. the Harleian reading And westward in the mynde and in memorye may safely be regarded as the scribe' emendation of the defective reading of most manuscripts, And on (or in) the westward in memory. Professor Tatlock in the study in which he discredited the Harleian text as a whole was inclined to accept its authority in this passage. But the reading, And on the gate westerward in memorye, which has been found in a few scattered manuscripts, is more likely to have been what Chaucer wrote, and would explain easily the corrupted forms which the line is preserved. Similarly the greater number of unique Harleian readings appear on examination to be emendtions, and many of them can be traced to the scribe's deslike of headless, or ninesyllable, lines There remain, however, a few pasages in which it is hard not to follow the Harleian text. In KnT, I, 2037, where all the printed manscripts have the obvious blunder sertres (or a varient thereof), the Harleian reads correctly sterres, which all editors adopt (except Koch, who emends to cercles). Again in Gen Prol, I 485, And swich he was ypreved afte sithes all the manuscripts except the Harleian read preved, to the decided impairment of the rhythm. In this case Professor Liddell, whose definitely announced policy was to "boycott the Harleian," adopted its reading, as he did also in KnT, I, 3104, And he hire serveth also gentilly (where all the other printed manuscripts read so). On the other hand in KnT, I, 2892, Mr Liddell read Upon thise stedes grete and white, rejecting the relief afforded by the Harleian text (that weren grete and white), though the other reading compels us to accent upon unnaturally on the first syllable and to pronounce the final -e of thise, which is usually silent. Possibly the correct reading of this line is Upon thise steedes grete and lilye whyte, which is found in MS. Cardigan. Again in KnT, I, 3071, Mr. Liddel reads I rede we make of sorwes two, with objectionable ryhthm and questionable haitus, and refuses to insert that on the sole authority of the Harleian. It is difficult for any editor to proceed consistently, and improbable that any two editors would always agree, in delaing with these readings. In the present edition they are accepted sparingly, and only when the alternative readings are so unsatisfactory, or those of the Harleian manuscript so intrinsically superior, as to justify the risk. In its wholesale correction of headless lines the editor has not followed the Harleian scribe, for there is abundant evidence that Chaucer wrote them in both his decasyllabic and his octosyllabic verse. But in lines where the rhythm is otherwise objectionable or open to question the help of the Harleian manuscript has sometimes been accepted, and special considerations have sometimes entered into the editors decision. Thu in Gen Prol, I, 752, the Harleian reading, For to have been a marchal in an halle, has been adopted in place of the shorter For to been of the other manuscripts, not simply because of the headless line, but because of the possibility that the Harleian reading preserves, or restores, the good old use of the perfect infinitive to express action contrary to fact. In the case of all doubtful readings the editor has tried to give special consideration to old grammatical forms or idioms which might have been lost or corrupted by the scribes.

The presence of correct unique readings in he Harleian copy may be explained either on the theory of emendation, or on that of contamination with some good lost manuscript, and there is other evidene that the Harleian text is derived in part from a source which belonged to type A. It is perhaps even possible that Harleian preserved some good readings which were coincidently corrupted in the A manuscripts and in the remaining manuscripts of type B. But of course the chances of this are slight.

The problem of unique readings arises sometimes with superior manuscripts, like the Elelsmere copy of the Canterbury Tales or the Cambridge Gg copy of the Parliament of Fowls. In the ease of Ellesmere the editor has had no such means of testing them as was afforded for the Harleian manuscript by Professor Tatlock's study. The Chicago collations, when published, will show just how much scattered support such readings may have. But from the evidence furnished by printed texts and the editor's collation of the Cardigan and Morgan manuscripts it does not appear that they are to be accepted without scrutiny on the bare authority off Ellesmere. That manuscript, though superior to all others, has its proportion of errors, some of which it shares with other manuscripts of the a group. It therefore cannot be regarded as an independent witness to the original text; nor do its peculiar readings look like revisions by the author. It does, however, preserve some lines, apparently genuine, and marginal glosses, very likely due to Chaucer, which are not found in any of the other published texts. These passages, at least, it seems to have derived from a good copy outside its immediate source and now unknown. There is consequently justification for considering its unique reading, and the editor has accepted them in a very few cases, especially where they preserve good old forms or idioms that might have been lost through scribal corruption. Examples of the cases where this consideraton has affected the decision are KnT, I, 1176, wistest; KnT, I, 1573, after he (rest, afterward he with variants); KnT, I, 1260, witen (rest, woot, wote, etc.); MLT, II, 336, hastifliche (rest, hastiliche, hastily). In mere matters of orthography, when verbal variants are not involved, the Ellesmere copy has been followed, as representing a good scribal tradition. But throughout all Chaucer's works, as explained below, the spellings of the manuscripts have been corrected for grammatical accuracy and for the adjustment of rimes.

The question of the authority of a superior manuscript arises again in connection with the Parliament of Fowls. The Combridge MS. Gg. 1.27, like the Ellesmere copy of the Canterbury Tales, belongs to the best group of authorities, and is commonly adopted as the basis of the text. But there are two opinions as to the value of its testimony when it stands alone or has very slight support from other manuscripts. It is not esay to decide this question. The present editor finds about twenty readings, either peculiar to Gg or having slight support in other manuscripts which clearly right or so strongly preferable to the critical text as practically to demand adoption. Some thirty-five more appear to deserve serious consideration, and a few of them have been hesitatingly adopted. Still other Gg readings would have a strong claim for adoption if the manuscript were known to be derived in any fashion from a source independent of all the rest. A few of its readings have been adopted for reasons connected with grammar or meter. Gg variant in mere phraselogy have been in nearly every case rejected, though some of them are tempting. The fact that the manuscript preserves the unique copy of the revised Prologue to the Legend of Good Women makes easier the assumption that it contains the author's corrections of the text of the Parliament. But the variants themselves do not seem to bear out this theory.

A textual problem fundamentally different from the offered by the Canterbury Tales or the Parliament is presented by the Troilus. In the Conterbury Tales, although there are numerous cases of correction, cancellation, or rearrangement, there is no thorouh-going and sysematic revision. In fact, far from having prepared a second edition, Chaucer never completed a first. But in the Troilus it is agreed that the manuscripts show either two or three distinct stages of composition. Details about the classificaton of the authorities are given below in the Textual Notes and need not be repeated here. The essential facts are that all scholars recognize a first version, a, which stands in many respects closest to the Italian original, and a second (or third) version, γ, which is preserved in the most correct and best authenticated manuscripts. A third form of the text, preserved in manuscripts not wholly distinct from those which contain a and γ, is held by Professors Root, as by his predecessor in the study of the problem, the late Sir William McCormick, to represent a separate version β, which those two scholars have conceived in different ways. More recently professor Root, who continued and completed McCormick's thorough and elaborate study of all the manuscripts, has arrived at the opinion that, β represents Chaucer's final revision—that is, the third stage of his text. While he recognizes the superiority of the best manuscripts, he holds that to arrive at Chaucer's authoritative version an editor would correct the γ text by, β readings wherever these are susceptible of sure determination. The description and classification of manuscripts by McCormick and Root the present edior has found to be thorough and trustworthy. It is, in fact, one of the most substantial achievment of Chaucerian scholarship. But even if two stages are recognized, that represented by the γ manuscripts has, in the opinion of the present editor, the best authority. The β readings have consequently not been accepted in this text, which is based consistently on the γ version. The reconstruction of γ has of course not been in itself always easy, since the γ manuscripts contain errors and omissions. Exclusive γ readings have been examined with special care because of the uncertainty whether they are due to Chaucer or a scribe. But the authority of the γ group, even when it stands alone, seems better to the present editor than it does to Mr. Root. It should be added, however, that the differences between the γ text and Mr. Root's, β version are few and unimportant.

The question of revision arises in relation to several other works of Chaucer besides the Troilus, but it nowehere else presents so serious a practical problem to the editor. In the case of several of the Canterbury Tales, it has been argued that Chaucer made over early poems for use in the collection. There is no question in editing, however, of a choice between versions. Similarly in the case of passages possibly unauthentic or canceled by the author, the editor has simply to decide whether and where to admit them to his text. In the Prologue to the Legend alone is there another instance of thorouh-going revision, resulting in parallel versions and in this case it is clear that both texts should be printed side by side, as has been done in most recent editions.

An editorial problem somewhat different from those far discussed is raised by the Book of the Duchess and, in less degree, by the House of Fame. It may be illustrated by some account of the character of the text in the former of these works. There are only four authorities—the Farfax, Bodley, and Tanner manuscripts, and Thynne's edition. Farfax and Bodley are, as usual, closely related, and in this poem they offer the best text, Thynne furnishes a number of good corrections of their readings. The critical text is easy to construct, and there are very few cases where a choice of readings is difficult. But there are many cases where the authorities agree in readings unsatisifactory in sense or in meter, and it is hard to decide how far an editor should go in mending such passages. It may be freely admitted that the manuscripts are late and none too trust-worthy. At the same time it should be remembered that some roughness of workmanship might be expected in so early a work as the book of the Duchess and in a meter of such free traditions as the English octosyllabic couplet. Headless lines were quite as natural there as in the decasyllabic verse, and extra syllables within the line are not hard to accept, though some of them may be due to scribes who supplied works to take the place of finl *-e's* they had wrongfully suppressed. Lines which lack an unaccented syllable in the middle are very unlikely to be right. For verses so constructed, with two abutting streses—a metrical type sometimes called Lydgatian because of its frequent occurence in Lydgate's poems—are almost unknown in those works of Chaucer of which good text is preserved. All these irregularities, which occur commonly in the Book of the Duchess, are easy to remove if an editor feels at liberty to emend his manuscripts at will. The present text is less freely corrected than Skeat's and for that reason less smooth in many places, as the editor is well aware. But one kind of emendation, the restoration of full grammatical forms apocopated in the manuscript to the detriment of the meter, is certainly justifiable and has been freely employed.

The editor of Chaucer, after he has settled the matter of authorities and readings and made his critical texts, still has to consider the question of grammatical rectification. For the best manuscripts contain many forms that are demonstrably incorrect—nouns and adjectives with meaningless final *-e's*, or strong preterites with the same ending incorrectly added in the singular number. These errors cannot be removed by a critical comparison of the manuscripts; they must be treated, if regulated at all, in the light of Middle English grammar. Fortunately the materials are abundant for constructing a grammar of Chaucer's dialect, and the inflections he employed are very fully and precisely known. It is therefore posible to correct with confidence most of the grammatical errors of the scribes. But the practice of editors in making such corrections has varied considerably. Skeat's general policy was to normalize both the spelling and the grammar of his texts, though he was not quite thorough or consistent in removing erroneous forms. The Globe editors differed one from another in their practice, but many incorrect endings were allowed to stand in their text. Professor Root, in his edition of the Troilus, though recognizing that numerous final *-e's* in his text did not represent a syllable, thought it most consistent with his purpose to follow the actual usage of his scribes. His method and that of the Globe edition is of course defensible, and it has its advantage, especially for an investigator of the history of English orthography. For many of the forms under discussion are not, strictly speaking, incorrect, but are rather specimens of a system of spelling divergent from the ordinary practice in Middle English. According to that system final *-e* may denote not only a pronounced final syllable but also, as in modern English, the long quantity of a preceding vowel (as in "hate," over against "hat"). This principle is doubtless to be recognized in some of the spellings of he Chaucerian scribes. In a small number of nouns and adjectives it is not certain whether Chaucer's nominative form had a final *-e'*, and in others he clearly used two forms, one with *-e'* and one without. Words of the latter sort are entered in the Glossary of this edition with a bracketed -e'(*e.g., bliss*(e), *cler*(e), and in the text the form which occurs in manuscript is usually preserved. But the editor's practice has probably not been perfectly consistent in this matter, and the final *-e'* may sometimes have been struck off when unpronounced in the verse. In the case of nouns in the dative construction it is sometimes difficult to decide whether to allow the inflectional *-e*' outside of the stereotyped or "petrified" phrases to which it is mainly restricted. Its use undoubtedly spread somewhat, even to cases other than the dative, but Chaucer's dative was usually without ending, nad the dative *e's* have been struck off in this text unless there was special reason for supposing them to have been preserved. Perhaps the influectional form that makes most trouble with regard to this matter of final *-È* is the second person singular of the imperative of strong verbs and of long-stemmed weak verbs of the first Anglo-Saxon conjugation. Strictly speaking these forms should have no ending (sing, send, heer, etc.). But they are commonly spelled with a final -e', and the ending is occasionally demanded by the rime or verse-rhythm. It can be accounted for as a subjunctive from used in a jussive sense, or as an ending which was developed in the imperative of the verbs mentioned above because of the analogy of the subjunctive and the other weak classes in the imperative. It would be defensible to keep such forms in the text when they occur in the manuscript. In this edition the practice is again not wholly consistent, but in most cases the -e's have been struck off and the correct historical forms restored. One other form, of frequent occurence, may be cited to illustrate this editorial problem. The possessive pronoune his, when used with a plural noun, frequenty takes a final -e (hise) in the best manuscripts. This is very common, almost regular, with the Ellesmere scribe. But the -e is not justified by the Anglo-Saxon form (his) and appears never, or almost never, to be pronounced in Chaucer's verse. It has been struct-off in the present edition. But since the form with -e clearly occurs in Middle English, an editor might with equal propriety allow it to stand where his manuscript has it.

In matters of spelling, apart from questions of inflection or dialect, the procedure of the editor has been conservative. The lack of any autograph manuscripts leaves us without an authoritative Chaucerian standard, and any attempt to construct such a standard (like that Professor Koch in his early edition of the Minor Poems) is sure to encounter many uncertainties. The ordinary critical method fails entirely at this point, since the scribes modified spelling rather freely in copying. A variety of practices is consequently open to the editor, ranging from the "diplomatic" reproduction of a given manuscript to the introduction of a new phonetic spelling of his own. For the purpose of teaching pronunciation and meter this last method would have its advantages, and it has been adopted with selected specimens of the verse (as, for example, with the whole Manciple's Tale in Dr. Plessow's edition). The present text, therefore, in the case of those works that are preserved in the best manuscripts, follows the spelling of the scribe where it is not absolutely or probably incorrect. Final -e's omitted in the manuscripts have not been supplied if they were elided or apocopated in the verse, but they have been restored when necessary to the meter. Grammatical errors, as already explained, and dialectal spellings, where not appropriate and presumably intentional, have been mended with care. But no effort has been made to introduce uniformity in less important matter's, such as the use of *o* and *e* or of i and y, or the doubling of long *o* and long *e*. Such slight modernization as has been adopted in printing will be explained below.

In the case of nearly all Chaucer's works it has been possible to follow this method of close adherence to the spelling of the manuscripts. Indeed such is the excellence and general agreement in these matters, of the Ellesmere copy of the *Canterbury Tales* and the Corpus and Campsall copies of the Triolus, that those manuscripts may be reasonably supposed to represent practices closely similar to Chaucer's own. But there are a few poems in which the masnucript of best verbal authority presents a dialectical or otherwise vagarious orthography. This is notably of the *Legend of Good Women*, where the Cambridge Gg manuscript is the only source of the revised text for the Prologue; and the case is similar with the parliament of Fowls and some of the short poems. Under such circumstances an editor to choose between printing a text of strange and un-Chaucerian appearance and making the spelling conform to Ellesmere and Corpus standards. The latter method seems decidedly preferable, and the orthography of the legend and of a number of the minor poems has accordingly been freely normalized.

Capitals have been used at the beginning of lines of verse. Capital F has been substituted for *ff*, which often takes the place of a majuscular sign in the manuscripts: *th* for the archaic "thorn" (*p*); and *j* for the capital *I* which sometimes represents it. The letters *u* and *v* have been adjusted to modern practice (use, virtue, love, for the manuscript spellings *vse, uertu, loue*). The apostrophe has been employed with *n*', *t*', and *th*', when the vowel of ne, to, and the (or *thee*) is elided before a following initial. Contractions, like the stroke which designates a final nasal, have been silently expanded unles there was real doubt about their meaning. In the case of words in on, oun (nacioun, condicioun, etc.) which are spelled very inconsistently and may be pronounced with the sound of either *o* or *ou*, it has been necessary to adopt an arbitrary practice. The ending is commonly abbreviated in the manuscript, sometimes with *m* (*n* with with an upper return stroke), sometimes with *n* or *u*. These signs are used inconsistently by the scribes. In the present text, when words of this class have their pronunciation determined by rime (as by such unambiguous rime-words as toun or oon), they are spelled accordingly. When two words of the *nacioun* (*nacion*) type rime with such other, *n* with the return stroke is expanded as *n*, and *n* or *u* wth the makron as *un*. When the scribes use both abbrevations in a single pair of rimewords (nacion: condiciou), as occasinally happens, both are normalized with the spelling *oun*.

In spacing (which varies greatly in the manuscripts) modern usage has been followed except Middle English appears to have had a different sense of unity. Thus upon, into therto, theron, withoute, also whose, nowher, and the participle compound with *y*-and *for* are regularly printed without spacing or hyphen. But combinations which were less clearly recognized as units (such as for sothe, but if, by cause, over al, in the sense of the German überall) are either hyphenated or separated entirely. In this second class of words consistency of practice has been hard to attain, just as in modern spelling there is considerable variation in the use of the hyphen.

To the foregoing explanation of editorial method may be added a word about the Textual Notes in the present edition. They contain accounts of the manuscripts and other authorities for the text of each work, with information about their relations, and lists of the more important variant readings. It was the editor's original plan to register much more fully than he has finally done in print. But various considerations—lack of space, the appearance of Professor Root's edition of the Troilus with full textual apparatus, and the announcement of Professor Manly's projected work on the Canterbury Tales—led him to reduce his citations to about one quarter of those originally collected. The selected list now printed is not intended to exhibit the characteristics of manuscripts or to supply adequate materials for textual investigation. Scholars having these interests in mind will naturally resort directly to the manuscripts or to complete reprints and repoductions. But it is hoped that the variants here given will be found to include such alternative readings as have any literary interest. The different versions of the Troilus have been recorded with some fulness; also rejected passages (including some that are spurious) from the Cannfferbury Tales. Some variants in phraselogy have been registered because they have a bearing on the poet's vocabulary. Finally, in a good many cases where the readings are doubtful the editor has supplied his readers with the material for testing his decisions.

❐

3

Indian Worlds in English

Factors contributing to the adoption of Indian words into, English are many and varied. First, it has been a natural' tendency with English to borrow words and this could not be checked by any official command. Many of the Indian words were adopted because they met a real need. Where English names cannot be easily found or coined to denote certain objects, actions or concepts, English readily borrowed from any of the languages in India. Thus, a good number of words like *calico, tussore, banian, pyjamas, suttee, juggernaut, bandicoot, mango, mongoose, betel, anaconda, catamaron* and many others had to be borrowed out of necessity. Again, words like *ryot* and *ryotwar* suggest more precise notions of land revenue in South India than does any of their English counterparts, cultivator, agriculturist and peasant. Besides these, many words were taken into English for the sake of picturesqueness and local colour. Another important factor is that the English are not free from pedantic show of familiarity with another language. They used some Indian words in their conversation, in their letters and in their speeches. English men of letters were not lagging behind in using Indian words in their writings. Travel-literature and adventure-narrating familiarized the English reading public with some of the Indian words. Milton himself knew some Indian words. Dryden evinced some interest in India and Indian words. Burke and Orme, in the eighteenth century, effectively used Indian words. Scott in his '*The Surgeon's Daughter*' made use of surprisingly large number or words of Indian origin. Robert Southey tried to assimilate and naturalize some Indian words into English. Of all, Kipling", Thackeray, E.M. Forster did much to familiarize the

English public with Indian words. In recent times, English writers were attracted to Indian philosophy. Chief of them are Aldous. Huxley and T. S. Eliot.

It would be interesting to note that some Indian words entered the English lexicon indirectly, long before the advent of British rule in India. These words, which entered English through Greek, Latin and French are few but full of history. They go back to 'the dim backward and abysm' of antiquity 'where Greek and Roman, traders ventured over land through Asia Minor and Persia in quest of ivory, spices and precious stones. From this ancient trade came words like *beryl, camphor, candy, ginger, mace, musk, pepper, rice, sandal, sugar, panther* and so on. Elizabethan writers like Marlowe and Shakespeare were quite familiar with these words and they used them figuratively, proverbially and sometimes as attributes.

In 1510, the Portuguese occupied Goa and from that date,-dominated the trade in the East throughout the following century. A kind of Portuguese-Indian lingua franca evolved in the Portuguese occupied areas along the sea coast. From this, a number of Indian words found their way into English, for example, *betel* from, Malayalam *vetilla* meaning simple leaf; *copra* from Malayalam *Koppara* meaning kernel of the coconut; *catamaron* from Tamil *Kattumaram* meaning binding wood, hence a raft; *curry* from Tamil *Kari* meaning sauce; *monsoon* originally from Arabic *mausim* meaning season; *palanquin* from Sanskrit Paryanka meaning bed; teak from Malayalam '*Tekka* and *verandah* from' Hindi *baranda* and so on.

In 1600, Queen Elizabeth granted a charter to the East India Company. From this historic date many words started entering the English language. They tell us the history of the 'historical and cultural relations of two races so dissimilar in their ways of life and thought as the English and the Indian. Indian words taken into English in the seventeenth century bear out the commercial nature of relations between England and India. Hundreds of words were borrowed in this century, but only a few survived; *calico, chintz, chuddar, tussore, bengal* (applied to piece-goods of different kinds) and such others. Words like *copra, .ginger, pepper, sugar, indigo* were once again borrowed, though they had already entered English by way of Latin and Greek. So they are called much-travelled words. Other words which have a bearing upon commerce are: banian (hindu trader), *coolie, bazar, godown, rupee, pice, mohur, pagoda,* guz, maund. viss. seer, tola and so on. Words like *brinjal* (From Malayalam, ultimately arom Sanskrit), *cutch, jaggery, dubash* (originally dobashi meaning .a man who knows two languages, hence an interpreter) belong to this century.

In the eighteenth century, the number of words borrowed is smaller than those of the seventeenth century. This was perhaps due to the fact the already-borrowed words were put to use in figurative and transferred senses. For example, in expressions like *Bengal-silk, mango-bird, Pagod-worship, dawk-bearers, cot-frame, cutcherry-list*, India rubber, *malabar-nut, Jaghir lands* and many other, words of Indian origin are used either attributively or combinatively. A number of derivative words came into use in this century; Indianize, *Islamism, nabobism, nabobish, nabobese* and so on. Some words were used in transferred or figurative meanings. For instance, *pagod* was used to mean a person superstitiously or extravagantly reverenced; *Indian* was also used to European who resides in India or who has returned from India; *nabob* was used to mean a person of high rank and great wealth,," specially one who has returned from India with large fortune acquired there. It was also used to mean a rich and luxury-loving-person.

While words relating to commerce are quite meagre in this century, political and military words are found in abundance. To this period belong words like, sepoy, sebundy (irregular native soldiery), telinga (a native soldier dressed and disciplined in quasi-European fashion. The term was frequently used in Bengal in the eighteenth century, because the first soldiers of that type came to Bengal from what was considered to be Telinga country *viz.* Madras), *loot, looty, pindari, dewani, subedar., naik, havildar jamedar* and so on. Further, things like *hookah, chillum, moutch, khedda* seem to have interested the Englishman of this century greatly.

In the nineteenth century there is a larger intake of Indian words. Attributive, derivative and figurative uses of already borrowed words have become more prominent. The word *cot* is used in expressions like *cot-bed, cot-arrangement; khaki* was used in expressions like *khaki-clad khaki-coloured, khaki-election;* hybrids like *gymkhana, mem-saheb, competition-wallah* are found.

The character of the words borrowed in this century is different from that of the words borrowed earlier. William Jones and Max Muller discovered new relation between Europe and India—on linguistic plane. The term *Indo-European* was first used in this century. Comparative grammar and Indology interested the Englishman of this century. Sanskrit words are freely used in philology; for example *guna, gunate* (verb) *sandhi, swarabhakti*. In striking contrast to the materialistic nature of the Indian contribution to English until now is the contribution of India to English on philosophic, religious and literary planes.

In the twentieth century, India's struggle for independence and the unique methods adopted for its achievement are indicated by such words as *Gandhism, hartal, khaddar, khilafat, Satyagraha, swadeshi, swaraj*. The First World War left its mark by contributing words like *blighty, cushy, cootie* and such others. Expressions like ack dum, *bundook, chello, chit, chitty, dekko, puggled* (from pagal) came into English through the lips of the armymen. In the Second World War, the Indian army to the general army slang, a few words like *chup* (silence; to 'keep chup'). But old borrowings are revived and given wider circulation. Among them are words ike *buckshee, charpoy, char* (cha), *dhobey* (noun and verb), *izzat, jildi, pukka, phut* (as in 'go phut'). Peculiarities of usage also are seen; an easy-going officer is said to be *cushy*; '*to get a god, chit*' means to earn the praise of the powers; *to do a jildi move* means to make a hasty retreat.

It would be of interest to note that a large number of English men of letters like Chaucer, Spenser, Shakespeare, Milton, Dryden put Indian words to effective use in their works. But none of these writers, who lived before the eighteenth century had any personal knowledge of India and Indian languages. From the eighteenth century onwards, we find writers who lived in India and had intimate knowledge of things in native surroundings. Two names stand odt most important in the—eighteenth century Robert Orme and Edmund Burke.

In the nineteenth century names like Southey, Macaulay, Thackeray, kipling, Edwin Arnold and Scott stand out as pre-eminent among those who used Indian words in their writings. Others are Lamb (banian day), Jane Austen (mohur, nobob palanquin), Thomas Moore (amrita, vina), Shelley (Hindoostan, pariah, champak), Carlyle (banyan tree, jungle, thug).

Walter Scott's *The Surgeon's Daughter* has a sprinkle of Indian words. Southey in his almost forgotten poem *The curse of Kehama* uses words like swarga, suras, asuras, amrita, devatas. Thackeray abundantly used Indian words in his novels. He bends Indian words into strange and humorous use and sometimes turns them into proper nouns. For naming some of his characters he resorts to names of Indian foodstuffs, drinks, fruits, ornaments and coins. Thus we find in his *Book of Snobs* names like Mr. Chutney, General Rice Curry, Mr. Mulligatawney, Mr. Punch, Miss Mac Toddy, Mr. Goldmore, Lady Mary Mango.

Kipling's interest in India is deeper than Thackeray's. He lived and moved among the Indians for many years. When he used Indian words, it was with a sense of ease and touch of familiarity. He breathed new life into certain words. For example Pukka was put to several uses as, Pukka job (permanent); pukka curry (hot); pukka house (stone, brick and mortar); pukka fever (malignant, dangerous); pukka poem (a real poem, not mere verse). There are several other words which, by the magic touch of Kipling's pen were roused into life.

In this way, we have surveyed briefly the story of Indian contribution to the English language. It indicates not only India's contribution to the civilization of England, but also the reaction of the English to the social, political, religious, philosophical life and thought or the Indians. It may be hoped that the friendly relations and the cultural link between England and India will be preserved to enrich the Indian element in the English language.

THE GROWTH OF VOCABULARY

The English language is the richest and has the most extensive vocabulary. Johnson's Dictionary records about 48,000 words; the Oxford Dictionary about 400,000. The enormous difference between the sizes of vocabulary of the two dictionaries is due to remarkable enlargement of English vocabulary from the days of Johnson. Language grows with knowledge and civilisation. As new ideas, new perceptions and new discoveries and inventions come up, it becomes inevitable to enlarge the vocabulary of the language.

There are chiefly two ways of increasing the wealth of words in any language. First is, as has been seen in the last chapter by borrowing words from foreign languages and naturalizing them. The English language has immense capacity to absorb foreign element into its fold. But foreign loan-words, indispensable as they are, have their limitations. The chief enrichment of the language is due to what is called the "genius of the language" to mint new words from its own resources. Several processes in this direction are at work in the English language. The scope and variety of the methods of word-building are remarkable. The modes of word formation can be classified as follows:

(a) by adding a prefix or suffix to existing words;

(b) by composition. Henry Bradley studies the growth of vocabulary broadly under three heads, deviation, root-creation and composition. Here is a more detailed classification of the modes of word-creation.

(c) by putting old words to new use without adding anything to them,

(1) Compound Word Formation. Compound word formation is a pattern of word-making in which two or more words are combined to express a new meaning or to describe an object. A variety of combinations have been tried in English. Some of the compounds are formed by prefixing one noun to another, as in *bookcase, railway, waterproof, housewife cupboard* and so on. Often the compound word expresses a meaning different from that of any of its components. No dne relates daisy with its 'components *days eye*. Nostril is a compound of nose+thyrl. Compound is a sort of brief description of things, and so we should not search for logical relation of the components with their compound word. The relation is to be inferred from the meaning, and the meaning from the context. The difference between *garden flower and flower garden* illustrates this. Similarly *home letters* are letters from home; *Home voyage* ir voyage back home, and *home* life is life at home.

There are compounds of adjective+noun, as *blackbird, hotbed* noun and adjective, as *penny-wise, purse-proud* and *grass-green*; of verb+adverb, as *break-up, knock-out, run-away;* of adverb and verb, as *overcome, inlay, understand, outlive* and. so on. One of the productive combinations is of verb and noun; the verb in this type is the imperative and noun is the object, as *pick-pocket, cut-purse, know-nothing, stop-gap, scare-crow, lack-lustre, tell-tale make-shift, scape-grace* and so on.

Sometimes, the components of a compound noun lose their original meaning. Thus, the old English *Godspel* (good tidings) has now become *Gospel*; Old English *husbonda* (house-dweller or cultivator) has become *husband*; the Poetical designation *day's eye* has now become *daisy*; *Holy day* has become *holiday* and *Christ's mass* has become *Christmas*.

There are other compounds which generally abound in poetry. They suggest images and often bear the mark of the personality of the writer. Shakespeare created compounds like "*Proud-pied April*", "*a heaven-kissing hill*", "*the world-without-end hour*". Spenser invented "*self-consuming care*", "*silver-dropping tears*", "*rosy-fingered morn.*" However, it should be mentioned that these compounds belong to the domain of poetry and have not passed into the language of the common man.

(2) By the Addition of Prefixes and Suffixes. One of the most productive methods of word-making is to create new words by adding prefixes and (or) suffixes to the root of the word. this is a very ancient and a rich source of enrichment of the language. The extensive use of this method in Old English is illustrated by the variety of expressions invented from the root word *God; god-bot* for atonement made to the church, *godcund* for divine, *godcundness* for divinity or sacred office, *godferht* for god fearing and, therefore, pious, *godgield* for idol, *godscyld* for impiety, *godspellbodung* for gospel preaching, *godspeltrahte* for gospel commentary, *godspr* for oracle, and so on. It should be noted the root and the prefixes here are of native origin. Anglo-Saxons made extensive use of this process and the words created by resorting to native resources are widely distributed through out the language.

The living prefixes and suffixes in Modern English are chiefly of three classes, native, Romanic mainly Latin and French and Greek. The native affixes were inherited from the Germanic group of languages and so are sometimes called Teutonic affixes.

Some of the much used native suffixes are—*dom,* as in *kingdom, freedom, boredom, Christendom,* "*swelldom*", as Thackeray uses it;—*ship* as in *worship, fellowship, ownership* and so on; *th* as in *length, breadth, width* and so on; Other suffixes for abstract nouns are—*ness* (*goodness, truthfulness, swiftness, bigness* but not *harness*); -ment (basement, sediment, government), -ism as in Communism, Socialism, pacifism, Nazism and the like. Quite frequently suffixes are used to make adjectives out of nouns; *-ly* as in *lordly, cowardly*; -y as in *healthy, wealthy, sticky, stuffy, sleepy; -less* as in *powerless, useless, careless*. Many of the suffixes enumerated here are of French origin and some of them are ultimately of Latin origin. The suffix—*ish* (Old English -isc) is quite fertile. At first it was added to indicate nations as in English, *Irish, Scottish, Danish* and so on. Later it was added to other nouns and adjectives as in *foolish, feverish, boyish, girlish, childish, bookish, biggish, greenish*. The suffix—er is extremely useful for formation of agent-nouns. At first it was used to make nouns out of other nouns, as in *Londoner*, *New Englander, hatter tinner*. Later it became the usual form to denote the agent noun formed from verbs; *hunter, doer, goer, maker, lover*. In recent times the suffix is used to indicate things and instruments, as in *slipper, rubber, typewriter, sleeper*.

Some of the most extensively used prefixes are ambi-, ante—, pre—, post—, con—, per—, inter,— extra—, super—, etc. The native prefix which is still in use is for—as in *forbid, forget, forgive, forlorn*. It is amazing to see words getting multiplied with the help of prefixes. Thus, the simple Latin root *vert* (to turn) has given, with the help of prefixes, *convert, pervent introvert, extrovert, retrovert, controvert, invert, subvert, divert, revert* etc. Similar is the fertility of the prefix *inter*—in modern times; *inter-collegiate, intercaste, interracial, interreligious, international, interplanetary*. F.T. Wood remarks, "the prevalence of the prefix inter—indicates a tendency to overleap, intellectually, narrowing boundaries and look towards wider horizons."

(3) Shortening and Abbreviation. Man seek comfort and ease in matters of oral communication too. In his search for ease he clips and shortens certain polysyllabic words or long phrases: The shortening promotes quicker utterance and relieves the speaker from the burden of speaking cumbersome phrases or words. Thus, *examination* is shortened into exam, *laboratory* into lab, *mathematics* into maths, *photograph* into photo, *bicycle* is conveniently called bike, tricycle is shortened into *trike*. Cumbersome *Parambulator* is shortened into *Param* and in rapid speech is syncopated into *Pram*.

Such abbreviations take place first in spoken English and pass into private documents like letters and in the third stage the abbreviated forms may become a part of the current vocabulary. It cannot be predicted whether a given abbreviated form attains literary status, if so, at what stage. But it is likely that many of such forms elevate themselves to higher status. The eighteenth century purists frowned upon words like *cab, mob,* which are shortened forms of *cabriolet* and *mobile vulgus* (fickle crowd). They regarded them as low class words and sure, they would have objected to words like bus from *omnibus, taxi* from *taximeter-cabriolet.* Many of the abbreviated forms have attained respectability, at least, at colloquial level.

Another variety of abbreviations is that by which a long and cumbersome Latin phras is reduced to one or two prominent words in the phrase. The words like *Quorum, Affidavit, veto* are the opening words instructions, oathtaking ceremonies in courts of law. Veto meaning 'I forbid' opens the Latin formula by which a monarch forbids an act of one of his ministers or his legislative body. *Status* quo is all what is left from the original *Statusque Ante bellum* (the state existing before war).

The third variety of abbreviation is that by which a long and frequent phrase is represented by the initial letters of each word in the phrase. In course of time the initials become more commonly used, both in spoken and written forms of language, than the actual full-length phrase. Thus we speak of B.A., M.A., M.P., M.LA., C.I.D., T.B., D.D.T., W.H.O., B.B.C., A.R.P., A.I.R., U.N.O. and so on. In all these cases the initials have remained so, distinguished by a pause in spoken form and a full stop in written form. But, there are some interesting instances, where the initials are combined to form a word and the word thus. formed is in wider use than the phrase that is represented by initials. The most recent examples of this type are Unesco, Unicef Nefa, Radar etc. How many of us Can recollect the phrases that these words stand for? In the Second World War a pipe-line was opened under the English channel to supply oil to the armies in France and the pipe-line was called by the initials P.L.U.T.O. (Pipe Line Under The Ocean). The initials are combined to form Pluto which reminds us of the god of the underworld.

(4) Old Words Put to New Use. This is one of the methods extensively used in the English language. Often, words with certain meanings are used in such a way that they give new meanings, not altogether unrelated to older ones. Almost all the words with more than one meaning come under this process. How a word can be made to extend its semantic sphere is illustrated by a word like *board*. This word stands for *(a)* plank of wood, *(b)* a table made of planks of wood, *(c)* food served on the table, *(d)* officials who sit around the table as in Board of Studies, *(e)* any plain surface whether made of wood or not, as in *notice-board black-board*. The word *pedant* in Shakespeare's time meant a school-master (a harm-less profession). But now its sphere is narrowed down by limiting its application. To day, a pedant is one who shows off his learning. Literary in Johnson's day was something related to 'alphabet' but now its meaning is changed to 'anything pertaining to literature'.

Closely related to the change of meaning is the change of the function of words. This is another variety of the process under discussion. Certainly, the noun *park* does not mean the same thing as the verb *to park* and similar is the difference between *pocket* and *to pocket*; between the *elbow* and *to elbow*, the *lip* and *to lip*; between a *wire* and *to wire*. In all these cases the change of meaning is accompanied by a change in the function of the words. Nouns are made verbs or verbs nouns only by putting old words to new use. The oscillation between nouns and verbs is more clearly seen in the following examples. *Brush* is at first a noun indicating an instrument and then' it is used as a verb *to brush* and again as a noun indicating the action of the instrument as in "your coat needs a *brush*". Similar are the fortunes of *smoke* which is first a noun (the smoke from the house), then a verb as in he is *smoking a pipe* and again another type of noun as in *let us have a smoke*. Wire is first a piece of metal and as a verb it means to telegraph and again as another noun it means a telegram. Words like *gossip, dart, faint* etc. belong to the same class. Obviously, this is one of the sources of enrichment of the English language.

(5) Words From Proper Names. It is entertaining to see how some words in the English language owe their origin to the names of some persons. Characters in fiction, like. Pickwick, Mrs. Malaprop Mrs. Gamp and Don Quixote are remembered in those words. Words from proper names are of every conceivable kind and the most of them fill a gap in the language. The adjective *maudlin* meaning tearful and sentimental comes from Magadelen, the surname of Mary of Magadelen, one of the disciples of Christ. She was, somehow, identified with the "woman who was a sinner" in Luke and so the word came to mean "penitent." *Tawdry* is from Saint Audrey. At Saint Audrey's fair cheap and coarse variety of lace was sold and hence the meaning of the word. The word mammet for a 'doll' had its origin in Mahomet in the Middle Ages, it was believed that Mohammedans worshipped Idols. So the name of the prophet became a synonym for idol or image and finally a doll. There is an interesting story behind the word *Franken Stein*. In Mrs. Shelley's novel, Franken Stein is the name of a physiologist who makes an artificial human being and endows with life. The creator of this monster is haunted by his creature and finally causes his death. From the name of the scientist the ,word is transferred to his creature and is used in modern times for any invention over which man has no control.

The word Guy is named after the notorious Guy Fawkes of gunpowder fame. On an anniversary of the Gun-powder plot a queerly dressed effigy of Guy Fawkes was carried in procession and so the word was first used to describe any strangely dressed man.

Justice Lynch of the United States, round about 1780, dispensed justice in an arbitrary fashion, without giving opportunity to the accused to explain themselves. His tyrannical practices gained notoriety and so today any summary treatment is called a Lynch law.

The history of the verb to *boycott* is better known. Round about 1880, Captain Boycott was an agent for the Irish estates of a certain English Lord. He gained notoriety for his tyrannical treatment of his tenants. The tenants finally organised a sort of strike against him, and got him removed by a kind of passive persecution which is known as *boycott*. Captain Boycott was the man to be boycotted.

Similarly words like *bedlam, bowedlerize, Sadism, Panicky,* etc., had their origins in proper names of either places or persons. A very recent word of this type is *Quisling* used to describe a traitor who betrays his country into the hands of the enemy. A Norwegian Nazi Captain Quisling helped the Germans in their invasion of Norway in 1940. Hence the meaning of the word—a person who treacherously intrigues against his motherland.

(6) Folk Etymology. This is about the common man's contribution to the English language. It is wrong to think that it is always the learned man that enriches the language. The man in the street has immense capacities to misunderstand foreign words or strange and unfamiliar native words. The result of such misunderstanding is corruption of the word into a new form. This process of misunderstanding followed by corruption is called folk-etymology. In its simplest' form folk-etymology operates by associating together words which have identical sounds and by showing often a fancied relation in the meaning of such words. Thus the word *asparagus* borrowed from Latin was transformed into *sparrowgrass* by an unconscious attempt to *associate* it with a compound of identical sounds. The word shamefaced was formerly *shamefast* which means *modest*. But the last syllable is associated with the pronunciation of *faced* and so a new word came into existence which now means not so much 'modest' as 'bashful and disconcerted'. *Cassimere* is simply the name of the Indian State *Kashmir*. The corrupted and transformed word now stands for a particular variety of fabric. Similar is the fate of the word *Calico* which was originally the name of a town in Southern India, *Calicut*. Now the word means a certain variety of coarse cloth. *Standard* was of French origin with the meaning "that which is *spread out*". In English it was associated with *stand* and it means "that which stands firm" or "is fixed". The parting form of salutation "*Goodbye*" is what remains of the original "God be with ye". *Jeopardy*, likewise is corruption of the French "Jeu Parte" which means an evenly matched game. Since such a game is fraught with risk and uncertainty, by modification, it has come to mean the risk. The word "helpmate" had its origin in misunderstanding.

(7) Telescoping. 'Param' was the real short form of Param-bulator. But in rapid speech there is a tendency to elide some vowels. In this case the first vowel *a* is elided and the consonants on either side are brought immediately close to each other. Some linguists call it syncopation. Other examples of this process are once < ones; else < eles; hence < henes; born < boren; shorn < sheren; forlorn < forloren. But the process is not productive, that is, it has not created new words to add to the vocabulary. On the other hand, it changes the form of old words into new spelling and pronunciation.

Sometimes two words are run together into one, as a result of the last, a syllable. This is also called telescoping. For example, the verbs to *do on, do off, do out,* lost one syllable each by the elision of *O* which perhaps looked cumbersome in rapid speech. So the new verbs are created as to *don, to doff, to dout*. The verbs *atone*, too, can be explained by this process; at+one atone;' but here no loss of vowel is involved.

(8) Portmanteau Words. This is a process in which a part of one word is added to a part of another word, to form a new word, which often gives the meaning of both the words merged together. An example will make it clear. Lewis Carroll combines a part of the word *gallop* with part of the word *triumph* to make *gallumph*, carrying the meaning of both the words. Thus, *tragedy* plus *comedy* came to be known as Tragicomedy; *melody* plus *drama* melodrama. The word *lunch* is said to have its origin in the combination of *lump* and *hunch*. *Lunch* is further subjected to this process with breakfast giving rise to *brunch* (meaning you are too late for breakfast and too early for lunch). Here are some more examples of portmanteau formation.

smoke and fog > smog

California and Texas > Caltex

Radio and gramophone > Radiogram

Electricity and Execution > Electrocution

Communist international > comintern

Europe and Asia > Eurasia.

(9) Metanalysis. This is closely related to telescoping and again, this is caused by careless pronunciation of phrases in rapid speech. When we don't care to pronounce distinctly the phrase at *home,* sounds *atome,* and *science and arts sound science en darts.* However, these new forms have not come into standard English. But certain words which have long been in use in Standard English owe their existence to this process. Thus, a nickname was originally *an ick name* meaning an additional name. In "*eke out one's earnings*" the old meaning is preserved. In slovenly pronunciation, the tendency is to add the last sound of the first word, to the first sound of the next word, or the *vice versa.* Thus *an ick name* came to be pronounced and then written a *nickname*, which is perfectly good English now. Here are some more examples of the operation of metanalysis.

a non paire (supreme) > an umpire

a naddir > an adder

a napron > an apron

a norange > an orange

(10) Back Formation. This is a kind of misunderstanding of words. Certain words in English have a false appearance of ending with well known suffixes. By removing the supposed suffixes, new words are formed and this is known as Back-formation. Some actual examples will make the process clearer. Thus, some of the nouns like the *beggar, pedlar, hawker, editor* give a false impression that the last syllable is an agent-noun suffix. Misled by last syllable, their verbal forms are made, to *beg*, to *peddle*, to *hawk*, to *edit*. Most agent-nouns are formed from their corresponding verbs, by the addition of -er or -or. But here the verbs are formed from the nouns. By a similar process, verbs like *darkle, grovel, sidle,* came into use from *darkling, grovelling, sidling*. In this case, the last syllable is taken for the present participle ending—ing. From the word *husht* which was originally an exclamation, the verb *hush* was formed. The old singular like *pease, chevise, skates* were mistaken for plurals, and so new singulars are formed, *pea, cherry* and *skate*. Often the ending—y is removed from words like *greedy, gloomy* to make abstract nouns *greed* and *gloom*. The process is extended to words like *cosy* and *lazy* and their verb-forms *cose* and *laze* are used by Kingsley. Following are some more examples of back-formation—

To televise < television; to peeve < peevish;

To audit < auditor; to donate < donation

to henpeck < henpecked

to sunburn < sunburnt.

(11) Imitation or Onomatopoeia. This process is called echoing words. This is a process by which a word is created, imitating in its sound the thing which it is intended to describe. A number of words, especially those which describe the kind of sound are imitative in character. Words like *bang, click, whizz, rumble, rattle, hiss* can be taken as representatives of this process. But it should be borne in mind, that this imitation of natural sound by human speech can never be perfect, nor can it be uniform in all languages. But it can be said that by various combinations of vowels and consonants, words carry certain associations or suggestions. For instance, long vowels suggest a slower movement than the shorter ones; *dong* carries deeper sound than *ding*. Words beginning with *qu* suggest shaking or trembling movement as in *quiver, quaver, quagmire, quacker;* words beginning with *ft* suggest a kind of inflation as the checks are made to inflate; *blow, blast, bloated, bladder, blubber,* and so on. Words with *fl* in initial position suggest sense of hurry as in *fly, flee, flash, flicker, fling. Sev* combinations suggest a sort of loud hysteric cry or scream, *screach, screak* and so on. A large number of words suggesting stability begin with *st* combination: *stop, stay, station, stable, stand, still, stage, statue.* As L. P. Smith observes, "This suggestive power is due partly to direct imitation of natural sounds, but more to the sounds of the vocal organs, and their analogy with the movements we wish to describe; an explosive sound describes an explosive movement, as in *blast* or *blow*, while a sound suddenly stopped suggests the stopped movement, and a prolonged sound a movement that is prolonged also."

(12) Deliberate Coinages. As civilization grows, the vocabulary too has to grow. As new things are discovered or invented new words are minted. Often new words are created as if from nowhere. Frequently we also find new words replacing the old and unsatisfactory words. Thus, the earliest name *Velocipede* has been replaced by the *bicycle*. The earliest *flying-machine* has been replaced by the present *aero-plane*, and likewise, *aviator* was replaced by *airman*. For most of the scientific terms, classical languages have proved a fertile source for the word-coiner. Scientists are happily not linguists and their words are made for convenience and expressiveness arid not for euphony. They have never shown any aversion to any kind of formation. Hybrids like *automobile, television* and *dictaphone* are readily accepted in the world of science. But in most cases, classical language supplied names for modern inventions; from Greek we have *oxygen, hydrogen, logic, biology, geology, psychology, geography, telephone, telegram, telegraph, photograph, astrology* and so on. From Latin we have *radiator, propellor, extempore* and so on.

❒

4

Language Change

The spelling of English, even in printed books was not finally standardized until the eighteenth century. With such freedom from restraint, especially before the eighteenth century, we must expect the history of spoken English to give evidence of drastic change; but the changes which took place were not all of the same kind.

(1) The most important kind of change tends to affect the realization of a phoneme in all its occurrences. Such changes, not usually being set in motion by any immediate, outside influence, are in this sense independent; they are often known as isolative internal changes. Thus, the ME realization of the phoneme in a word such as house had the sound [u:], which has generally become [aʊ] in modern English; similarly, the ME vowel phoneme having a value of the [a:] type, as in a word such as name, is in most cases realized as a kind of [eɪ] in PressE. Changes of this type apply particularly to the English vowel system, which underwent a remarkable evolution of values, known as the *Great Vowel Shift*, during the centuries preceding the modern period.

(2) Another kind of change which affects the realization of a phoneme is that which is brought about by the occurrence of phonemes in particualr contexts—a dependent change, often called *internal combinative*. Thus, the phonome in mice, having now the sound [aɪ], results from an earlier [i:] by means of an isolative change; but this [i:] sound in

[mi:s] arose as a result of a combinative process of vowel harmony, or i-mutation, through the stages [mu:si], [my:si], >[mi:s] where the change [u:] > [y:] can be explained by the fronting of [u:] under the influence of the [i:] of the following syllable. Such a combinative change belongs to OE, but a more recent change of this type is exemplifed by words such as swan. This word was probably pronounced [swan] in about 1600, but the [w] sound has rounded and retracted the vowel to give the modern form [swɐn]. The large majority of earlier [w] + [a] sequences have now given [w] + [ɐ], or [ɔ:], by reason of this combinative change affecting this particular sound sequence, *e.g.* want, quality, war, water, etc.

(3) Some changes are neither independent nor dependent upon the phonetic context; they may be said to be external to the main line of evolution. Thus, it was fashionable in Elizbethan times to pronounce such words as servant and heard with [ær] or [ar], perhaps originally a dialect form, rather than with [ɛr], the regular form of development; these words, with some exceptions such as clerk have reverted to the normal development of ME [ɛr],—[a:] rather than [a:]. It was also fashionable to pronounce the termination -ing as [ɪn], only now retained as a special form of affectation or of vulgar speech. Such changes, involving a change of distribution of phonemes among word and morpheme classes, do not affect the phonemic system of the language. The introduction of foreign words may, however, at least temporarily and in the speech of a restricted number of individuals, disturb the number of phonemes or their distribution as regards position in the word.

(4) In addition to changes of quality, there have also to be taken into account changes involving quantity and accentual pattern (stress). Thus, the vowel in such words as path, half, pass, still short three hundred years ago, is now long in the South of England. Or again, the vowels in good,

book and breath, death, once long, are now relatively short. Changes of accent are particularly striking in the case of words which have come into the language from French.

RATE AND ROUTE OF VOWEL CHANGE

The English vowels have been subject to more striking changes than have the consonants. This is not surprising, for a consonantal articulation usually involves an approximation of organs which can be felt; such an articulation tends to be more stable in that it is more easily identified and transmitted more exactly from one generation to another. Changes in the consonantal system comparatively rarely involve a modification of sound. Far more common is the type of distributional change involving the conferment of phonemic status on an existing sound (*e.g.* [v, ð, z], allophones of /f, θ, s/ in OE, later obtain contrastive, phonemic, significance), or the disappearance of an allophone (*e.g.* postvocalic [x] and [ç] in such words as brought and right were largely lost in the South of England by the seventeenth century) or the insertion of an existing phoneme in a particular class of words (*e.g.* the initial /h/ in words of French origin such as herb, homage). Whether it is a question of consonantal change, loss, or addition, it is usually possible to explain the type of modification which has taken place and the approximate period during which it occurred.

A modification of vowel quality will, however, result from very slight changes of tongue or lip position and there may be a series of imperceptible gradations before an appreciable quality change in evident (or is capable of being expressed by means of the Latin vowel letters). It is particularly difficult to assess rate and phonetic route of change in the case of those internal independent vowel changes which affect the realization of a phoneme throughout the language. It is known, for instance, that the modern homophones meet and meat had in ME different vowel forms, approximately of the value [e:] and [ɛ:]. The [e:] vowel of meet became [i:] by about 1500 and it might be postulated that by a process of gradual change the [ɛ:] of meat first closed to [e:] and then, by the eighteenth century, coalesced with the [i:] in meet. The available evidence, however, suggests that the change [ɛ: > i:] may not have been either simple or gradual, but that two pronunciations existed side by side for a long period (the conservative [ɛ:] beside another form [i:] which had resulted from an early coalescence with the meet vowel) and that it is the [i:] form which has in most cases survived. In other vowel changes, it may be agreed that the change was gradual, but it is difficult to date precisely the stages of development. thus, the modern /aɪ/ of time results from a ME [i:] value; it is clear that the change has been one of progressive, widening, diphthongization, but there may have been a period of incipient diphtongization when there was hesitation between the pure vowel [i:] and some such diphthong as [ɪi] or [əi]. It is well to remember, therefore, that at any particular time in history there are likely to be a number of different, coexistent, realizations of vowel phonemes, not only as between regions but also between generations and social groups. An example of such variety in modern English is provided by the diphthong in the word home, which in the South of England may be rendered as [əu] by yonger generation and something more like [ou] by the older people. The speech of any community may, therefore, be said to reflect the pronunciation of the previous century and to anticipate that of the next.

SOUND CHANGE AND THE LINGUISTIC SYSTEM

It is convenient to study sound change in terms of the development of particular phonemes or sounds, but it is misleading to ignore the relationship of the sound units to the system within which they function and which may, in fact, not be changing. In other words, although there may be considerable qualitative changes, the number and pattern of the terms within the system may show relative stability. The ME /i:/ phoneme, for instance, is now realized as [aɪ], but there is still a phonemic opposition which contrasts such words as time, team, tame, term, tomb, etc., and, in any case, a new phoneme /i:/ has emerged in words of the team type. On the other hand, the system may change because a sound, without itself changing, may receive a new, phonemic, value, *e.g.* the sound [ŋ] has always existed in English as a realization of /n/ followed by the velars /k/ or /g/, but when the final /g/ in a word like sing was no longer pronounced, /ŋ/ contrasted significantly with /n/ and /m/.

Since the system of our language consists of a framework of significant oppositions by means of which we communicate, it may be assumed that there is a tendency for the system to remain stable, the loss of an opposition involving a possibility of confusion. In fact, of course, the redundancy of English is such that some degree of neutralization of phonemes is easily tolerated: thus, to-day, few speakers in the South of England distinguish saw and sore by means of an opposition /ɔ:/ - /əɔ/, yet the loss of the /əɔ/ diphthong is no impediment to communication. An example of an earlier coalescence of vowel phonemes in that illustrated by the homophony of meet and meat. On the other hand, new oppositions may emerge in the language, *e.g.* the phonemes /v, ð, z, ŋ/, as we have seen. Nevertheless, despite the adjustments in the number of phonemes which have taken place, the history of the English sound system display, over the last 1,000 years, a considerable degree of stability.

Though the relationships within the system may tend to remain stable, a change of phonetic realization of any phoneme is likely to have qualitative repercussions throughout the system. Such a disturbance may be observed in modern English. The phonetic relationship of the vowel phonemes in set and sat, in one type of pronunciation, is of a front vowel between half-close and half-open to a front vowel between half-open and open. If, however, the vowel of sat has a closer articulation than that described, that of set must be raised, too. Alternatively, if the vowel phoneme of sat is realized as a front open vowel, as in many English regional dialects, the vocalic area in which the phoneme of set can be realized becomes more extensive; in fact, in those kinds of English where this occurs, the vowel in set tends to be a half-open variety. Such considerations of the phonetic relationship of ponemes have a relevance in the historical, diachronic, study of English.

Although, therefore, it is often convenient in diachronic studies to investigate the development of individual phonemes in terms of the quality of their realization, it is clear that many sound changes can be explained only by reference to a readjustment of the phonetic relationships of the phonemes of the system as a whole, Moreover, any particualr point in the development of a language's sound system is not simply to be considered as a stage in the process of change of a number of sound units but rather as the presentation of the functioning of a system at a certain historical moment. The primary significance of the sounds of modern English is their function in the system of to-day; in the same way, the English sound of 1600 are to be viewed in terms not only of their past and future forms but also of their contemporary, synchronic, relationships and functions.

Some sound changes are, indeed, the result of an influence which applies to the system as a whole. A prosodic, or supra-segmental, feature such as the stress-accent provides an example of this kind. English has always possessed a strong stress-accent, certain syllables of a word or utterance being made more prominent than their neighbours because of, amongst other things, the greater force with which they are said. Those drastic changes of vowel quality known as the Great Vowel Shift mainly affect vowels in accented syllables. But vowels in most unaccented syllables (especially those in word final positions) have undergone, in the last thousand years, an equally striking, though different, type of change. Henry Sweet has called OE the period of full endings, stanas being realized as ['sta:nas]; ME, the period of levelled endings, when stones was pronounced ['stɔ:nəs]; and eModE and later English, the period of lost endings, when stones is [sto:nz]; [stəunz]. There is, therefore, a general tendency for all unaccented vowels to shorten (if long) and to gravitate towards the weak centralized vowels [ɪ] or [ə], or sometimes [u], if not to disappear altogether. This fact accounts for the high frequency of occurrence of [ɪ] and [ə] in PresE and for the complete elision of many vowels in unaccented syllables in rapid colloquial speech, *e.g.* suppose [s'pəuz], probably ['prɐbblɪ].

Our conclusions will, therefore, be based on information mostly of an indirect kind; yet such is the agreement generally amongst the various types of evidence that the broad lines of sound change can be conjectured with reasonable certainty:

(1) **Theoretical Paths of Development.** If in dealing with the changing realization of a particular phoneme we can be reasonably sure of its sound value at two points in hisotry, we can, from our knowledge of phonetic possibilities and probabilites, infer theoretically the intervening stages of development. We can, of course, be sure of the pronunciation of PresE. If, then, the evidence suggested unequivocally that, of instance, the vowel in home was pronounced as [a:] in OE, the development to be described and accounted for would be [a:] > [aʊ]. It is likely that the articulation has always involved the back, rather than the front, of the tongue; the change has clearly meant a closing of the tongue position, to which at some stage there has been added a gliding (diphthonga) movement. We might, therefore, postulate such developments as [a: > aʊ > ɔʊ > oʊ > əʊ] or [a: >ɔ: > o: > oʊ > əʊ]. The available evidence will then confirm or refute the hypothesis—in this case the second solution being more in keeping with the information. Such recognition of phonetic probabilities will always be implicit in the tracing of change. It must be considered unlikely they [a:] on its way to [oʊ] or [əʊ] would have passed through a stage of front articulation, without any combinative influence.

(2) **Old English.** It is most important in an investigation of the development of English sounds over the last thousand years that the pronunciation of OE should be established with some certainty. If this can be done, we shall have a 'starting point' for the phonetic route of change to PresE. The term old English, however, spans a period of some four hundred years from about A.D. 700 to A.D. 1100. Morevoer, the invasion of the Angles, Saxons, and Jutes in the fifth and sixth centuries introduced four separate varieties of English: the Angles, in the Midlands, north-east England,

and the south of Scotland, using types of English known as Mercian and Northumbrian (or, in general terms, Anglian); the Saxons, in the south and south-west, using the West-Saxon dialect; and the Jutes, settling mainly in the region of Kent and using a dialect called Kentish. Of the four dialects, West-Saxon, which was to become a kind of standard language, is the one about which most is known from the extant texts. In its later form—that in use between about A.D. 900 and A.D. 1100—it is referred to as Classical OE.

The broad lines of the pronunciation of this language can be conjectured from a comparison of the development of the other members of the West Germanic group of languages to which it is related. But by far the most explicit evidence concerning its sounds is to be inferred from the alphabet in which it is written. The earlier Runic spelling was replaced by a form of the Latin alphabet. This alphabet was probably introduced into the country in the seventh century by Irish missionaries. It can be assumed, therefore, that the sounds of OE were represented as far as possible by the Latin letters with their Latin values, with some modifications of an Irish kind. A great deal is known about the pronunciation of Vulgar Latin, whose sound system had much in common with that of modern Italian. If an Italian, knowing no English, were to-day asked to write down with his own spelling the PresE pronunciation of the world milk, [mɪlk], he would have no difficulty in representing the first sound, which he could spell as m; the vowel [ɪ] might, however, seem to him to resemble the sound he would write in Italian as e rather than as i; and 'dark' [l] would appear to have a back vowel glide accompanying it, requiring a spelling such as ol; and, since he has no k letter, he would spell the final [k] as c. His transcription of the word might, therefore, be meolc, which is, in fact, a West-Saxon spelling of the word now written milk. This is a fortuitous example and must not be taken to suggest that OE was pronounced in the same way as PresE. But it does demonstrate the OE spellings, which may appear to be very different, are often less surprising when we keep in mind the Latin values originally attached to the letters.

Sometimes the simple forms of the Latin alphabet were evidently inadequate for representing the English sound; thus, the joined form æ was used to symbolize a sound between C[a] and C[ɛ]; the sounds [θ] and [ð] were writing in the earlier manuscripts as th initially and d medially and finally in a word, and later as ð or the rune þ, regardless of the sound's position in the word or its voiced or voiceless quality; the rune p frequently replaced the earlier u or uu. The vowel values of the OE system were particualrly difficult to represent with the five Latin vowel letters. Sometimes the spelling used will hesitate between two letters: thus, the vowel of mann, probably of a C[a] or [ɐ] quality, is written either with a or o, indicating a vowel between the open central unrounded value of the Lain letter a and the back half-open to half-close rounded value of o. Unaccented vowels, too, already beginning to be obscured and levelled, presented a problem to the scribes, the Latin alphabet offering no way of showing a central vowel of the [ə] type. Unaccented æ, e and i soon begin to the written as e and unaccented a, u, o later tend to be used indifferently, indicating that the vowel distinction was being lost. A diphthong such as the one written as ea must probably be interpreted as a glide to a central [ə] quality.

Quantity is often shown in the case of vowels by doubling the letter or by the use of an accent and in the case of consonants by doubling the letter. The stress-accent in a word is also sometimes shown by the use of a mark; but, in any case, it is agreed, from a comparison of the West Germanic languages, that the word accent in OE fell generally on the first syllable of words, with the exception of certain compounds.

The written form of OE provides us, therefore, with considerable information concerning the language's pronunciation; we have a working hypothesis from which to begin our investigations. The study of later forms of English will often, in fact, confirm that the OE pronunciation postulated from the spelling and the comparison of Germanic languages in the only one from which later forms can be expected to have developed.

(3) **Middle English.** Spelling forms can also help us to deduce the pronunciation of the ME period, roughly A.D. 1100-1450. Generally speaking, it may be said that the letters still had their Latin values and that those letters which were written were meant to be sounded. Thus, the initial k is a word such as knokke was still pronounced and the vowel in time would have an [i] quality. This persistence of Latin values in spelling was no doubt due to the influence of the Church, which was still the centre of teaching and writing, and the absence of a thoroughly standardized spelling accounts for its predominatly phonetic character. However, English spelling was modified by French influences. Notably, the French ch spelling was introduced to represent the [tʃ] sound in a word such as chin (formerly spelt cinn), where the new spelling form indicates no change of pronunciation; in addition ou, or ow, represents the sound [u], formerly written u, *e.g.* hous, in OE hus. The simple u spelling was retained to express both the French sound [y] in words like duke and fortune and the OE short [u] sound, though this latter sound is often written as o, especially when juxtaposed to letters of the w, m, n type, *e.g.* wonne rather than wunne, to avoid confusion between the letter shapes.

Rhymes, too, have their value, especially as, in this period, they are likely to have been satisfactory to the ear as well as to the eye—in the whole of Chaucer's work, for instance, there are very few rhymes which appear to involve the pairing of different vowel sounds. Nevertheless, evidence from rhymes is valueless unless it is possible to be certain, from other sources of evidence, of the pronunciation of one member of the pair. Thus, the Chaucerian rhyme par cas: : was, because we can be sure that the French word cas had a vowel of the [a] quality, is evidence to confirm the view that the [w] of was had not yet retracted and rounded the vowel to [ɐ] and, the final s in the two words being still likely to represent [s], that the word was probably pronounced [was].

Again, words imported from French can give us information concerning the timing of sound changes. Thus, French words such as age and couch, which we know from French sources had [a:] and [u:] at the time of their introduction into English, fell in with the English vowel development [a:] > [eɪ] and [u:] > [aʊ] in words like name and house; we can conclude, therefore, that at the time the French words came into the language the [a:] and [u:] vowels had not begun their change.

Moreover after the ME period, as we shall see, a great deal of direct evidence is available to us, so that our conjectures from about 1500 onwards can be made with considerable certainty. We my often, therefore, be able to deduce from our knowledge of pronunciation in the sixteenth century the stage probably reached in the ME period in the development of a sound from OE. The OE [i:] sound in time, for example, was beginning to be diphthongized generally very early in the sixteenth century. It is reasonable to suppose (even if other evidence to support the theory did not exist) that time still had a relatively pure [i:] for much of the ME period.

Finally, the metre of verse reveals the stress accent of words. It is for this reason that we know that French words, in Chaucer's verse, generally retained their original accentual pattern, *e.g.* courage [ku'ra:dʒə], and that the accent shift in these cases is a phenomenon of at least late ME.

(4) **Early Modern English.** The same sources of evidence which we have already considered remain available for the eModE period, roughly A.D. 1450-1600. The introduction of printing brought standardization of spelling and already the spoken and written forms of the language were beginning to diverge. But individuals, especially in their private correspondence, often used spellings of a largely phonetic kind, in the same unsophisticated and logical way that children still do. If a modern child writes He must have gone as He must of gone, he is only representing the phonetic identity of the weak forms of have and of ([əv]), an identity which he will learn to ignore when he adopts the conventional spelling distinction. In the same way, if fifteenth- and sixteenth-century spellings show the word sweet occasionally written as swit, it may be assumed that this original ME [e:] was by now so close that it could be represented by i with its Latin value. Or again, the spelling form sarvant instead of servant reflects an open type of vowel in the first syllable which was current throughout the eModE period in such words. Moreover, the conventional adoption of an unphonetic spelling can sometimes provides us with positive evidence as to its value: thus, when words like delight (formerly delite) began to be spelt with gh, this spelling form gh clearly no longer had the consonantal fricative value which it had formerly represented in light, since there never was a consonantal sound between the vowel and final [t] is delight. We may conclude, therefore, that gh no longer had its former phonetic significance in words such as light.

Care must, of course, be taken to identify the increasing number of learned or technical spellings adopted by printers. The initial letter group gh in ghost (OE gast) indicates no change in pronunciation—goose was also sometimes spelt ghoose in this period. Again, spellings which aim at revealing the etymology (true or false) of a word must usually be discarded as phonetically valueless, *e.g.* debt, island. It is above all from the writings of individuals that some general indications concerning sound changes may be gathered and used to supplement evidence derived from other sources.

Rhymes, too, continue to be useful as complementary evidence. A rhyme such as night: : white confirms the view that postvocalic gh no longer had a consonantal value; or again, can: : swan suggests that the rounding of [a] after [w] had not yet taken place. Yet, just as in the case of ME, rhymes must be treated with caution, more particularly as eye-rhymes were doubtless beginning to become more prevalent. There is, however, in Elizabethan literature, additional evidence afforded by the frequent use of puns, which usually rely for their effect upon similarities, if not identities, of phonetic value. Shakespeare, for instance, plays on the phonetic identity of such pairs as suitor, shooter (both capable of being pronounced [ʃu:tər] and known, none (both [no:n}); such puns suggest that the pronunciation of the two words was commonly sufficiently close to make an immediate impression upon an audience.

The most important and fruitful evidence for this period, is, however, of a direct kind. It is provided by the published works of the contemporary grammarians, orthoepists, and schoolmasters. They are of unequal value and their statements have often to be interpreted in the light of other evidence; yet they provide us with the first direct descriptive accounts of the pronunciation of English. From the sixteenth century ownards, ours conclusions rely more and more on their descriptive statements and less on clues of an indirect kind.Sometimes there appears to be a conflict between the phonetic probabilities, the statements of grammarians, and evidence from other sources. Frequently the solution must be that there existed at any time a variety of current pronunciations, resulting from differences of dialect, generation, fashion, and place in society, in the same way that a description of PresE (even that of a restricted area such as the south of England) would have to take into account a large number of variants.

MODIFICATIONS IN THE ENGLISH SYSTEM

1. **Distribution of Phonemes.** The similarities of the systems given abve may obscure the fact that the same sound, especially as far as the vowels are concerned, may occur in different categories of words according to the period. Thus [u:], now in food, occurred in OE in words such as town; [i:], now in team, occurred in OE in time. The following summary shows some of the most striking changes affecting the vowel quality used in particular word categories

		OE	ME	eModE	PresE
time	.	i:	i:	əi	aɪ
sweet	.	e:	e:	i:	i:
clean	.	æ:	ɛ:	e: (or [i:])	i:
stone	.	a:	ɔ:	o:	əʊ
name	.	a	a:	ɛ:	eɪ
moon	.	o:	o:	u:	u:
house	.	u:	u:	əu	aʊ
love	.	ʊ	ʊ	ɤ	ʌ(or[ä])

2. **Vowel Changes.** Several trends become apparent from a study of quality changes:

(a) OE long vowels have closed or diphthongized; on the other hand, PresE [əʊ] and [eɪ] show signs of monophthongization.

(b) Certain phonemic qualitative oppositions have coalesced, *e.g.* OE /e:/ and /æ:/; the orginally separate diphthongs of day and way; the diphthong of know with the originally pure vowel of no; the diphthongs of day, way with the former pure vowel of name; OE /y:, y/ with /i:, ɪ/ (or /ɛ/).

(c) Short vowels, with the notable exceptions of the OE /a, æ/ (and the short diphthong /ɛə/) in open syllables and ME /ʊ/, have remained relatively stable.

(d) Rounded front vowels have been lost, *e.g.* OE /y:, y/ and earlier /ϕ:, ϕ/.

(e) The loss of post-vocalic [r] in the eighteenth century gave rise to the PresE centring diphthongs /ɪə, ɛə, ʊə/, the pure vowel /a:/ and introduced /a:, ɔ:/ into new categories of words (cart, port).

(f) Vowles under weak accent are increasingly obscured to [ə] or [ɪ], or are elided.

(g) Changes of quantity affected certain phonemes in particular contexts or sets of words, *e.g.* lengthening of OE /a, æ, ɛə/ in open syllables and of ME /a/ + /f, θ, s/; and shortening of ME /o:/ in words like good, book, blood, and to ME /ɛ:/ in such words as breath, death, head.

3. **Consonant Changes.** Changes in the consonantal system are less striking, but the following may be noted:

(a) Double (or long) consonants within words were lost by late ME; certain other consonant clusters cease to be tolerated, *e.g.* /hl, hr, hn/ by ME and /kn, gn, wr/ in the eModE period; post-vocalic /r/ was lost in the south-east of England in the eighteenth century.

(b) Allophones of certain phonemes have been lost, *e.g.* the [ɣ] allophone of /g/ in late OE and the [x, ç] allophones of /h/ in eModE.

(c) New phonemes have emerged, *e.g.* /tʃ, d3/ in OE, /v, ð, z/ in ME, and /Ŋ, 3/ in eModE; in addition, /h/ is used initially in words of French origin where, originally, no [h] sound was pronounced (habit, herb, humble, etc).

THE PRESENT-DAY SITUATION

The English are today particularly sensitive to variations in the pronunication of their language. The 'wrong accent' may still be an impediemnt to social intercourse or to advancement of entry in certain professions. Such extreme sensitivity is apparently not paralleled in any other country or even in other parts of the English-speaking world. There are those who claim, from an elocution standpoint, that modern speech is becoming increasingly slovenly, full of 'mumbling and mangled vowels and missing consonants'. Alexander Gil and others made the same kind of complaint in the seventeenth century. There is, in fact, no evidence to suggest that the degree of obscuration and elision, often characteristic of a dynamic stress language such as English, is markedly greater now than it has been for four centuries. Of more significance—social as well as linguistic—is the attitude which regards a certain set of sound values as more acceptable, even more 'beautiful' than another. Judgments of this kind suggest that there is a standard for comparison; and it is clear that such a standard pronunciation does exist, although it has never been explicity imposed by any official body. A consideration of the origins and present nature of this unofficial standard goes some way towards explaining the controversies and emotions which it arouses at the present day.

(1) Great prestige is still attached to this implicitly accepted social standard of pronunciation. Often called Received Pronunciation (RP), the term suggesting that it is the result of a social judgment rather than of an official decision as to what is 'correct' or 'wrong', it has become more widely known and accepted through the advent of radio. The BBC formerly recommended this form of pronunciation for its announcers mainly because it was the type which was most widely understood and which excited least prejudice of a regional kind. Indeed, attempts to use announcers who had a mild regional accent provoked protests even from the region whose accent was used. Thus, RP often became identified in the public mind with 'BBC English'. This special position occupied by RP, basically educated Southern British English, has led to its being the form of pronunciation most commonly described in books on the phonetics of British English and traditionally taught to foreigners.

(2) Nevertheless, it cannot be said that RP is any longer the exclusive property of a particular social stratum. This change is due partly to the influence of radio in constantly bringing the accent to the ears of the whole nation, but also, in considerable measure, to the modifications which are taking place in the structure of English society. Just as the sharp divisions between classes are beginning to disappear, so the more marked characteristics of regional speech and, in the London region, the popular forms of pronunciation, are tending to be modified in the direction of RP, which is equated with the 'correct' pronunciation of English. This tendency does not, as yet, mean that regional forms of pronunciation show signs of disappearing, but it has to be recognized that those who wish, for any reason, to modify their speech have models of RP always readily available to their ears while, at the same time, the social inhibitions concerning movement between classes,

which were formerly so strongly operative, no longer, in the face of the standardization of society as a whole, exert the same pressure.

Moreover, it must be remarked that some members of the present younger generation reject RP because of its association with the 'Establishment' in the same way that they question the validity of other forms of traditional authority. For them a real or assumed regional or popular accent has a greater (and less committed) prestige. It is too early to predict whether such attitudes will have any lasting effect upon the future development of the pronunciation of English. But, if this tendency were to become more widespread and permanent, the result could be that, within the next century, RP might be so diluted that it could lose its historic identity and that a new standard with a wider popular and regional base would emerge. Such a change is made more likely through the recent more permissive attitude of the BBC (and of the commerical television companies) in their choice of announcers, several of whom now have markedly non-RP or non-British accents.

(3) Certain types of regional pronunciation are, indeed, firmly established. Some, especially Scottish English speech, are universally accepted; others, particularly the popular forms of pronunciation used in large towns such as London, Liverpool, or Birmingham, are generally characterized as ugly by those (especially of the older generations) who do not use them. This rejection of certain sounds used in speech is not, of course, a matter of the sounds themselves: thus, [paɪnt] may be acceptable if it means pint, but 'ugly' if it means paint. It rather a reflection of the social cannotations of speech which, though they have lost some of their force, have by no means disappeared. Indeed, RP itself can be a handicap if used in inappropriate social situation, since it may be taken as a mark of affectation or a desire to emphasize social superiority. It may be said,

too, that if improved communications and radio have spread the availability of RP, these same influences have rendered other forms of pronunciation less remote and strange. An American pronunciation of English, for instance, is now completely accepted in Britain; this was not the case at the time when the first sound films were shown in this country, an American pronunciation then being considered strange and even difficult to understand. Speakers of RP are becoming increasingly aware of the fact that their type of pronunciation is one which is used by only a very small part of the English-speaking world.

(4) A comparison to two regional or social types of pronunciation will reveal differences of several kinds:

(a) The system, *i.e.* the number of distinctive (phonemic) terms operating, may be the same, but the phonetic realizations of the phonemes may be different: *e.g.* the RP opposition between the vowels of bet and bat may be maintained, but the realization of both vowels is much more open than in RP so that the sound of /æ/ may come near to that of one type of RP /ʌ/ or when, as in Cockney, an allophone [?] in unaccented positions represents /t/ and often /k/ or /p/ or when the final allophone of /l/ is [l] rather than [ɫ].

(b) The system may be different, *i.e.* the number of oppositions may be smaller or greater: *e.g.* the RP /æ/ - /a:/ opposition may not be present in those Ulster or Scottish forms which do not distinguish Sam and psalm; or when RP /aɪ/ homophones, as in side and sighed may be differentiated qualitatively or quantitatively, as in some types of Scottish English; or when, as in some forms of RP, /a:/ levels with /aɪ/ and /aʊ/ before /ə/ or when the presence of /g/ after /ŋ/ in such world as sing deprives [ŋ] of its phonemic status.

(c) The system may be the same, but the incidence of phonemes in words is different: *e.g.*, in those Northern forms which have the RP opposition /u:/ - /ʊ/, but nevertheless us /u:/ in book, took, etc., or when /ɐ/ is used instead of /ʌ/ is one, among, etc., though the opposition /ɐ/ - /ʌ/ exists; or when the choice of phoneme is associated with the habits of different generations, *e.g.* /ɔ:/ for /ɐ/ in off, cloth, cross, etc., or /eɪ/ for /ɪ/ in Monday, holiday, etc.

(5) It is possible to make some classification of the various kinds of British English pronunciation in the light of the regional and social criteria mentioned. Features of regional pronunciation, without any contamination from RP, will be fo8und in highly educated and less educated speech (to be distinguished briefly as educated regional and popular regional); lack of conventional education will often, in addition, reveal itself by the use of non-standard grammatical and lexical forms. On the other hand, a regional pronunciation may be termed modified when it has adopted certain characteristics of RP, *e.g.* the adoption of the RP [a:] in words such as ask, after, path rather than [a]. In the case of the speech of the Greater London pupulation, there are a great number of gradations to be noted amongst the popular regional forms, through educated regional to RP; such varying mixtures of regional and RP are typical of the suburban districts.

Within RP itself it is convenient to distinguish three main types: the conservative RP forms used by the other generati n and, traditionally, by certain professions or social groups; the general RP forms most commonly in use and typified by the pronunciation adopted by the BBC; and the advanced RP forms mainly used by young people of exclusive social groups—mostly of the upper classes, but also, for prestige value, in certain professional circles. In its most exaggerated variety, this last type would usually by judged 'affected' by other RP speakers, in the same way that all RP types are liable to be considered affected by those who use unmodified regional speech. Advanced pronunciations, however, whenever they are not the result of temporary fashion, may well indicate the way in which the RP system is developing and be adopted in the future as general RP, *e.g.* the originally advanced ('affected') diphthong in home, involving increased centralization and a tendency towards monophthongization, seems likely to become general in a very short time.

These various types of British English pronunciation may be summarized as follows:

Regional	(Reg)	Received	(RP)
educated	(educ)	conservative	(cons)
popular	(pop)	general	(gen)
modified	(mod)	advanced	(adv)

(6) Finally, it has to be recognized that the role of British RP in the English-speaking world has changed very considerably in the last century. Over 300 million people now speak English as a first language, and of this number native RP speakers form only a minute proportion; the majority of English speakers use some form of American pronunciation. However, despite the discrepancy in numbers, RP continues for historical reasons to serve a model in many parts of the world, and, if a model is used at all, the choice is still effectively between RP and American pronunciation.

OLD ENGLISH PERIOD

After the Teutonic tribes had made themselves masters of the greater part of south Britain the English language came into existence as a separate idiom. The settlers spoke dialects which were very much allied, and from the fusion of their dialect resulted the English language. The earliest inhabitants of Britain during the time of the

Roman occupation from 55 B.C. to 410 A.D. spoke a language known as Celtic. The Celtic language must have received Latin element into its fold from the speech of the Roman soldiery. The history of the English language begins with the settlement of the three Germanic tribes, Angles, Saxons and Jutes in the sixth century. The coming of these tribes to Britain brought the Celts into contact with them and the contact influenced the languages of the Germanic tribes. In the area extending north-word from the Thames the Angles settled themselves. The Jutes settled in Kent and the Saxons settled in the rest of England south of the Thames. But the South-West of England was still occupied by the Celtic tribes. The Celts called their Germanic conquerors Saxons indiscriminately and the areas occupied by them was called Saxonia. But soon the Angle came into use and was applied to all the three Germanic tribes in general. The word English is derived from the name of Angles and was applied without distinction to the languages of all the Germanic tribes. Much later, England came into use from name of Angles. Old English was the language which emerged from the fusion of the dialects spoken by the invading Germanic tribes.

The Old English period extends from 450 to 1100. This period is known as the period of full inflexions. This period is described as the period of levelled or weakened inflexions since the inflexions which had began to weaken or become blurred towards the end of the Old English Period, became very much reduced during this period.

The Dialects of Old English

The three Teutonic tribes who settled in Britain spoke dialects which were more or less diverse. These tribes could no doubt understand each other, but there was no common tongue, and no common written language. Old English had four principal dialects Northmbrian, Mercian, West Saxon and Kentish. Northumbrian and Mercian were the dialects of the Angles and are often classed together and called Anglian. West Saxon represents the language of the Saxons and Kentish that of the Jutes.

Northumbrian was the first dialect to produce a literature. A rich body of old English poetry was produced in this dialect towards the end of the seventh century and in the beginning of the eighth century. But Northumbrian could not long retain its pre-eminence. During the reign of Alfred the Great in the West Saxon kingdom, West Saxon became the standard literary language of England. Even the older Northumbrian poetry was recopied into standard West Saxon Speech. Nearly all of Old English literature is preserved in manuscripts transcribed in this dialect. It is for this reason that West Saxon has been made the basis of the study of Old English.

Characteristics of Old English

No language is spoken or written in the same form through centuries. Language is a natural growth, partly mental and partly physical. It follows, therefore, that a language is undergoing constant change. The history of English language since its inception has been one of the continuous development. Hence, although Modern English has been derived from Old English by a regular process of change, Old English has quite respect of a foreign language. The language of Alfred seems to be quite different from Modern English, Old English has evolved into Modern English through gradual changes in pronunciation, spelling, grammar and vocabulary.

A page of Old English presents a look of strangeness to the modern reader because of its employment of certain symbols which are no longer in use today. Old English made use of two symbols xo and p to represent the sound of 'th'. These two symbols are no more used in Modern English. Old English represented the vowel sound as in words man, hat and so on, by the symbol ae. Much of the strange appearance of Old English is due to the frequent appearance of this symbol. Similarly 'sh' sound is represented by 'Sc' in old English as for example Sceap (Sheep), biscop (bishop), Likewise 'K' sound is always represented by c, as for example in words like cynn (Kin), nacod (Naked). In general it may be said that in pronunciation Old English has no silent syllable and its spelling is more or less phonetic, that is to say, its letters represents its sounds quite closely.

In Old English script there are seven vowel symbols- a, e, i, o, u, y and the digraph ae which is called 'ash'.

All the seven vowels represent either long or short sounds. Long vowels are marked by the sign, placed over vowels *e.g.*, a, e etc. The short vowels are pronounced almost as they are pronounced in Modern English. The pronunciation of some of the Old English vowels are indicated below:

OE a	Pronounced like the 'a' of father.
" oe	Pronounced like the 'a' of hat.
" oe	Pronounced like the 'ai' of air.
" i	Pronounced like the 'i' of machine.
" u	Pronounced like the 'u' of put.
" u	Pronounced like the 'oo' of food.

The Old English consonants have mostly the same sounds as in Modern English, but some call for comment. The letter 'h' is more strongly pronounced than it is in Modern English. The letter C has mostly a K-sound, SC the sound of modern 'Sh' and the combination 'Cg' the sounds of 'j' of judge. The letter r is trilled in all positions as in Modern Scotch. Old English script does not have the letter V, f serves for the sounds of both f and V. Old English alphabets contains two symbols P, called thorn and called 'eth' to represent the sound of th; P represents the sound of th in thin an δ the sounds of th in this, when we read Old English we must remember that each symbol is pronounced. In this sense, Old English is phonetic in character.

Therefore we can summarize by saying that Old English is essentially phonetic in character. There are no silent sounds and no superflous symbols, nor are the existing symbols made to overstram too much. In the course of time, Old English test its phonetic nature, especially from the middle English period. Two important characteristics of Old English are the phonetic changes known as graduation and mutation. Modern English have a bearing of these phonetic and sound changes. Gradation is a change in vowel sounds of principal parts of verbs according to whether they occur in a stressed or unstressed syllable. The vowel changes that we find in these old English verbs were due to shifting of stress long ago in the history of the Indo-European group if languages. But the changes in vowel sound in the root syllable of the verb is gradation. The verbs in which this gradation takes place are called strong verbs and the verbs which cannot make past tense by such a change in vowel but of adding suffix 'ed' are called weak verbs. This gradation is also called ablant. A similar change took place in the root syllable of the verb when a suffix was added to it in order to make a or a participle. As examples we may take the following verbs:

Present	*Past*	*Past Participle*
drifan (drive)	draf (drove)	drifen (driven)
radan (ride)	rad (rode)	riden (ridden)
writan (to write)	wrat (wrote)	writan (written)

The more important phonetic change in Old English was mutation, sometimes called amlaut. It should be more strictly called as i-mutation. It is a process in which, in early Old English vowels in accented syllables were modified through the influence of an i or j in the next syllable. The i or j that caused the change totally disappeared at the later stage. This is a very complicated sound change which had a good deal of living interest for modern student. It explains certain anomalies in Modern English. The following are the vowels changes that took place:

Short back vowels	*Short back dispththongs*
a > e	ea > ie
oe > e	eo > ie
o > e	io > ie,
u > y	

It will be noticed that what happened was that the back-vowels were changed to front vowels.

Grammar is the most striking characteristic that distinguishes Old English from the Modern English. It is an inflected language though not so highly inflected as the classical languages like Sanskrit, Latin and Greek. It stands a little more than half way along the linguistic road leading Indo-European synthesis to Modern English analysis. Modern English had dropped almost all the inflexions and has devised other means of expressing grammatical relations. In short Modern English is an analytic language, while Old English is a synthetic one.

A language is said to be in the synthetical stage when it expresses the grammatical relations of words by adding some suffixes to the stems of nouns, adjectives, pronouns and verbs. A language is free from such inflexional endings as far as possible and in their place makes free use of other devices like prepositions and other auxiliary words is said to be in the analytic stage. From this point of view Modern English is analytical. In its Grammar, Old English resembles Modern English. The nature of Old English grammar can be gathered by looking at the inflexions of its nouns, adjectives, pronouns, verbs, and so on.

Old English nouns have two numbers-Singular and Plural, three genders–masculine, feminine and neuter. The system of genders is irrational, because it is not dependent upon the consideration of sex. Where as what we call gender in Modern English is based on sex. Therefore, in Modern English all males are said to be Masculine, Females Feminine and things without life are called Neuter. But in Old English, as in Latin, it is not on sex or absence of sex but on the forms that a noun assumes in the course of its declension. Thus in Old English here (army) is Masculine, Wynn (joy) is faminine, wif (woman) is Neuter and wifman (woman) is Masculine perhaps the second element in the compound is Masculine Strangely mona (moon) is Masculine and sunne (sun) is Feminine.

Another peculiarity of Old English is the adjective like nouns have gender. The adjective takes the gender of the noun with which it is associated.

There are four cases-nominative, genetive, dative, accusative. The system of declension is very intricate.

The Old English noun is inflected according to its number and case. It has chiefly four cases and the endings of these vary with different nouns. There are two chief declensions and a consonant declension. Vowel declension is called strong declension and consonant declension is called weak declension. Whether a noun takes one or the other of the two declension depends upon whether the stem of the noun ended in Germanic in a vowel on in a consonant. The following examples will suffice to understand the nature of the declension of the nouns:

(1) Masculine-a Stem (Stan Stone)

	Singular	*Plural*
Nominative	Stan	Stan-as
Genetive	Stanes	Stan-a
Dative	Stan-e	Stan-um
Accusative	Stan	Stan-as

(2) Feminine O Stem:– giefu (gift)

	Singular	*Plural*
Nominative	gief-u	gief-a
Genetive	gief-e	gief-a
Dative	gief-e	gief-um
Accusative	gief-e	gief-a

(3) Masculine Consonant Stem:– flunta (hunter)

	Singular	*Plural*
Nominative	hunt-a	hunt-um
Genetive	hunt-on	hunt-ena
Dative	hunt-an	hunt-um
Accusative	hunt-an	hunt-an

It is a evident by thus how complicated the inflexions of the Old English noun is. Modern English has discarded most of the case endings except the Genetive case ending.

In Old English adjective, there is a two-fold declension one of them is the strong declension used with nouns when they are not accompanied by a definite article or a demonstrative pronoun. For instance 'god mann' (good man) is strong declension. The other is the weak declension used with nouns accompanied by a definite article. Thus, god a mann (the good man) is a weak declension. Further complication of the adjective in Old English adjective is that it is declined according to number, gender and case. In Modern English the adjectival remains undeclined whatever number, gender and case it is associated with. Such elimination of the complex adjectival inflexion gives a great advantage to the English language, over many other Indo-European languages.

A definite article is inflected according to gender, number and case. Like modern German, Old English had a fully inflected definite article. The little word 'the' assumed twelve different forms according to the gender, number and case of the noun.

Old English had two classes of verbs strong and weak which have passed even in Modern English and are known as regular and irregular verbs. There were only two tenses by inflexion past and present. The present generally served also a future (We go there next month) but million and scullan (will and shall) were occasionally used and their use foreshadowed future developments. In the strong verbs the change of tense is indicated by a modification in their root-vowel as in 'sing, sang, sung'. In the weak verbs such a change in tense is indicated by the addition of suffix. It is estimated that Old English has a few over three hundred strong verbs. Based on the gradation of the vowel they assume, they are classified into six classes and to those six is added a seventh class of verbs called reduplicating verbs. They may be illustrated by the following verbs :–

	Present		*Preterite*	*Preterite*	*Past*
			Singular	*Plural*	*Participle*
1.	drifon	(drive)	draf	difon	drifen.
2.	cheooan	(choose)	ceas	curon	coren
3.	helpan	(help)	healp	hulpon	holpen
4.	beran	(bear)	boer	boeron	boren
5.	sprecan	(speak)	spoec	sproecon	sprecan

In Modern English many of the characteristics of the verb are preserved with some modifications. Old English has distinct forms of the personal pronouns practically for all genders, persons and cases. Instead of two numbers, singular and plural, it has an intermediate number called the dual number, which represents two things. The existence of the dual form in addition to the plural is an unnecessary complication in language and so it has disappeared in Modern English.

After gaining the knowledge of Old English grammar, pronunciations, dialects we must learn about the language of Old English in prose and poetry. The presentation of a good prose style is always with the efforts made by the generations of writers. Old English prose lacks lucidity, simplicity and easy flow, it is often clumsy and unwieldy. But in some of the passages we find an impassioned prose of real merit. Of course the poetic style of the Old English, on the contrary has a great claim. It is marked by a leisurely movement, repetition of ideas and words, alliteration, an abundant use of compounds and synonyms. In Old English poetry there are twenty four synonyms for sea and including compound words and figurative expressions, the number of terms for sea must be at least a hundred.

LEXICAL BORROWING FOLLOWING THE RENAISSANCE

By superimposing the grammatical patterns of one language upon those of another we can determine some of the main grammatical difficulties involved in learning the second language. We find for example that there is agreement in number and gender between noun and adjective in French, but not so in English that the modifier comes before the noun in English, whereas it usually comes after it in French, United Nation giving *Nations Unies, some fresh air/de l'air frais*.

This gives us only the feature which each grammar lacks or possesses in relation to the other. Differential grammar is not, as some practitioners of it would have us believe, simply a matter of superimposing an outline of the grammar of one language on that of another. What is required is a special type of description which accounts for all types of differences and equivalences.

To begin with, we must distinguish between what may be said and what must be said. When a French learner speaks English he is forced into making certain distinctions that he has always ignored in the grammar of his own language. The grammar of English forces him to decide on whether he is referring to a state or an action, whether the action is incomplete and continuous or simply habitual. In his own language, he does not, for example, have to make the distinction between a person who plays the piano regularly as a hobby or profession and one who happens to be playing on the piano at any given moment: the utterance *Il joue du piano* covers all such situations. In English, however, the distinction is compulsory, and the French learner must get into the habit of making it, for in one case he will have to say *He plays the piano*, and in the other, He is playing the piano. It is not that he is unable to make this distinction in his own language for he can distinguish *Il joue du piano from Il est en train de jouer due piano*; it is that he is not forced to make the distinction.

Secondly, in what must be said, we must distinguish unique forms from alternate ones. The grammar of our native language may provide a number of different ways of saying the same thing. Only one of these may be possible in the second language. Conversely, a single form in the native language may be equivalent to a number of different forms in the second language. For example, the adverb well in He spoke well of you may be equivalent to an adverb in French (Il a tre's bien parle' de vous) or it may be equivalent to a noun (*Il a dit du bien de vous*).

Although the examples we shall use are of the obligatory type, a complete differential grammar would also show what choices exist in each of the four grammatical categories—(1) the systems of the grammar, (2) the structures of the grammar, (3) the grammatical classes, and (4) the grammatical units.

Differences in System

Not all languages have the same grammatical systems. Some languages have no cases, for example. A French learner of German has to get used to the whole idea of case inflection in nouns—nominative, genitive, dative and accusative—in addition to the use of the right case in the right place.

Languages with the same systems, however, do not use them in the same way. An English learner of French knows that both English and French have a passive voice; but he must learn to avoid equating one with the other, for an English passive may be equivalent to the French "pronominal voice". (E. *It's not done* / F. *Ça ne se fait pas.*)

Not only do different languages have different inflectional categories, but the same category may function differently in one language from the way it does in the other, so that the function of number, case, person and tense is different in each language.

Of the differences with the systems of the verb, let us take as an example the use of tense in English and French. The fact that English and French have many tenses in common does not mean that these are equivalent. Both English and French have a simple present tense, but the English present may often be equivalent to the French perfect, future, or future perfect:

I hear he's coming	= E. PRESENT/F.PERFECT
	= J' *ai appris qu'il viendra.*
I hope he comes.	= E. PRESENT/F. FUTURE
	= J' *espere qu'il viendra.*
After we finish.	= E. PRESENT/F. FUTURE
	= *Apres que nous aurons fini.*

PERFECT

Both English and French have simple past tenses, but the English simple past is often the equivalent of the French imperfect, subjunctive, or present perfect:

He said he knew.	= E. PAST/F. IMPERFECT
	= II a dit qu'il le savait.
It's time he shut up	= E. PAST/F. SUBJECTIVE
	= II est temps qu'il *se taise.*
I saw him yesterday.	= E. PAST/F. PRES. PERF.
	= Je l' *ai vu hier.*

Conversely, if we were to take the French tenses as a starting-point, we would find a similar lack of equivalence with those of English. For example:

F. PRESENT	E. PERFECT
Nous le connaisions depuis des anness.	We've known him for years.

Differences in Structure

Languages differ in the way they put words and phrases together. They differ in the order and interdependence of their items. A description of the structural differences between two languages will show such things as diffferences in word-order. For example, although adverbs are used in both French and English they do not always occupy the same relative position in the sentence.

F. II repond *toujours en francais.*	/E. He always answers in French.
F. J' aime beaucoup le the.	*/E. I like ead very much.*

A differential description will also show the differences in the type of interdependence of words in the sentence. In French, the tag-question is completely independent; in English, it depends on the main verb and must agree with it. A French learner of English must get used to making this agreement.

In the following example, note how the French *n'estce pas* always remains the same, being independent from the main clause with which it is used. On the other hand, the English equivalent is a dependent group which always has to agree with the main clause.

II est prêt, n'est-ce pas?	He's ready, isn't he?
II etait prêt, n'est-ce pas?	He was ready, wasn't he?
II sera prêt, n'est-ce pas?	He will be ready, won't he?
II semble prêt, n'est-ce pas?	He seems ready, doesn't he?
II semblait prêt, n' est-ce pas?	He seemed ready, didn't he?
II n'est pas prêt, n'est-ce pas?	He isn't ready, is he?
II n'etait pas prêt, n'est-ce pas?	He wasn't ready, was he?
II ne sera pas prêt, n' est-ce pas?	He won't be ready, will be?
II ne semble pas prêt, n'est-ce pas?	He doesn't seem ready he?
II ne semblait pas prêt, n'est-ce pas?	He didn't seem ready, did he?

Different Classes

Although most languages have such word-classes or parts of speech as nouns, verbs and adjectives, the number of classes is not necessarily the same for all languages.

In languages with the same number of word-classes, each class does not necessarily do the same work as its counterpart in other languages. And in actual use, a word (*e.g.*a verb) may be equivalent in one language to a word belonging to an entirely different part of speech, in another language. This sort of equivalence is called transposition.

A French verb, for example, may be equivalent to an English adverb, or adjective, or noun:

II ne tardera pas a rentrer.	F. VERB/E ADVERBE He 'll soon be back.
Des qu'on essaied' êtrearbitraire.	F. VERB/E. NOUN Any attempt to be arbitrary.

A French noun may be equivalent to an English adjective:

Au débuts du 19e siécle. F. NOUN/E. ADJECTIVE In the early 19th century.

And some French nouns are equivalent to English phrasal verbs:

Attention! F. NOUN/E. PHRASAL VERB Look out!

Different Units

Words phrases, sentences, etc., are the units of grammar. Not all languages have the same sort or the same number. Those that exist in both languages do not always correspond. A word in the first language may be equivalent to a phrase in the second, as when the English word agenda is equated to the French *ordre du jour*; or when the German word *druckfertig* has to be rendered into English as ready for printing.

Some of the difference may form a pattern, as may be seen by comparing English phrasal verbs with their french and German equivalents. Examine, for example, the following:

F. VERB	*E. PHRASAL VERB*		*G. PREPOSITION*	
Entrez.	Come in.	Go in.	Herein.	Hinein.
Sortez.	Come out.	Go out.	Heraus.	Hinaus.
Montez.	Come up.	Go up.	Herauf.	Hinauf.
Descendez.	Come down.	Go down.	Herunter.	Hinunter.

Many French verbs are equivalent to an English verb followed by some sort of modifier, giving such combinations as phrasal verbs. The structure of phrasal verbs enables English to make distinctions like the one between come in and go in which the French single verbs like entrer do not reveal.

The most important word units in a language are its structure words—its articles, prepositions etc. Althouth these are limited in number, they are found in almost every utterance. Structure words of the first language, however, are not always equivalent to those of the second. For example, although the English structure word come is equivalent to the French partitive du in a few of its uses, it must very often be equated with other French structure words such as:

en	Give me some	Donnez m'*en*
un	Some fool has...	Un imbecile a...
quelque	For some time	Pendant *quelque* tems
environ	Some forty persons	Environ une quarantaine
certains	*Some say* that....	*Certains* disent que...

Structure words, however, are limited in number, forming part, as they do, of a closed system. If the word is not a structure word, it is part of an unlimited series required a different technique of differential description. This is the function of lexicology.

Differential Lexicology

By far the most numerous items which distinguish one language from another are the items of vocabulary. Some of these may have the same form in both languages, but differ in content; or they may have different forms and the same conent. The vocabulary of both languages may be compared from these two points of view: *(1)* equivalence in their forms of expression, and *(2)* equivalence in meaning, or content.

EXPRESSION EQUIVALENCE

Words with similar expression forms in both languages may be described as to *(1)* what they stand for (their reference), and *(2)* the combinations, or collocations, into which they enter.

Refernece of Cognates

If a word has the same form in both languages, it may *(i)* have the same referent, *(ii)* have different referents, or *(iii)* have some referents in common.

(i) A few words, like jeep in French and English, which look and sound alike in both languages may also refer to the same thing.

(ii) There may be a number of words which look and sound alike in both languages but which refers to different things. The word car in French has not the same referent as it has in English.

(iii) Many of the words which look and sound alike have some referents which are the same and some which are different. The word administration which look in English and French sometimes refers to the same thing. It sometimes, however, refers to something different. In business texts, for example, administration in French is equivalent to management in English. When the reference is not external but internal, reference to feelings or thoughts, the analysis of common and different referents is necessarily more complex.

Collocation of Cognates

Cognates vary greatly in the combintions which each language allows them to enter. The German word Winter may seem like a close cognate of English winter, but in German, winter cannot be "around the corner" it can only be ''at the door" (*vor der Tür*). Even identical geographical place names may have collocations which are quite different. The word Rome may refer to the same city in English and French; but to find the French equivalent of the collocation *When in Rome do as the Romans do*, one would have to consider howling with the wolves.

Yet in the actual use of the language, homophones and homographs can be more a peril than a help. In order to use them safely, one has to go to all the trouble of learning the cases in which they are cognates and the cases in which they are not; and when they are similar, to what extent they are similar. For example, English hound and German hund are similar in form and meaning. But in order to use the English word correctly, the German learner has to forget about the word hound and learn word dog, the usual equivalent of German Hand.

There are many such confusing similarity between genetically related languages like English and German, languages that once have been identical and still are classed in the same family. But each language develops in its own way and undergoes different influences, so that what was once the same has become different in pronunciation, spelling or meaning.

There is also a great number of confusing similarities between languages which have been in close contact, languages like English and French. Although thousands of English words have been imported from the French language, few are now identical with their French counterparts. The reason is that only part of the meaning may have been imported in the first place, or the meaning may have changed and developed in a different direction from the original. Moreover the imported words has to be fitted into a different phonetic, grammatical and semantic structure.

A third case is where the cognate has been imported from a common language. Words like sugar—sucre—Zucker, coffee—cafe'—Kaffee, tea the'—Tee imported ultimately from the Near and Far East; may differ in spelling and pronunciation but have a number of formal and semantic elements in common.

CONTENT EQUIVALENCE

If two words are different in expression-form in both languages, they may likewise be analysed according to what they refer to and how they combine with other words, that is, according to *(1)* the reference of the counterparts in the other language, and *(2)* the collocations ino which these counterparts enter.

1. **Reference of Counterparts.** If the two words are different in their form of expression, they may be identical in reference. The English word *cod* and the French word morue refer to the same fish. This one-to-one equivalence is popularly supposed to exist between all the words of both languages. And this is what many learners expect to be taught when they study a foreign langauge or when they look up words in a bilingual dictionary.

   What is usually the case, however, is that the content equivalence is only partial, that a word in one language has a number of counterparts in the other. The English word head, for example, has a number of counterparts in French, since it covers an area of content which is only partly equivalent to that covered by the French téte, as a glance at the following list will reveal:

	téte	(of a person)
	chevet	(of a bed)
	face	(of a coin)
	pomme	(of a cane)
head =	bout	(of a match)

haut bout	(of a table)
directeur	(of an organization)
mousse	(on beer)
rubrique	(title)

Similarly, the French makes a distinction between rivers which flow into the sea (fleuve) and those which do not (riviére); for English they are all rivers. It is this unexpected and seemingly unreasonable difference in grouping of referents that is responsible for so many of the errors in second language learning. When a German learner of English says "Close the door, please; there's a train." He has no reason to believe that the concepts of train and draught should not have a single label in English as they do in German, where the word Zug covers both.

2. **Collocation of Counterparts.** Even when the counterparts are equivalent, however, the equivalence rarely extends to the complete range of collocations into which each word may enter. The English verb laugh may be the counterpart of the French rire and the German lachen; but when we laugh up our sleeve in English we laugh in our beard in French (dons sa barbe), and in our first in German (*ins Fäustchen*).

   Differences in range of collocations have not been determined for any two languages. There have been studies of deceptive cognates, useful treatments of certain areas of content in two languages, and a large number of isolated instances unearthed in the compilation of some of the more complete bilingual dictionaries.

   All the above differences in vocabulary, grammar and pronunciation do not add up to a complete differential analysis. This is because all levels of language work together as a whole. In the final analysis, what must be known is how each language, working as a system of systems, differs in the production of complete utterances in any given situation. One language may require a long utterance, and in the same situation another language may require not more than a word or simply a gesture. It is a matter of style.

No differential analysis of two languages can be complete unless it includes *(1)* such differences in the contents of the responses to convenional situations. And since responses may themselves be made through diferent levels in each language, vocabulary, grammar, or pronunciation, the description must include *(2)* the differences in the levels of expression.

It is not sufficient to know that words and phrases in two languages may differ in content. These words and phrases appear in different sequences which may relate differently to the same situation. In all sorts of everyday situations involving such things as requests and courtesy, giving and getting, what is normally said in one language does not correspond in either form or conent to what may be said, in the same circumstances, in another. For example, if a German speaker offers a stranger his seat, he will probably begin and end the act with what might be interpreted as please (bitte). No so in English, where he may begin with a slight gesture or remark and end with a Not at all or That's quite all right.

Equivalents lie often in entirely different levels of language. It may be a matter of vocabulary in one language and of grammar in another, of grammar in one language and of phonetics in another. Because each language is absolutely free to represent what it likes with its structure words, inflections, and parts of speech, in any level or combination whatever, the differential analysis of two languages can be a highly complex affair. Such an analysis, however, is necessary if we are to get a picture of the internal problems of foreign-language learning.

NEW LEXICAL ITEMS

The creation of new lexical items is partly because of necessity and partly because of fashion. Necessity arises when a word is lost for linguistic reasons, such as attrition or homonymic clash. Obviously a new one must take its place. Similarly, if the meaning of a word is 'devalued', another one must be put in the gap left by the devalued one. And new inventions such as radar, laser and penicillin require new words. But at other times new words arise purely through fashion.New words spring up alongside older words. At the first, these new alternatives may be regarded as slang, but in course of time many of them become increasingly common. For example, words such as pot, hash, grass are becoming increasingly common.

The continual infiltration of new lexical items is a normal and healthy trend. It testifies to the essential productivity of language–the ability to say new things and deal with new situations.

New lexical items can be assigned to two main classes: items created from resources within the language (internal borrowing) and items created from outside sources (external borrowing).

'When any part of the strucutre of a language is changed by importation of features, whether from some other part of the language or from some external source, the imported features are said to be borrowed'. We distinguish between two types of borrowings: external and internal on the basis of the source of the borrowing.

External Borrowing

Under the heading of external borrowings come those from one dialect to another (dialectical borrowings), those from an earlier stage of the same language (archaisms), and those from the languages (loans). It is very frequent for a language to borrow lexical items from related dialects (regional, social, occupational) for various reason, distinctive meanings, humour, or pleasant or unpleasant connotations of one sort or another.

Borrowing is a very common linguistic phenomenon. In all probability, no language is completely free of borrowed forms.

Languages change through the influence of other languages. Some languages borrow too largely, other only to a limited extent. For example, in English over half of its lexicon is borrowed; in Albaniam, on the other hand, only a few hundred words are thought to have entered the lexicon through borrowing. In periods of mass borrowing, such as Italianism in Elizabethan England or Anglicansim in twentieth century India, entire sectors of vocabulary may become saturated with loan-words. Prestige is the decisive factor in any borrowing.

Borrowing is never a linguistic necessity, since it is always possible to extend and modify the use of existing lexical items to meet new communication needs. A common cause of lexical borrowing is the need to find words for objects, concepts, and places. It is easier to borrow an existing terms from another language than to make one up. The paths of lexical borrowing reflect to a certain extent the paths of cultural influence. For example, Hindi has borrowed from English words as radio, television, telephone, rail, signal, platform, guard, conductor, and so forth. Similarly the influence of Italian music and art can be seen in Italian: opera, tempo. English through these words borrowed from piano, sonata, sonnet, fresco, etc. A large portion of the Arabic words in English pertain to the realm of science: zero, cipher, zenith, alchemy, algebra, nadir, alcohol, etc. Government and other terms that came to English from French include crown power, state, reign, country, peer, court, duke, duchess, prince, sovereign, minister, chancellor, council, authority, parliament, baron; borrowed terms related to military matters are battle, army, war, peace, office, lieutenant, navy, admiral, soldier, sergeant, troops, arms, armour, gallant, company, force.

French borrowings can also be seen in English religious, moral and legal vocabulary. A large number of French borrowing is there in English, because in England for a pretty long time French was the prestige language. and the use of French words in English conversation became a common practice, especially after the Norman Conquest of England in 1066.

Latin and Greek had great prestige in the world of scholarship during the middle Ages. Consequently Latin and Greek have provided

English with the richest resource for borrowing. Most of the words borrowed from Latin and Greek and learned words and the list of such words may run to many thousands. Even the names of many scholarly disciplines are borrowed from the classical language: sociology, psychology, anthropology, philosophy, philology, biology. Many words in English are forms with Latin morpheme ex-'out of form': exact, exaggerate, exalt, exclude, explain, explicit, explode, explore, export, extend, extinct, extort, etc. Similarly ex-husband and ex-wife are the examples of Latin ex prefixed to Germanic forms. Lexical borrowing in English is sometimes of such complexity that a word may be derived simultaneously from two or more different sources. The words typhoon, for example, is derived possibly from as many as three different sources: Urdu toofan (storm) Greek Typhoon, and Cantonese daal fung (big wind).

Semantic borrowing is more elusive, and more difficult to trace, for example, the semantic influence of Judaeo-Christianity on Greek. The lexical form of angel (Fr. ange, Ger. Engel, Rus. angel) is derived from Greek aggelos, but the concept itself is borrowed from Hebrew. Semantic borrowing is a process virtually impossible to forestall. Usually it occurs in one of the two forms: either meaning of an existing word is changed and then new meaning replaces the old one completely, or the old meaning continues to exist along side the new meaning. As an example of the second type, we can take the word red which has become synonymous with socialist and especially communist since the Russian Revolution. As an example of the first type can be cited dialectic which can now-a-days only with difficulty be used in the original sense of 'lexical' disputation'. Traumatic used to refer to physical shock; but this meaning has been superseded by 'a disturbing experience affecting the mind.' In British English snag meant 'a trunk or large branch of a tree embedded in the bottom of a river' until the meaning 'obstacle' was borrowed from American English, which eventually eclipsed the earlier meaning altogether.

Semantic borrowing will be particularly frequent where there is an intimate connection between two languages. This happened, for instance, in the early Christian Church where Hebrew exercised a powerful influence on Greek, and the latter on Latin. It is now happening in the language of sports, which in many countries, is saturated with Anglicanism.

Internal Borrowing

Internal borrowing frequently start out as slang, which later becomes accepted, such as the word snob, squabble, hard up. Bird, now becoming acceptable in meaning of 'girl', is perhaps borrowed from the word 'bribe'. A common type of internal borrowing is the adoption of proper names, as the words sandwich from Lord sandwich, the first person to eat his meat between two slices of bread.

Nevertheless, the following methods of forming new items are important in English:

(a) Affixation—New words can be created by adding prefixes, such as de-, self-, anti- (defence, self-service, antithesis), or suffixes, such as-ise,

(b) Analogy—*e.g.* motorway after railway.

(c) Blends (or Contamination)—Blends occur when two existing words are combined into a new one. They are sometimes called 'portmanteau' words, after the statement of Humpty-Dumpty in Alice Through the Looking Glass: 'You see it's like a portmanteau–there are two meanings packed up into one word.

e.g. smog<smoke and fog

Brunch>brekafast and lunch

(d) Compounds–Two existing words are sometimes juxtaposed to form a new compound lexical item:

e.g. break into

salesman

(e) Shortening–Long words are shortend to form new ones:

e.g. Pram<perambulator

bus<omnibus

LIST OF SYMBOLS FOR WORDS

The word list given below contains a number of words collected during the field-work. Single words and compounds are listed on the basis of informant's use during my data collection. Compounding in the present list gives a complete idea of the compounding system of the language. Grammatical positions of the words are not listed against them because of a few uncertainties in their categories. (See Lipika : 1971). The list is arranged alphabetically according the Devnagari alphabet system, *i.e.*, A, a, i, u. e, o, k, kh (x), g, ng, hng, c, j (z), t, tb, hl, d, n, hn, p, ph, b, m, hm, l, v. s,and h. Some of the symbols and abbreviations used are as follows :

A	=	Λ
ng	=	η
V	=	Verb
N	=	Noun

∫ oblique between the words is used in case of by-form or dialectal variations in the Thadou speaking area.

A — (dash) is used between words and morphemes in case of compounding.

Tonal symbols are used as given in the phonology. Words in coats ( ) are optinally used.

Aké?	=	'half, broken'
Akéu	=	'empty, naked (human being)
Akòp	=	'pair'
Agéi	=	'rim of basket'
Agéi/gèi-sáng	=	'delay'
Agó	=	'to wither (plants etc.)'
Angái	=	'nature, usual'

Acům	=	'birth of animal'
Azi/Azò	=	'reason, cause'
Athù	=	'sour'
Àn	=	'meal, food'
Àn-kÀm	=	'mustered-leaf'
Àn-cÀng	=	'rice'
Abȯn(cā)	=	'all'
Amå	=	'he (himself), she (herself)'
Amå-ā	=	'his, her'
Amå-hő	=	'they'
Amå-hő-ā	=	'their'
Ahī-lè	=	'if so, then'
ā	=	'upto, (locative)'
a?	=	'fowl'
å?-tùi	=	'egg'
å?-nóu	=	'chicken'
å?-sī	=	'star'
ài	=	'a particular festival'
ài	=	'jungle ginger'
ài	=	'crab'
át	=	'to reap, to saw'
ī-tī	=	'how'
ī-tī-lè	=	'when'
in	=	'house'

in-cùng	=	'roof'
in-hlÀng-nī	=	'day before yesterday'
in-sùn	=	'rafter'
in-vá/piÁ-pā	=	'sparrow'
ī-pī	=	'what'
ū	=	'elder'
ū-pā	=	'elder-brother'
ū-nū	=	'elder-sister'
ūi-cā	=	'dog'
ùm	=	'to fence'
u̇m	=	'gourd'
u̇hm	=	'to stay (remain)'
e?/é	=	'dung'
éng	=	'yellow'
éng-ból	=	'to tese, punish'
ō	=	'echo'
ȯ?	=	'to be cought in trap'
ȯi	=	'belly'
ȯi/nūm	=	'to agree (hold the same opinion)'
ȯi-mð	=	'to accuse'
ȯp	=	'chest'
ðm	=	'to boil'
kĀ/kėimá	=	'I (myself)'
kÀng	=	'to dry (like water) up, to fry'

kÀp(N)	=	'cry'
ká (V)	=	'to cry'
kÀm	=	'mouth'
kÀhm	=	'to set trap'
kÀl-òu	=	'to climb-down'
ká	=	'to open (mouth, wound)'
kái	=	'to drag (backward), 'pull'
kài/kÀi	=	'to lead (an animal)'
kāi-ku̇ng	=	'cry-fish'
kāng	=	'wheel, a game with a particular type of bean'
káng	=	'white'
káng-kùi	=	'rake'
kắhn/sÀm-ei	=	'to bind (hair)'
kām-sÀn	=	'fire (an old term)'
ki	=	'horn'
ki?	=	'again'
ki?-zÀl	=	'to unfold'
kíu-cȯng	=	'elbow'
kíel	=	'famine'
kícåt	=	'afraid of'
kixòp	=	'to gather, come together'
kingÀm	=	'to fix on'
kin	=	'to cringe'

kīl = 'curl (of hari)'

kil = 'hair clip, to fasten with nail'

kīsėl = 'hide (act of)'

kú/kő = 'grave, earthen hole'

ku̇o/kó = 'nine'

ku̇ng = 'handle'

kūm = 'to descend'

kùm = 'spoon-shaped'

ku̇hm = 'year'

kūl = 'circle'

kèi = 'I'

ké/kèi-ā = 'my'

kéi/hó (excl.) = 'we'

eihó (incl.) = 'we'

kéi-hó-ā (excl.) = 'our'

éi-hó-ā (excl.) = 'our'

kéipī = 'lion'

kéng = 'leg'

kéng-kò? = 'shoe'

kéng-cùt/còt = 'slipper'

kéng-kò? {sim / xúi} = 'cobler'

kéng-còng = 'ankle'

kéng-tò = 'sole of foot'

kéng-pòī	=	'tœ'
kéng-pháng	=	'foot'
kél-ngúi	=	'sheep, lamb'
kél-ngúi- cing	=	'shepherd'
kél-cÀl (M)	=	'he goat'
kél-pī (F)	=	'she goat'
kél-līm	=	'a part of varandah (Lit. goat part)'
kēl-bī/kÀl-bī	=	'rung'
kó	=	'to point (indicate direction)'
kó	=	'poincer'
kói	=	'who' (cf. kòi = to embrace).
kói-sèt	=	'to arrange'
kó?	=	'anywherelse'
kó?	=	'to get sour'
kóu (N)	=	'to call (ask a person to come)'
kòu (V)	=	—do—
kòu	=	'the big green dragon'
kòng	=	'boat, box'
kòng	=	'disc'
kòt	=	'wet'
kòt	=	'crooked (not straight)'
kòt	=	'door'
kòt-cing	=	'upper wood of the door'
kòt-pī/kiel-kòt	=	'gate'

kòt-xùm/sāng-kil	=	'base of the door'
kòt-hlá/uī-còt	=	'window'
kòt-pè	=	'leaf of the door'
kòt-bil	=	'handle of the door'
kòp	=	'turban'
kòl-bù?	=	'maze'
kòl-bù-thèi	=	'pomegranate'
kòl-bùl	=	'temple (of Ear)'
xÀ-zùm	=	'chin'
xÀ-mùl	=	'beard'
xÀng-tòu	=	'to grow', 'to prosper'
xÀng-phèi	=	'the upper part of the the central house (on the south)'
xÀt/xèt	=	'one'
xÀp	=	'hump back insect'
xÀp	=	'to lay head on the pillow'
xå	=	'to wake-up'
xå?	=	'to hit the target'
xá	=	'louse (of cloth)'
xā	=	'bitter'
xå	=	'lock'
xá-xūm	=	'to shut'
xāp	=	'span'
xá mèn/pò?-kól	=	'tomato'

xȋ	=	'to tie'
xī	=	'bead'
xī-mū	=	'necklace'
xȋe	=	'to peel'
xiel	=	'side of hip'
(Àn)-xing	=	'to cool'
xu᷄	=	'smoke'
xú (V) xút (N)	=	'cough'
xū/xō	=	'village'
xúi/xói	=	'bee'
xúi-zu᷄	=	'honey'
xùi	=	'to sew, tailor'
xùi/zèp	=	'art of stitching'
zém-xùi	=	'to embroid'
xú.ng	=	'drum'
(A) xúng/hām	=	'to chirp'
xút	=	'to scratch'
xút/xòt	=	'hand'
xùt {ngòng / cóng}	=	'wrist'
xùt-zèm	=	'ring'
xùt-zùng	=	'finger'
xùt-pLàng	=	'palm'
xùt-bè?	=	'to clap'

xú.p	=	'knee'
xùp-káng/xúp-kàng	=	'patella'
xʊ́m	=	'supporting pillar'
xúl- {zin / cē}	=	'to travel'
xúl-zin̄	=	'traveller'
xė?	=	'to spin (thread)'
xél	=	'to change, alter'
xēl	=	'to miss (the target)'
xó	=	'to pierce'
xò	=	'fist (a measurement)'
xō.tāl	=	'heel'
xó-dò?	=	'to skin'
xó-lèng/xó-thèi	=	'shuttle'
xót-sù?-xáw	=	'reins'
xón	=	'to weave (cloth)'
xōn	=	'jar (of water)'
xóm	=	'to gather'
xòl	=	'to save (put aside for future)'
gÀng	=	'fast, quick'
gÀn-Àn	=	'fodder'
gÀm	=	'wild land'
gÀm-màng	=	'jungle, woods'
gĀmÀt	=	'to catch (go and catch)'

gĀmlā	=	'far away'
gĀlà	=	'to get (go and get)'
gâ	=	'fruit'
gà	=	'handle of spade or axe'
gái	=	'pregnant'
gài	=	'to get conceived (to get pregnant)'
gál-(mī)	=	'enemy'
gi	=	'heavy (in weight)'
gi	=	'demarcation'
gièl	=	'to think'
giei-zing	=	'to long for'
ging	=	'rumble'
gí el-mÀl	=	'pen'
ging-mó	=	'to suspect'
git-cā	=	'a part, type of sparrow'
gin	=	'fear'
gil/gil-zÀng	=	'guts (intestine)'
gu̇	=	'bone'
gū?	=	'to steal'
gu̇/gô	=	'rain' (cf. gu/go=bamboo)
gó/gu	=	'bamboo'
góAzū	=	'to rain'
gūcá	=	'thief'
gu̇p	=	'six'

gůol/ȏi = 'friend'

gůl-blēm = 'triangular snake'

gůl-hłá = 'green snake (with wings)'

gůl-pī = 'pithon'

gůl-sům = 'lazy snake'

gůl-só? = 'cobra'

gèi = 'late'

gèi-sáng = 'delay'

gó = 'to dry'

gŏu = 'to roast, wealth'

gòu = 'to set on fire'

gō-dál = 'a winnowing basket'

gót/pbòu = 'to dry (in sun or on fire)'

gót = 'to rub'

gót-i.à = 'the place where things are made dry'

gól = 'fencing-bars'

gól-và = 'to celebrate'

ngÀm = 'do dare (challenge)'

ngÀm = 'courage'

ngÀl = 'aggressive'

ngÀl-Àng = 'bore'

ngå = 'fish'

ngái = 'to like and love (human)'

ngài/zà = 'to hear, to listen'

ngài/dèi = 'to need'

ngài / ngè - dÀm = 'to forgive'

ngái/ngài-lůt = 'to love (mother to child)'

ngíen = 'metal'

ngim = 'clean, bare handed'

ngèi/phé/bīng = 'cheek'

ngél = 'to shift (winnow)'

ngȯl = 'exhausted'

ngȯi-sà? = 'to tame'

ngȯng = 'neck'

ngȯl = 'to abstain (from eating)'

(Àn)-ngȯl = 'to tast (food)'

cĀ - nū(F) / −pā(M) = 'daughter, son' (Lit. child)

nÀng = 'alone'

nÀngèng = 'metel bell (small)'

cĀnéi/Abing = 'to bear (child)'

nĀpòm = 'to carry (baby in the lap)'

nɑ́u-zÀng = 'bangle'

cÀl-páng = 'forehead'

càng (V) / càng (N) = 'ambush'

cạng/céng	=	'the bamboo joint'
cáng-át	=	'harvest'
cáng-tè?-gái	=	'dragon fly'
cáng-sāl	=	'granary'
cī	=	'salt' (cf. ci = horn)
cî	=	'to shut (mouth)'
ci	=	'wisdom'
cī (V) cit (N)	=	'to sneeze'
cīeng	=	'rupee'
ciheng	=	'clever, wise'
cihn	=	'to preserve'
cīng/vèt-tůp	=	'to watch'
cī-xū/cī-cū	=	'that'
cīnī	=	'sugar'
cil	=	'spittle'
cī-hi/hīcē	=	'this'
cù?/cù	=	'to bite (like a snake)'
cù	=	'rainy season'
cúng, cùng-lÀm	=	'up on' (*cf.* over–Ac u ng)
cùt	=	'to tread'
cūt	=	'to bundle'
cū-lè	=	'and'
cū-zóu-lè	=	'then, after that'

cún-dỏ?	=	'to lift up'
cùp	=	'to strike (with fist)'
cúm	=	'fist (for beating)'
cùl	=	'faded colour'
cēng	=	'to wear (pant, etc.)'
céng	=	'to dwell, live ac'
cèng	=	'hanging bridge'
cēn (N)	=	'settlement'
cèng (V) cén (N)	=	'to put on (pant, etc.)'
céng	=	'joint (of the body)'
cèp/cēp	=	'to smoke, to suck'
cép	=	'to suck (the breast)'
cēp-tÀn	=	'to circumcise'
cèm-kúng	=	'dull of knife'
cèm-kòn	=	'scimitar'
cèm-cā/tÀng-súl	=	'knife'
cèm-zām	=	'sword'
cèm-póng	=	'dao'
co/lå꞉	=	'to dig (the root)'
cò?/pē	=	'to move (stire)'
côi	=	'to hold (inanimates)'
còu/cò	=	'to challenge (to a contest)'
còn/kin	=	'to contract'
cóp	=	'to kiss'

cōp	=	'lungs'
còp-tōu/cùng-còp	=	'to jump up'
còp-kài	=	'to jump across'
còp-xúp	=	'to jump over'
còm	=	'another'
còm	=	'short (things)'
cȭm	=	'to loot a house'
còl-hAng	=	'high platform by the side of southern wall'
cȭl	=	'tired'
còl	=	'baking powder'
zÀng	=	'straight'
zá/zÀ-kòm	=	'kneepit'
zá	=	'itching, irritation'
zÀvám/dūm-vā́m	=	'cigarette ash'
zá/zĀxÀt	=	'hundred'
zā́/(N)	=	'respect'
zå/(V)	=	'to respect'
zâng	=	'elevated'
zāng	=	'plain'
zā́ng	=	'light (in weight)'
zâng-tḗl	=	'hair knot'
zāng-sī́l	=	'yak'
zān	=	'night'

zān-hī/zān-nī	=	'yesterday'
zál-lái-hlà/zál-phèi	=	'middle portion of a hanging shelf on the fire place'
zál-cùng-nū	=	'upper portion of a hanging shelf on the fire place'
zī-pā (M) zī-pū (F)	=	'spouse'
zi?	=	'bud'
zin-lÀm	=	'foot-path'
zip	=	'to hum'
zí el/zél	=	'to roll up'
zīl	=	'to learn'
zù	=	'rice beer'
zū-xá	=	'wine'
zūng	=	'root'
zù-cā	=	'mouse'
zùn	=	'to dissolve, melt'
zùn-thá (V)	=	'to urinate'
zū-bī	=	'nut (coco)'
zú?-mÀng	=	'to sell away' (T)
zè?	=	'untouchable, prohibited'
zè in	=	'because'
zèn	=	'to nurse'
zò?	=	'to sell'

zṓ	=	‘rather’
zŏ́/zóu	=	‘victory, complete’
zóu	=	‘to conquer’
zóu	=	‘after (in time)’
zó-ná?	=	‘defeat’
zōu	=	‘to tell a lie, false’
zōu-sèi	=	‘to tell a lie (utter falsehood)’
zṓu	=	‘thick forest’
zṓu-lèi	=	‘jhum field’
zóng	=	‘monkey’
zòng	=	‘also’
zól	=	‘rafter, bar’
tÀng	=	‘big lizard’
tĀng	=	‘to roll (oneself)’
tÀn	=	‘to cut’
tÀn	=	‘to break (as a rope)’
tå?	=	‘hard’
tâ?	=	‘fact, reality’
tā?	=	‘tune’
tâ?-sÀn	=	‘to believe, trust’
tái	=	‘waist (front part)’
tái-må?	=	‘crore’
tā́o	=	‘to pray’
tā́o/tú?-sÁt	=	‘to howl’

ting	=	'cane, cane string'
ting-ngòl	=	'stick (of wood)'
ti-zāt	=	'arraid or'
tin	=	'nail'
ti-pụ̀m	=	'body'
ti-bù?	=	'smoking pipe with water inside' (hubble-bubble)
til-kīlát	=	'to castrate'
til-xȏu	=	'to encourage'
tù-nū (F) —pâ(M)	=	'grand-daughter/son, sister's child'
tú/vù	=	'to burry (a thing)'
tù-phùl	=	'hoe'
tù?	=	'fist'
tù?	=	'to measure (with fist)'
tù?	=	'to hold (animates)'
tù?-xù?	=	'back part of the neck'
tú?-cā	=	'knotted hair'
tùi-kāi	=	'the let-out of water from the roof, top'
tí-kīnóng	=	'wave (of water)'
tùi-zAp	=	'to swim'
tùi-tèng	=	'the green dragon'
(A) túi-thà?	=	'to batch (egg)'

tī-páhn	=	'moss, swamp'
tùi-ném	=	'tank'
tūn/tū-bin	=	'now'
tė?	=	'old age'
tè?	=	'to beat'
té?/té	=	'to invite'
tēkå?	=	'parallel, to compare'
tėp	=	'to taste (eat a sample)'
tém/tíem	=	'to measure'
tém-nå?	=	'invitation'
tòu-nà?	=	'seat'
tò-kà-cúl	=	'full pant'
tò-kå-síi/tò-kå-síng	=	'half pant'
tòng	=	'measurement (one hem)'
tòng (V)	=	'to work'
tò (N)	=	'work'
tóng	=	'waterfall'
tőng	=	'drum (of tin)'
tòng-Am	=	'the seat made of bamboo and the hide'
tót	=	'to cut joke'
tòt	=	'to carry (on head)'
tő-phé	=	'buttocks'
tóm	=	'to cover (parcel, pillow etc.)'

tòm {dÀn / dén} = 'the back side room'

tòm̈-phə̃ɨ = 'reed'

thÀt = 'kill'

thÀt = 'to sacrifice'

thĀhlóm = 'weak'

thÀm = 'to touch (contact)'

thÀl-cÀng = 'arrow, bow'

thå = 'to itch'

thá = 'energy'

(tu̇i) thå/thå = 'to lay (an egg)'

thā? = 'to see off'

thá? = 'new'

thāo = 'fat (grease)'

thāo-mèi = 'earthen-lamp'

tháng = 'trap'

tháp = 'inner sole lining'

thāl = 'to fill (liquid)'

thi?/chî = 'iron' (cf. thi-blood, thi=evening)

thi?xiéng = 'blacksmith'

thi = 'death'

thī-sÀn = 'blood'

thi-lùng = 'corpus'

thī-ngèng = 'dam'

thing-át	=	‘to saw’
thing-gó	=	‘dry wood’
thing-cÀng mái	=	‘papaya’
thíng-phùng	=	‘ginger plant’
thing-phùng	=	‘tree’
thing-tùm	=	‘beam, log of wood’
thim/thip	=	‘calm quiet’
thīm	=	‘darkness’
thù?	=	‘to revenge’
thū?	=	‘deep’
thủ	=	‘sour’
thû	=	‘rotten’
thū-tÁn	=	‘to decide’
thú-pè?	=	‘to advise’
thù-mòp	=	‘messenger’
thùn	=	‘to fill in’
thùm	=	‘three’
thūm	=	‘to ask for’
thé	=	‘to spread (seed)’
thei	=	‘can (be able)’
thêi-tùi	=	‘juice’
thêi-thùp	=	‘apple’
thêi-hlùm	=	‘*naspati*’
thíem-xÀt	=	‘some’

thòu-hle = 'big fly'

thò-dò? = 'to get up (arise)'

thőu-sí? = 'fly (insect)'

thòt = 'to send (someting)'

dÀm-lòu = 'Not well (ill)'

dÀm-sȧ? = 'to cure (an ailment)'

dȧ? = 'gong'

dȧ?-dùl = 'brinjal'

dȧ î-(tui) = 'dew'

dái-dḗp = 'lizard'

dāi-pàng = 'fore-head'

dāk/mél = 'mail (post)'

di? = 'right (borrect)'

di-lȗt = 'to wince'

dieng = 'potter'

ding (v) }
din (n) } = 'to stand up'

diÁl/tuf-xAng-líem = 'sea'

diĂl-sūn = 'to kneel (both knees)'

dúng = 'length'

dùm = 'sky'

dūm = 'tobacco'

deī/dū = 'like, want'

dè? = 'forbid, to oppose, bargain'

dèt	=	'firm'
dò?	=	'visible'
dól/dói	=	'to aim at (gun or arrow)'
dő̃i	=	'magic'
dóng	=	'young age, soft'
dòng/dò?	=	'to ask'
dón	=	'off-shoot of tree or bamboo'
dóhn	=	'to drink'
dòp	=	'lift (raise)'
dòp/cóɨ	=	'to carry (in hand)'
dóp/ló	=	'a flat basket of bamboo'
dòm	=	'carry (in hand hangingly)'
dòm-(káng)	=	'to lift up'
dōhá-ból	=	'to deceive'
nÀng/nÀng-má	=	'you (singular)'
nÀng-ā/Àng-in	=	'your (singular)'
nÀng-bó ā	=	'your (plural)'
nÀng-hó	=	'you (plural)'
nĀm	=	'tribe'
là?	=	'ache, pain'
nâ	=	'leaf (du-wish branch)'
nā́?	=	'ribs'
ná?/nà?	=	'nose'
nā́i	=	'near'

ná?-hài/ó-ci?	=	‘to snore’
nắ?-gů	=	‘ribs’
ná-cÀng	=	‘palantine’
nài- {xúm / ngÀm}	=	‘to approach (come near)’
nál (n)	=	‘slippery, smooth’
nàl (v)	=	‘to slip (lose footing)’
nâ-vól-hing	=	‘locust tree’
nī	=	‘two’
nī-vĕ́i/viè-nī	=	‘two rounds, twice’
ni?	=	‘skirt, under-wear’
(nÀp)-nīt	=	‘to blow (nose)’
(nī-xó	=	‘day’
nī-gui	=	‘sun-beam’
nīen	=	‘dirty’
ning	=	‘rotten’
ning	=	‘corner’
nīhlà	=	‘evening’
nī-sĀ-và?/nī-và?	=	‘sunlight’
nū	=	‘mother’
nù	=	‘to paint’
nūi-sÀt/nūi-zát	=	‘to laugh at’
nùng	=	‘behind, after’
nùng-zū	=	‘to follow’

nùngâ:?	=	'maiden'
nùngà?	=	'mother's sister'
nùng-kòi/kòi-kit	=	'to put back'
nùng-dèl	=	'to chase (persue with the intention to catch)'
nùng-loù/séi-lèp	=	'to deny (knowledge)'
nǘm	=	'comfort'
nùm-sá	=	'to enjoy (the company)'
nū-mè/kói-yè	=	'want, admit (one's fault or error)'
né?né	=	'lip'
né/né	=	'to push'
né?níe	=	'to eat'
nèi	=	'to own (possess, to have)'
nēu	=	'small, low'
né?1/nḗ?l-dī	=	'sand'
nēm	=	'soft, gentle'
nél	=	'argument'
nò?	=	'to get irritated'
nṓ-xů̀m/bù-lú	=	'attack'
nóng	=	'pleces'
nṓi-mů?	=	'nipple'
nṓi-mÀng	=	'to erase'
nṓu-nèi/Àsó	=	'to bear'
nɒ̀t	=	'to clean'

nót	=	'to polish, to rub'
nòl/tát	=	'to sharpen, to grate'
pĀngóng	=	'widower'
pĀng	=	'round granary of bomoo mat'
pĀng-sà?	=	'to weave (basket etc.)'
pĀtxá̆.o/pĀt-zÀng	=	'thread'
pĀt-xè?	=	'to spin'
pĀt-còn	=	'the carded cotton's balls'
pĀt-tú̆i	=	'raw thread'
pĀsĀl/pūsĀl	=	'man, young-man, male'
pá	=	'mushroom'
pā	=	'father'
pâ	=	'thin (inanimate)'
pȧ?	=	'the inner part of flower'
pá̆i/cèm-pái	=	'sheath'
pái-cā	=	'big chisel'
pái-pà?	=	'the besket which is used for bringing fish'
pát	=	'pond'
pát-lè/dő̆p-lèi	=	'marsh'
pī	=	'grand-mother'
pī	=	'mother (animal)'
pí̆Al	=	'to avoid'
píeng	=	'to shout'

pî en/pî ng	=	'birth (of child)'
pū	=	'grand-father'
pùm-tōn	=	'guava tree'
pùl/hlĀmÀng	=	'to fall off (fruits etc), decay'
pé?/hing-pé?	=	'wooden plank, flat'
pè?	=	'to kick'
pē?	=	'hotness of chilly etc. (sense)'
pē	=	'to give'
pel	=	'offer'
péng	=	'daffodils, reed'
pé?/pèt	=	'to bite (as a dog)'
pèl	=	'mixed'
pėl	=	'rat trap'
pò?	=	'to carry (a baby-anywa)'
(tbi) pòt	=	'to bleed'
pòn/pun	=	'cloth'
pón-xóng	=	'loom'
pón-sōp	=	'washer-man'
pón-thùp	=	'thick cloth'
pón-hlè?	=	'light thin cloth'
pól	=	'mixed colour'
pòl	=	'to mix rice and curry'
pòl	=	'straw'
phÀn	=	'terracing'

phÀn-sâ	=	'to knit'
phÀ-mā̆i	=	'granery (ȍut of the village)'
phÀl-bī	=	'winter'
phÀl-pi?	=	'to allow'
phÀl } - mit sù? }	=	'to extinguish'
phà?	=	'leprosy'
phá	=	'good'
phít/phúi	=	'to drag frontward or feet)' to lead'
phù	=	'bundle'
phùn-/cò-ci	=	'to complain'
phúl	=	'boiling of milk'
phè	=	'to flicker (like fire etc.)'
phé?	=	'flesh, meat'
phè?	=	'to braid (hair)'
phòi-pī	=	'blanket like cloth'
phòn	=	'rough'
phón	=	'bubble'
phón-dò?	=	'to declare'
bÀng	=	'similar'
bÀt/pÀlá?	=	'to borrow'
bā?	=	'bat'
bà?	=	'hair'

bà?-cē? = 'scissors'

bái-bè? = 'nightingale'

bāng = 'to stop'

băng = 'wall'

báng-tòm = 'back side wall'

báng-lái = 'partition wall (mid one)'

bát-pùt = 'carry (on shoulder)'

bán = 'arm'

báhn = 'after, follow'

bí = 'the thatching straws'

bī = 'target'

biè = 'to strike (with hand), to slap'

biém = 'round, circular'

bièm = 'a big basket of bamboo'

bièl-xiéng = 'copper, modeller'

bièl-hléng = 'small plate'

bītÀl = 'a small bundle of thatching grass'

bil/bil-kúl = 'ear'

bil-bà = 'ear-ring'

bù? = 'food'

hù? = 'hat'

bú?/vĀ-bú? = 'nest'

bū?/bū = 'ice, ball'

bū?/bÀng = 'snow, ice'

bú?-lut	=	'dirt in the eye'
búl	=	'starting point'
bè/bè?	=	'to cling'
bèi-zin	=	'without'
bèng	=	'basket'
béng	=	'bat'
be-pī	=	'bean creaper'
bèl	=	'to get assylum'
bó	=	'to pick out, dig out'
bò?	=	'crookedly swollem'
bó?	=	'dirt'
bó-sè	=	'dirty (ground)'
bóng	=	'cow (both male and female)'
bóng-cÀl	=	'bull'
bóng-pī	=	'caw'
bóng-nōu	=	'calf'
bóng-nói	=	'milk'
bóng-nói-kÀn	=	'curd, butter-milk'
bóng-thíng	=	'a particular tree'
bòt-kè?/sÁt-kè?	=	'to tear, rip (cloth)'
bòn/buón	=	'mud'
bóm	=	'sub-clan'
ból	=	'to-do'
ból-zòu/tòng-zòa	=	'to finish'

ból-lòu	=	'to deny (orders)'
ból-så?	=	'to compell (force)'
bŏ́l	=	'lake'
mĀxĀgå	=	'walnut'
mĀxèl/phÀgā	=	'to over take, to get at'
mĀng	=	'to use'
mĀng-núm	=	'to enjoy'
mĀng	=	'to disappear'
mĀn-så?	=	'to lose (something)'
mĀl	=	'leg'
mĀl-phēi	=	'thigh'
mĀlcā	=	'chilly'
mĀ-sÀng (in)	=	'before'
mĀḗsi	=	'to predict, foretell'
mái	=	'face'
mái-púng	=	'water-melon, pumpkin'
mái-mÀm/mòm	=	'spider'
mī	=	'person, man'
mīzóng	=	'harlot (male)'
mīt	=	'eye'
mīt-xú?-mùl	=	'eye-brow'
mit-mùl	=	'eye-lashes'
mit-vùn	=	'eye-lid'
min	=	'name'

min-sa?	=	'to name (give name)'
mî n/mihn	=	'to get ripen (fruit etc.)'
mū	=	'hawk, kite'
mû/mûm	=	'bud'
mʉ́	=	'to find (Lit. to see)'
mʉ́	=	'to visit'
mʉ́-:ói	=	'to find out (easily)'
mʉ́/vét	=	'to see'
mù?	=	'point, bull-eye'
mūthòng	=	'vulture, eagle'
mūlūkòl	=	'kite'
mū-ván-lài	=	'kite'
mú-mòng	=	'horizon'
mùt	=	'to blow (mouth)'
mùn	=	'place'
mūn-thɛ́?	=	'broom'
mūm/mû	=	'bud'
mùl	=	'feather'
(sĀ)-mùl	=	'wool'
mʉ́ol-mól	=	'mountain'
mʉ́ol-kòt	=	'high mountain pass'
mɛ́i	=	'cloud'
mêi	=	'tail'
mèi	=	'fire'

mèi-ām	=	'unburn'
mèi-kȧ?	=	'to burn (int.)'
mèi-kóng	=	'flame'
mèi-xú?	=	'smoke'
mèi-cē	=	'ashes'
mèi-thái	=	'widow'
mèi-hòl	=	'coal (charcoal)'
méng-cā	=	'cat'
méAl-mā	=	'opponent'
muóu-(pùi)	=	'bride' (Lit. go and take)
mòt	=	'banana'
móhn	=	'to decay (inside rotten)'
mól	=	'faded colour'
mól	=	'blunt'
mol	=	'stick'
lAng	=	'appearance'
lĀng	=	'reverse'
lÀm	=	'path'
lÀl	=	'glory'
lȧ	=	'to take'
lȧ	=	'away'
(hùng)-lȧ	=	'to get (come and get)'
lȧ?	=	'to wear (shirt etc.)'
lȧ	=	'among'

lȧ = 'to pick up (from ground)'

lȧ-lút = 'take inside'

lȧi = 'to dig'

lȧi = 'middle'

lâng-vȧ /phÀt-vèt = 'a small box with mirror'

lām = 'to dance'

lám = 'a measurement of both of hands including body'

lī = 'four'

li? = 'dead'

li = 'round circle'

lí́e/lḗ = 'shadow'

lí́e/lé = 'to taste (with tongue)'

iėi = 'earth'

lē-xȧ- {pón / pè?} = 'paper'

lėng-kòu/liėg-kòu = 'shoulder'

lėng = 'to fly'

lėn = 'fly (insect)'

lèn = 'tired'

lėl = 'to lose (the game, battle)'

ló = 'vomit'

lō = 'to earn'

lō-sȧ = 'to name after (somebody)'

lò (V)	=	'shift through (flour etc.)'
lő (N)	=	'strainer'
lò-pī	=	'a bamboo mat (with edges high)'
lò	=	'to shake (something) (Tr.)'
lòi-nū	=	'to plaster, colour'
loù	=	'medicine'
lòu/pó	=	'not'
lòu-vin	=	'without (only abstract nouns)'
lőu	=	'field'
phái-lőu	=	'plain field'
thing-lőu	=	'jhum'
mā o-lo ú	=	'bamboo field'
lőu-kài/xòi	=	'to plough'
lőu-kivát	=	'to mow the grass/field'
lőu-th úl/lőu-thùl	=	'onion'
lōng	=	'corpus'
lòng-kái	=	'a tall basket'
lól-(hóm)	=	'throat'
lól-gūi	=	'neck'
lól-cē ng	=	'the neck rib'
lól-xóη/-dihn	=	'to gargle'
hlĀging	=	'loose'
hlÀng	=	'down (south)'

hlÀng-kībÁng/
cÀn-kibÀng = 'equally divided'

hlÀbei = 'lost'

hlÀbei-zān = 'the darkest night of the month'

hlÀbei-mĀsĀ zān = 'a day after dark night'

hlÀlùt = 'to dip into, sink'

hlà-lùt = 'sunk'

hlÀvȧ = 'moonlight'

hlÀsēt = 'humiliation'

hlȧ = 'wing'

hlȧ i (V) = 'to run'

hlȧ i (N) = 'run'

hlȧ i = 'to chew'

hlái-mÀng = 'to run away, to flee'

hlȧ ng = 'hill'

hli = 'to fold (sticks, arms)'

hling = 'full'

hlit = 'to strain (shift through strainer)'

hlim = 'spindal'

hlim-hlȧ = 'to forsake'

hlú? = 'to fall down'

hlú? = 'to faint, collapse'

hlù = 'hump of cow etc.'

hlùt/tùt = 'to hold'

hlùug	=	'to arrive'
hlûm	=	'to sink, so inside and vanish'
hlùm	=	'sweet'
hlûm-pe?	=	'upto the end'
hlèi-bò?	=	'to break (a strick)'
hlèi-hlá	=	'to pour out (water)'
hlèt-nóng	=	'to change (money)'
hlén	=	'to choose'
hlèp	=	'to fold (cloth, rope, paper etc.)'
hlèp-hlá	=	'to cheat (by giving temptation)'
hlém	=	'to betray (a person)'
hló/hlòp	=	'wet'
hló	=	'to get swept by water, drown'
(nʊ́i)-hló	=	'to mild (a cow)'
hlʊ́u	=	'to last (stay is condition)'
hlông	=	'flour'
hlòp	=	'to transport'
hlòm-cā/thiem-cā	=	'a few'
vÀ-à?/vān-gá	=	'crow'
vÀ-cā	=	'stream'
vÀ-cā/va	=	'bird'
vÀng	=	'hole (in roof or wall)'
vÀtót	=	'duck'
vá	=	'satisfied'

vȧ	=	‘crawl’
vâ	=	‘to leak’
vắ	=	‘to serve (food)’
vá	=	‘to walk’
vá?	=	‘light, bright’
vá?	=	‘to feed’
vái	=	‘post-morning’
(xō)-và?	=	‘dawn’
vắi	=	‘bundle (esp. of cloths)’
(A)-vái	=	‘breadth’
vā i/cĀgā	=	‘poor’
vài-cát	=	‘poverty’
vắng-bò?	=	‘to bless’
váu̇-à?	=	‘skylark’
ván-ging	=	‘thunder, sky-sound’
vā n-kitbin	=	‘thunder-bolt’
vā n-cùng	=	‘heaven’
vùt	=	‘to dig (a hole)’
vùt-vái	=	‘dust’ lei-vai (KT)
vùt-hóm	=	‘to break, open’
vùn	=	‘skin’
(sĀ)-vùn	=	‘hide (of animal), leather’
vúl	=	‘rope, necklace’
vĕ́	=	‘to cover with lion cloth (male)’

vè (V)	=	'to look at'
vèt (N)	=	'sight'
vèi	=	'left (side)'
vȏu	=	'to shave, cut hair'
vòt	=	'cold (things)'
vōt	=	'leach'
vòm	=	'block'
vòm-pī	=	'bear'
sĀkòl	=	'mule, horse'
sĀkhī	=	'dear'
sĀgi	=	'seven'
sĀgó?-kèu	=	'naked'
sÀng	=	'younger (brother or sister)'
snÀgán	=	'donkey'
sĀcùng	=	'rhinoceros'
sĀzū	=	'stage'
sĂt	=	'heat'
sÀt	=	'to pull (rope etc.)'
sĀnà	=	'gold'
sĀnÁ-xéng	=	'goldsmith'
sÀp	=	'to call'
sÀp-sét	=	'to curse'
sĀ-bèng/sĀ-dèl	=	'to hunt (for game)'
sÀm	=	'hair (of head)'

sÀm-thi = 'comb'

sĀthlè? = 'very hot (sense)'

sà? = 'to construct, northern'

sà?-(à?) = 'to cackle (as a hen)'

sā = 'animal (esp. wild)'

sá/sȃ = 'meat'

sà = 'hot'

sái-pī = 'elephant'

sái-há = 'ivory'

sái-há = 'to whistle'

sáo = 'long'

sāng = 'to accept'

sáng = 'thousand, high'

sáng-sōm = 'ten thousand'

sáng-zā = 'lakh'

sāng-kil = 'the supporting slab of the door'

sàngxól = 'shirt'

sáng-lòu/lÀ-lóu = 'to refuse (orferings)'

sắt = 'to strike (with weapon)'

sām-bù?/hóng-cā = 'varandah, porch'

si? = 'edge'

sȋ = 'limeseed'

si = 'to prick'

sī = 'clutch (of animal)'

siél	=	'to hide (something)'
sīng	=	'to shut (eyes)'
sīng	=	'to cover (the food)'
sīm	=	'to fold (hand-fist etc.)'
sim	=	'to attach and kill, to shake'
síem-phá/xȋeng-phà	=	'to repair (tools etc.)'
sím/sēm/xòp	=	'to abound, to form (a team)'
síl/seÁl	=	'mithun'
sil	=	'to put on (unsewen cloth)'
sil/cíeng	=	'to wear pant etc.'
sil-(théng)	=	'to wash'
sù?/sú	=	'to pound the earth by the side a wall or peg'
sù/sép	=	'to winnow'
sùt	=	'pestle'
sù?/cùp	=	'to knock (the door)'
sù?/-cá/sò?-cá	=	'aquit (find innocent)'
sù?/-cá (v) sò?-cát (n)	=	'escape'
sù?/-zĀ-cát/zūm-sò	=	'to insult'
sù?-táng	=	'to check (flow of blood, water)'
sù?/sù?-tùm	=	'pestle'
sù?/-thóu/sú-hÀl	=	'to call (attention)'
sù?-thíem	=	'to clean'

sù?-hlù	=	'to knock down (something)'
sú?- hlóm (n) sú?- hlóm (v)	=	'less, decrease'
sù?-nói	=	'to kneel (on one knee)'
sù?pè?/vò?-pè?	=	'to flatten'
sù?-mil	=	'to forget'
sū-lùng-háng	=	'to pinch, annoy'
sù?-séi (v)	=	'to destroy'
sú?-sét (n)	=	'destruction'
sút-pī	=	'the pole on the front door'
sūn	=	'noon'
sūn-Án	=	'noon-meal'
sūn-kaÁl/sōn-kól	=	'the three legged fire place'
sùhm	=	'money, coins'
sùm	=	'mortar'
sùm-dóng	=	'to trade, to barter'
sūmèng	=	'gold' (Literally yellow metal)
sùm-sÀn	=	'cooper' (Red metal)
súm-hèi/aÀng-bóng	=	'to grind'
sè?	=	'hammer, Mason's tools for cutting bricks'
sé?	=	'to throw'
sèi	=	'to say, tell'
sèi-si?	=	'to inform'

sép	=	'to winnow'
sèp-hlá	=	'to drop (without support)'
sèm	=	'to butcher'
sēmáng	=	'minister'
só	=	'servant'
sò?lú	=	'goose berry'
só/sòu	=	'to happen'
sòu	=	'pulse'
sōu	=	'ten'
sòm	=	'dormitory'
sōm-lĀ-xÀt	=	'eleven'
sōm-lÀ-nī	=	'twelve'
sōm-lĀ-thùm	=	'thirteen'
sōm-lĀ-kúo	=	'nineteen'
sōm-nī	=	'twenty'
sōm-n̄i-lÀ-xÀt	=	'twentyone'
sōm-thùm	=	'thirty'
h̤Àgiĕl/hĀgèl	=	'to grit (teeth)'
hÀm/hÀm-pā?	=	'grass'
hÀnī	=	'gums'
hÀl	=	'to mix sugar in liquid'
hÀvā́i	=	'pulses'
há	=	'tooth'
hÁ-xòng	=	'fang'

hÁ-pī	=	'molar-tooth'
hÁ-tủ	=	'front teeth'
hÁ-bÀł	=	'broken teeth'
há-giṇ	=	'loud'
há-ngèi	=	'melody'
hâ (v) hái (v)	=	'open (eyes)'
hà?	=	'armlet'
hài (n)	=	'breath'
hǻi (v)	=	'breathe'
hāi	=	'glass, bottle'
hāi-(thèi)	=	'mango (fruit)'
hàu	=	'rich'
háo	=	'to yawn'
háng	=	'courageous, brave'
háng/há	=	'blackish man'
hát	=	'strong'
hāp	=	'to bark'
hi-ā/hilái-yā	=	'here'
hí engè/hing	=	'yes'
hing	=	'greenery'
hit	=	'louse'
hit/mē	=	'child-louse'
hit-túi	=	'egg louse'

hil	=	'to teach'
hil-cen	=	'to explain'
hīm/hēm	=	'sharp'
hú?	=	'to protect'
hù	=	'guess'
húi/hùi	=	'wind'
húi-nùng	=	'to blow wind'
hùng	=	'to come'
hūt	=	'worm'
hē?	=	'to appeal'
hè?	=	'to squeeze'
hè/hét	=	'to know'
hèi-cá	=	'axe'
hèu	=	'to strip off (branches etc.)'
héu	=	'needle'
héu-bil	=	'eye of needle'
hét	=	'to understand'
hèt	=	'to put in the basket'
hèt/hÀn	=	'the bamboo skin'
hém	=	'glacier'
hēm	=	'pointed'
hèl-si/hÀl-si	=	'the bamboo fibre'
hò?	=	'skin of (plants, paddy etc.)'
hő?	=	'drainage'

hő? = 'to shout'

(thing)-hò? = 'bark (of three)'

hòi = 'pretty'

hōi = 'to drive cattle'

hòu = 'to worship'

hòng = 'to open'

hòng-cā = 'gate'

hói-á = 'where'

hóu-līm = 'to chatter'

hópá/hlő-pā = 'to pass by'

hō-pài = 'through'

hòng = 'to look after the field'

hòn = 'to order'

hōn = 'garden'

hōm = 'hole, hollow'

hóm = 'to share'

5

Phonetics and Phonology

Phonetics is the scientific study of the production, transmission and reception of speech sounds. It studies the medium of spoken language. Touching upon physiology and physics, phonetics is now a pure science that studies speech processes, including the anatomy, neurology and pathology of speech, as well as the articulation, description, classification, production and perception of speech sounds. It looks at speech from three distinct but interdependent viewpoints : it studies the speech organs, which produce sounds of language; it studies waves, the physical form in which sounds are transmitted through the air from one person to another; and it studies the way in which human beings perceive sounds through the medium of the ear.

Phonetics studies the defining characteristics of all human vocal noise, and concentrates its attention on those sounds which occur in the languages of the world. In other words, phoneticians try to study how the various organs of speech–the lungs, the larynx, the soft palate, the tongue and the lip–function in the production of speech. They also attempt to offer articulatory descriptions of various sounds by describing the air-stream-mechanism and the phonatory and articulatory processes involved. Acoustic phoneticians examine the physical nature of sounds and analyse the speech waves with the help of various instruments.

BRANCHES OF PHONETICS

The Study of phonetics can be divided into three main branches : Acoustic, Auditory and Articulatory.

1. **Acoustic Phonetics.** Acoustic phonetics is the study of the physical properties of speech sounds such as frequency and amplitude in their transmission. Acoustic phoneticians analyse the speech waves with the help of instruments; they attempt to describe the physical properties of the stream of sound that issues forth from the mouth of a speaker.

   It is in the field of acoustic phonetics that the most striking developments have taken place since the Second World War. Complex sound waves produced in speech can be analysed into their component frequencies and relative amplitudes. Considerable progress has also been made in speech-synthesis. Acoustic anaylsis has confirmed (if confirmation was needed) that speech is not made up of a sequence of discrete sounds. The articulatory features of rounding of voice of nasality, of obstruction and of friction can also be identified acoustically. Acoustic phonetics has achieved a good deal of success in matters of the study of the sound of vowels, but regarding consonants it has not reached final conclusions.

2. **Auditory Phonetics.** Auditory phonetics is the study of hearing and the perception of speech sounds. It studies different auditory impressions of quality, pitch and loudness of sounds. The auditory classification of speech-sounds has not yet been carried to a decisive phase. At the present time, phonetics can be regarded as being made up of two main branches : articulatory and acoustic phonetics.

   In a book like this, it would not be of any significant use to go into the details of acoustic and auditory phonetics. The results of acoustic and auditory phonetics need very minute observations and great scientific and technical expertise, and are often puzzling. These branches use instruments which cannot be used easily outside a laboratory, and cannot be transported successfully from one place to another. Hence the easiest approach to observations about speech is the traditional and most common approach of articulatory phonetics.

3. **Articulatory Phonetics.** Articulatory phonetics recognizes that speech is produced by some kinds of sound-making apparatus inside the human body, and that specific sounds may be related to specific movement of the apparatus. Hence it is the study of movement of the speech organs in the articulation of speech. Speech is produced by the movements of the organs of speech–lungs, larynx, soft palate, tongue, teeth and lips. The knowledege of the organs of speech, their relation to each other, and the way in which they are used while speaking, provides a sound basis for the classification of sounds of human languages.

HISTORY OF PHONETICS

The ancient Hindu Rishis who composed the Vedas, must have been in the knowledge of phonetics. The Vedas were to be chanted and pronounced very accurately. To mispronounce a Vedic **mantra** or **richa** was regarded as a sin of the first order. Even the classification and arrangement of sounds and their formation in **varnas** in Sanskrit give an evidence of a sound phonetic base of this language. In the works of Panini (400 B.C. ?) Patanjali (2nd Century A.D.), etc., we can have some concrete and outstanding evidence of the ancient phonetics of India. At about the same time the Greeks and the Romans had also made language and speech the subject of serious study.

Early Studies. Besides the Indians, the Greeks, the Romans, the Egyptians, and the Arabs also took interest in speech around the seventh century A.D. in connection with the Koran and Arabic studies leading to the developmetns in lexicography (dictionary making), the study of pronounciation, and language history. The Buddhist missonaries contributed to the study of the phonetics of Chinese and Japanese from as early as the fifth century A.D., and the

Christain missionaries contributed towards the study of not only Greek, Roman and Hebrew but also of a number of languages whose written forms did not exist.

The Sixteenth Century. Some of the first writers whose work was concerned with the relation between the sounds of English and those of another language were John Palgrave (Lesclarcissement de la langue Francoyse, 1530). William Salesbury (Dictionary in English and Welshe, 1547), Thomas Smith (De rectaet emendata linguae anglicae scriptone, 1568), John Hart (Orthogaphie, 1569), John Wallis (Grammatical Linguae Angliacane, 1563). Special mention must be made of Hart and Wallis. Besides making out his case for spelling reform and proposing a revised system, Hart took a keen interest in the description of the organs of speech, defined vowels and consonants and noted the aspiration of voiceless plosives. Wallis intended his Grammer to help foreigners to learn English more easily and also to enable his countrymen to understand more thoroughly the true nature of their language. A work of wider scope than Wallis' is Bishop John Wilkins' work who wrote Essay toward a Real Character and a Philosophical Language (1668). Wilkins also describes the functions of the speech organs, and offers a general classification of the sounds articulated by them. He offers suggestions for a phonetic alphabet.

The Seventeenth Century. Among the seventeenth-century phoneticians the most important name is that of Christopher Cooper. His work on English pronunciation was first published in 1685 Grammatica linguae Anicanae, with an English edition appearing in 1687 (The English Teacher, or The Discovery of the Art of Teaching an Learning the English Tongue). Cooper wanted to describe, and prescribe rules for, the pronunciaton of English for 'Gentlemen, Ladies, Merchants, Tradesmen, Schools and Strangers. His aim was to describe English as it existed and not to reform its spelling.

The Eighteenth Century. The work done in the seventeenth century was continued in the eighteenth, but it lost its original spirit. The Eighteenth-century writers were deeply interested in the production of dictionaries to stabilize and standardize the language. The Dictionaries of Samuel Johnson (1755), Thomas Sheridan (1780), and John Walker (1791), are noteworthy contributions of this age. Some of the scholars in this age confused phonetics with rhetoric. And it was not until the nineteenth century that a clear distinction was made between the aesthetic judgments and the phonetic analysis.

The Nineteenth Century. Since the Renaissance the elocutionists, language teachers, spelling reformers, shorthand inventors, auxiliary language enthusiasts, and missionaries have taken interest in phonetics. But it was at the beginning of the nineteenth century that phonetics received a real boost with the discovery of the ancient Indian phoneticians mentioned in the preceding paragraphs.In England Alexander J. Ellis (1814-90) presented to English children as well as to foreigners, an alphabet (phonotype, 1847). He also developed other types of alphabet notably Glossic and Palaeotype. In 1867 Alexander Melvile Bell set out to classify all the sounds capable of being articulated by the human speech organs and to allot a systematic and related series of symbols to the sounds. By the end of the nineteenth century the developments in physiology and acoustics, and the accompanying progress in instrumentation (as demonstrated by Alexander Bell's system of Visible Speech), had stimulated a considerable amount of experimental research into all branches of phonetics. Also in the late nineteeth century scholars like Henry Sweet attempted at producing a phonetic alphabet; and the international phonetic Alphabet, which is still the system in general use, came to be formulated in 1889.

The Twentieth Century. In the present century phonetics has developed immensely into various branches and is mature enough to claim an independent status as a discipline. Already some linguists have talked about **linguistic** sciences–by which they mean phonetics and linguistics the former dealing with the general properties of human sound making the latter with those properties which are of importance in the system of a particular language. The focus of interest in this century has been to find out accurate and precise ways of the modern age. Spectographs, oscillographs, sound-monitoring machines, tape-recorders, and a number of other electronic **devices** developed by communications engineering have been greatly helpful in studying sounds. The aim of phonetics now-a-days is not to provide a notation : it is to analyse speech into its basic units, which may thereafter be transcribed in some way. Hence the phonetic description is primary : a notation secondary. The contribution of Danial Jones, Abercrombie, Gimson in Britain and of Roman Jakobson, Morris Halle, Chomsky, Trager and Smith in the United States, besides a host of European and Russian scholars, to the study of speech-sounds is of considerable significance.

PHONEME

Learning to speak a foreign language is the acquiring of an ability to express oneself in different sounds and different words through the use of a different grammer. Any sounds, words or items of grammar of the foreign language may or may not have counterparts in the native language. And these counterparts may have meanings, or content, which are similar to or considerably different from those of the other language.

Since such similarities and differences may be used as foundations for language-teaching methods, it is important to know what they are and how they may be analysed. They include those similarities and differences in pronunciation, grammer, vocabulary and usage between the first language and the second. An analysis of these results in differential descriptions of the two languages.

Differential description is of particular interest to language teaching because many of the difficulties in learning a second language are due to the fact that it differs from the first. So that if we subtract the characteristics of the first language from those of the second, what presumably remains is a list of the learner's difficulties.

If the description of a single language is a highly complex affair, the differential description of two languages is more than twice as complex. It involves not only the analysis of two languages, but a comparison of the differences in separate items and of the way they work together.

Comparing the phonetics and phonology of two languages involves not only the phonemes themselves but also their variants, the way they work together and the patterns superimposed upon them in complete utterances. It therefore involves differences in *(1)* articulation, *(2)* catenation, *(3)* rhythm, and *(4)* intonation.

DIFFERENCES IN ARTICULATION

In analysing differences in articulation we determine which phonemes of the second language do not exist in the first and which onces are simply pronounced differently. This is done for both *(1)* the vowels, and *(2)* the consonants.

Vowel Phonemes. Taking the vowels of English (RP) and Standard French as an example, we first make a table of the vowel articulations in each language. By putting these tables side by side, we can see at a glance which vowels are lacking in each language. This gives some idea of the differences in pronunciation.

When we examine the table, we find that French lacks the following English vowels and diphthongs: /3/ bird, /^/ bud, /æ/ bad, /1/ bid, /D/ put, /ou/ boat, /ei/ bate, /ai/ bite, /au/ bough, /oi/ boy; these are the ones which would have to be learnt by native French speakers learning English. On other hand, English lacks the following French vowel phonemes: /o/ tôt, /e/ thé, /y/ lune, /o/ feu, /œ/ boeuf; these are the ones which, along with the nasals, give English speakers difficulty when they learn French.

But the solution is not so simple as that. A comparison of the diagrams of lip and tongue positions of French and English shows that the differences largely a matter of degree. Both English and French have the /ɛ/ sound but in English it is located between the French /ɛ/ and /e/ sounds.

And the English sound is further apart in tongue position from the French sound than are the two different phonemes, the French / / and the English. /^, which were listed as separate phonemes to be learned. The difference here, however, is mostly in lip position; so that if a French learner of English spreads his lips when he utters his sound / / as in comme, he gets acceptable equivalent of the English sound /^/ as in come; or he gets an equally good approximation by retracting his tongue when uttering the /a/ the battle to sound like the English word but.

Secondly, although a sound may not exist as a phoneme in the mother tongue, certain words may nevertheless contain a close approximation to it. French, for example, does not have the English phonemes /ai/ as in eye or /ei/ as in bay, but it does have in many of its words certain combinations of sounds which come very close to the pronunciation of the English phonemes, words like ail /aj/ and abeille /ej/, which can be used as starting points; likewise with French beurre and Southern British burr. Any two languages are bound to contain a number of similar approximations.

Consonant Phonemes. In comparing the consonants of two languages, it is convenient, for ease of comparison, to arrange them into a single table:

If we look at the table of consonants, we find the same sort of differences as we did in comparing the vowels of the two languages. We find for example, that French does not have the phonemes /θ/ and /∂/ as in thin and this; and English lacks the French phoneme / / as in huit.

But as we have seen in the case of the vowels, a simple comparison of phonemes does not reveal all the differences, and difficulties. For example, both English and French have an /r/ phoneme, but in English it is a glide and in French it is a fricative or a trill. And this difference is sufficient to make the sound one of the most difficult to master for the English or French learner studying the other's language. An added complication is that there are different varieties or /r/ in French; there is the fricative or breathed / / the rolled guttural /R/ (uvular trill) and the trilled alveolar (gum-ridge) /r/. A further example are the phonemes /n/, /l/, /t/, and /d/, which exist both in English and in French but are not pronounced in the same way, since in French the tongue is here more advanced than it is in English. But what the table does not reveal is the fact that there are words in English in which these sounds are pronounced with the tongue touching the teeth as it does in French, words like health, where the following dental /θ/ causes the advance of the tongue as far as the teeth.

A similar table of German and English sounds would show that English has no /ç/ phoneme as found in German words like Chemie, ich, manches, Mäidchen. But that does not mean that English speakers never make the sound; for they often pronunce it is the first sound of words like huge and hue. The reason they have difficulty with the German sound is not because of the sound itself but because of its position in the word. In German it occurs before or after the vowel; in English, always before. For a similar reason it is difficult for English speakers to begin a word with the sound / /; for speakers of some African languages this is by no means difficult, for there are many words in these languages which begin with such a sound. In English, although the sound is very frequent at the end of words like long, hang, and sing, it never occurs at the beginning. Many mistakes in pronunciation are due, not to the fact that the sound or phoneme does not exist in the language being learned, but to the fact that it does not exist in the same positions. When a North German says that he likes the English pubs /p ^ ps/, it is not because he lacks a /b/ phoneme in his language, but because the final /-b/ in his language is always devoiced and becomes a /-p/, or something very close to it.

Comparative tables cannot reveal everything about the exact quality of each sound. For instance, they do not show the essential difference between English and French stop consonants. They do not reveal the fact, for example, that English initial voiceless stops are followed by a puff of air and that French stops are not, except in marginal and emphatic speech and in interjections like hop and hep. These differences in quality could be put into the table, however, by making it more complicated and by using a more detailed or narrower notation; but the tables would then not be limited to a comparative list of phonemes (the sounds which made; difference to the code of the language) but would include all speech sounds which made a difference to the ear.

Speech sounds themselves, however, do not give the whole picture. What is equally important for the comprehension of the language is the way the sounds work together.

DIFFERENCES IN CATENATION

Catenation involves the answers to three main questions: *(1)* What combinations of sounds does each language permit? *(2)* What changes occur in each language when different sounds come together? *(3)* How does each language separate or join together its words and phrases?

Combinations Permitted

Two languages may differ considerably in the combinations they permit; this may be a great source of difficulty in learning to pronounce a sound language. For example, English, French, and Russian have the sounds /f/, /s/, /j/, but the English or French learner of Russian has difficulty in combining them into Russian words.

Not only the combinations themselves are different, but so are the positions in which they occur. There is, for example, a big difference in English in the number of combinations permitted before stressed vowels and the number allowed after them; there is also in Russian. But those permitted before the vowel in Russian are not the same as those permitted before the vowel in English; so that it is easy for an English speaker to end a word in /-ts/ as in the word cats, but harder for him to begin a word with /ts/, as he will need to, if he happens to the learning Russian. For the same reason, Spanish learners of English will pronounce the word steak as /estek/ and drugstore as /drogestor/; for although Spanish has the combination / -st/ after a stressed vowel it does not have it before one, and never begins a word with /st-/.

In differential phonetics, therefore, a distinction must be made between combinations permitted before the stressed vowel and those allowed after it. As an example let us take those consonant combinations of English (RP) which occur before the stressed vowel or begin a word, tabulate them, and then superimpose on the table the consonant combinations of Spanish (Castilian) which can occur before the stressed vowel or begin a word. (see table.)

When we look at the table, the first thing that strikes us is that English permits more consonant combinations than does Spanish, that those which are permitted in Spanish are limited to single consonant plus /l/ or /r/, and that of the English combinations not permitted in Spanish, must begin with an /s/, accounting for the Spanish pronunciation of words like steak, as we have seen above.

Combinations Causing Sound Changes

Different languages react differently when two or more of their speech sounds come together. When two sounds come together, one of them may change so as to become more similar to its neighbour (Assimilation). It may do so in two ways: It may change its voicing, as when /n/ + /s/ in the word pens is pronounced /penz/ (voice assimilation); or it may change its position in the mouth so as to have

	p	b	t	d	k	g	θ	■	f	v	s	z	f	3	tf	d3	m	n	l	pl	kl	r	pr	kr	h	j	w	kw
p																			E/S			E/S				E		
b																			E/S			E/S				E		
t																						E/S				E	E	
d																						E/S				E	E	
k																			E/S			E/S				E	E	
g																			E			E/S						
θ																						E/S					E	
■																												
f																			E/S			E/S				E		
v																										E		
s	E		E		E				F								E	E	E	E	E	E	E	E		E	E	E
z																												
f																						E/S						
3																												
tf																										E		
d3																										E		
m																										E		
n																												
Q																										E		
l																												
r																										E		
h																												
j																												
w																												

Initial Consonant Combinations in English (E) and Spanish (S) a place nearer to its neighbour, as when the /n/ of tenth touches the teeth because that is the place of the neighbouring /θ/ (place assimilation).

But which sound influences which? The influence may go in two directions: it may go forward, changing the sound that follows, as when pens is pronounced /penz/ (progressive assimilation); or it may go backward, changing the sound that precedes, as when alveolar /n/ becomes dental in tenth (regressive assimilation). With the same combination of sounds, one language may use one type, and another language, the other type. One language may assimilate in one direction; another language, in another. Although English and French make use of both forward and backward assimilation, English often goes forward in situations where French goes in the opposite direction; so that a French person learning English is likely to apply his backward tending type of assimilation to the language he is learning and say /∂izbuk/ for this book, and /teig∂ is/ for take this. On the other hand, English learners of French, failing to apply this very type of assimilation tends to say /absolyma/ absolument for the usual / apsolyma/ and pronounce medicine with a voiced instead of a devoiced [d].

When two or more sounds come together, languages differ in the tolerance with which they may let one of them drop (elision). A word like clothes, especially in such combinations as clothes closet will generally be uttered without /∂/ as /klouzklazit/, and waistcoat without /t/ as /weiskout/. Elision in some languages may depend on whether or not. The syllable is stressed. In English, for example, in unstressed syllables /h/ is often not pronounced; the sentence, he had his hat at the hotel in normal speech, might be /i -ed iz 'hat et di ot'el/.

Linking and Separating Words

Languages differ in the way they link together or separate words and phrases. The rules of liaison in French are well known to those who have studied the language in school, *e.g.* les étres /lezetr/, but les hêtres /hezεtr/ English has a different system of linking. It has three linking glides : /^{w}/, /^{j}/ and /^{r}/, two /^{w}/ oranges, three /^{s}/ apples, more /^{T}/ apples. French speakers of English, who do not use this system of glide-linking in their language, often seem to be adding an / h/: two /h/ oranges, three/h/apples.

The differences in junction or juncture, between languages are not always easy to analyse because so many different elements come under this rather abstract and very general notion—special linking sounds, as we have just seen, special separating sounds like the glottal stop in German, stress and intonation patterns, and even time, have all been suggested as elements. In test sentences like Not all blackboards are blackboards, what separates the word blackboards from being identical to blackboards may be the stress pattern, intonation pattern, co-articulation (pronouncing /k/ and /b/ together), pause, or any combination of these factors. And this combination may differ from one language to the next.

DIFFERENCES IN RHYTHM

Of all differences in the pronunciation of two languages, rhythm is often the most noticeable. Faulty rhythm in English is perhaps responsible for more misunderstanding than any other feature.

What makes a differential description of rhythm complicated is that in some languages, like English, it is closely connected with a number of different factors. For examples, as an English phrase increases in length, the number of syllables per beat of rhythm naturally increases, and this changes the stress of the words involved.

Examine the series:

It's an 'old 'house.

It's a 'nice old 'house.

Tt's a 'very nice old 'house.

Tt's a 'very, very nice old 'house.

Notice how the word-stress shifts from old to nice to very. In French, on the other hand, the stress is much more predictable. It is most often at the end of the word, phrase, or sentence—except when certain words are emphasized, as they frequently are in conversation.

DIFFERENCES IN INTONATION

Some pairs of languages have much greater differences in intonation than others. A Welshman is most easily recognized by his intonation—that is, when he uses the intonation patterns of his own language in English sentences.

When making a differential description of intonation patterns, it is necessary to show, not only which patterns exist in each language, but also and for what they are used. The first task is difficult enough and it is hampered by lack of standard principles of analysis and of a standard notation.

The second task of giving a content or meaning to each intonation pattern is much more difficult, for a sentence structure may be used with a number of different intonation patterns. And intonation patterns may add special subtleties to the contexts in which they are used.

The importance of a phoneme then, lies not in the actual configuration of its sound-waves, but merely in the difference between this configuration and the configurations of all the other phonemes of the same language. Only the phonemes of a language are relevant to its structure, that is, to the work it does. A description of the non-distinctive features might be of great interest but for this it would have to be more complete and more copius than any that have so far been made since every utterance contains by definition at least one syllabic phoneme, the simplest way to describe the phonetic structure of a language is to state which non-syllabic phonemes or groups of non-syllabic phonemes (clusters) appear in the three possible positions : **Initial**, before the first syllabic of an utterance; final, after the last syllabic of an utterance and medial between syllabics. In this respect the dipthonge and tripthong play in English the same part as do the simple vowels; it is precisely this fact that compels us to class them as compounds phonemes and not as mere successions of phonemes.

A phoneme is a range of sound which is perceived by the native speakers of a language as a single, distinctive unit and functions as such in the stream of speech. The distinctive sequences of sounds are only very imperfectly represented in alphabetic writing in which the same phoneme may be represented by a variety of spellings. But before proceeding to speak about the visual representation of English phonemes we have to describe them phonetically and label their properly. To describe the phoneme as sounds three complementary classifications are useful, that is articulatory, acoustic or auditory and description of the phoneme.

An articulatory description of a phoneme specifies the mechanism which generates the sound. Articulatory descriptions are, in essence the recipes for making particular sounds and are based on the fact that human beings make use of a limited mechanism to produce the sound of speech. The human vocal apparatus consists of relatively few parts which can be brought together or held apart or otherwise, modified to take on various shapes. This provides a flexible system capable of producing a large variety of different sounds. In every language, however, the number of significant sound discriminations (phonemes) is limited and they can be described phonetically by analysing the mechanism of speech.

The syllabic semivowel [u] does not occur initially or finally : it occurs medially only before [t, k, d, s, f, m, l] as in put, took, mood, pass, push, room, pull. Of the vowels only [a :] and [O :] and the unstressed [s] and (i) occur at the end of the word. In southern British and some forms of American English the vowel and dipthongs merge with a following [v] in final position and before consonants into special types of articulation. Structurally, we may either set up these equivalences where [r] was troded as a pre-final and second pre-final or we may simply say that the syllabics are peculiar in adding an [r] before a syllabic stirring, fearing, curing caring, sparing, boring]. In either case with other than a post-final are rare: weird, larid are structurally peculiar word; so in own. Although [i, e, E, O, a] occur before [r] as in spirit, merit, carry, sorry, curry, they do not appear before the equivalent of a final or anti-consonantal [r].

The vowel [O :] does not occur before [g] and the vowel [a :] does not occur after the unitral non-syllabic [W]. Before prefinal [l] the only permitted dipthongs and among these first two occur only when [d] follows as in field, wild, old, colt. Before pre-final [n] only [aj, aw] occur with any freedom, as in pint, mount, bind, bound occur where [t] follows, as in point. The tripthongs [juw] differs from ordinary combinations of [j] plus vowel or dipthong [yank, year, Yale] in that it occurs after initial consonants are in pue, cew, beauty, gules, few, hew, view, muse, and after the clusters (sp, st, sk) as in spew, stew, skew. The triphthory does not occur after initial and consonant plus [l].

The structural pattern differs greatly in different languages and leads us to recognize different types of compound phonemes, German, for instance, has, on the whole, a structural scheme much like that of English, but with some striking differences. The voiced stops and spirants [b, d, g, v, z] never occur in final position. The initial groups can be simply described only if one takes the affricate combinations [pf, ts] as compound phoneme. The only dipthongs are the simplicity of structure in this respect, leads phoneticians to transcribe them rather. The French system differs not only as to the particular clusters but also in more general respect. The dipthongs are rising. The greatest difference is in the use of the vowel phoneme whose occurence is governed largely by the phonetic pattern, so that it may be said to play the part of a secondary rather than of primary phoneme.

An entirely different system appears in a language. The structure groups the phoenemes into five sets : the vowels [a a, e, i, i : u, o :]; these are the only syllabic phonemes, consonants of four types : stops [p, t, k], spirants [S, h], nasals [m, n], semivowels [j, w]. The initial possibilities are, no consonant, any one consonant; stop spirant or nasal plus semivowel; spirant plus stop; spirant plus stop plus semivowel. The only final possibility is one consonant. While English is especially rich in consonant clusters, it is easy to find others. Final clusters foreign to English appear.

Once we have defined the phonemes as the smallest units which make a difference in meaning we can usually define each individual phoneme according to the part it plays in the structural pattern leads us to recognize also compound phonemes; which resemble successions of other phonemes, but play the part of a simple phoneme and that very slight acoustic differences, such as in English the syllabic-strees on [l, n] or the greater tensity of [j, w] compared to syllabic [i, u] may give rise to separate phonemes. The phonemes so defined are the units of signating, the meaningful forms of a language can be described as arrangements of primary and secondary phonemes. This task has been neglected by linguists and very imperfectly performed by amateurs, who confuse phonemes with printed letters.

Therefore in conclusion we can say that we have studied the sounds of speech in three ways. Phonetics in the strict sense—that is laboratory phonetics gives us a purely acoustic or physiological description. It reveals only the gross acoustic features. The laboratory phonetician usually singles out for study some features which his lay knowledge recognizes as characteristics of a phoneme. *Practical Phonetics* is an art or skill, not a science, the practical phonetician frankly accepts his everday recognition of phonemic units and tries to tell how the speaker produces them. The term phonology is sometimes placed in contrast with the two forms of phonetics: phonology pays no heed to the acoustic nature of the phonemes, but merely accepts them as distinct units. It defines each phoneme by its role in the structure of speech forms. It is important to remember that practical phonetics and phonology presuppose a knowledge of meanings; without this knowledge we could not ascertain the phonemic features.

The description of language, then, begins with phonology, which defines each phonemes and states what combinations occur. Any combination of phonemes that occurs in a language, is *pronunciable in* this language and is *phonetic form*. The combination [ni nu] for instance is unpronounciable in English but the combination [men] is pronunciable and in a phonetic form.

FEATURES OF PHONEME

A phoneme may, be thought of as the smallest contrastive linguistic unit which may bring about a change of meaning. It is possible to establish the phonemes of a language by means of a process of commutations or the discovery of minimal pairs, *i.e.* pairs of words which are different in respect of only one sound segment. The series of words pin, bin, tin, din, kin, chin, gin, fin, thin, sin, shin, win supplies us with twelve words which are distinguished simply by a change in the first (consonantal) element of the sound sequence. These elements of contrastive significance, or phonemes, we may symbolize as /p, b, t, d, k, tʃ, d3, f, θ, s, ʃ, w/. But other sounds sequences will show other consonantal oppositions, *e.g.*:

(1) tame, dame, game, lame, maim, name, adding /g, l, m, n/ to our inventory;

(2) pot, tot, cot, lot, yacht, hot, rot, adding /j, h, r/;

(3) pie, tie, buy, thigh, thy, vie, adding /ð, v/;

(4) two, do, who, woo, zoo, adding /z/.

Such comparative procedures reveal twenty-two consonantal phonemes capable of contrastive function initially in a word.

It is not sufficient, however, to consider merely one position in the word. Possibilities of phonemic opposition have to be investigated in medial and final positions as well as in the initial. If this is done in English, we discover in medial positions another consonantal phoneme, /3/, cf. the word oppositions letter, leather, leisure or seater, seeker, Caesar, seizure. This phoneme /3/ does not occur in intial positions and is rare (*e.g.* in rouge) in final positions. Moreover, in fianl positions, we do not find /h/ or /r/, and it is questionable whether we should consider /w, j/ as separate, final contrastive units. We do, however, find one more phoneme that is common in medial and final positions but unknown initially, *viz.*, /ŋ/, cf. simmer, sinner, singer or some, son, sung.

Such an analysis of the consonantal phonemes of English will give us a total to twenty-four phonemes, of which four (/h, r, 2, ŋ/) are of restricted occurrence—or six, if /w, j/ are not admitted finally. Similar procedures may be used to establish the vowel phonemes of English.

The final inventories of vowel and consonant phonemes will constitute a statement of the total oppositions in all positions in the word or syllable; when any particular place in the word or syllable is taken into consideration, the number of terms in the series of oppositions is likely to be more restricted.

It is important to emphasize the fact that it is frequently possible to make several different statements of the phonemic structure of a language, all of which may be equally valid from a logical standpoint. The solution chosen will be the one which is most convenient as regards the use to which the phonemic analysis is to be put. Thus, one solution might be appropriate when it is a question of teaching a language to a particular group of foreigners, when similarities and differences between two languages may need to be underlined; another solution might be appropriate if it is a question of using the phonemic analysis as a basis for an orthography, when social considerations (*i.e.*, for example, relations of the people with other countries have particular ortho-graphic conventions) have to be taken into account. Even without such considerations, discrepancies in analysis frequently arise in the case of such sound combinations as affricates (*e.g.* [tʃ, d3, tr, dr]) and diphthongs (*e.g.* [eɪ, əʊ, aɪ, eɪ, aʊ]), which may be treated as single phonemes or combinations of two. Such problems concerning English will be dealt with briefly when vowels and consonants are considered in detail.

Up to now we haveobtained an inventory of phonemes for English which is no more than a set of relationship or oppositions. The essence of the phoneme /p/. for instance, is that it is not /t/ or /k/ or /s/, etc. This is a negative definition, which it is desirable to amplify by means of positive information of a phonetic type. Thus, we may say that /p/ is, from a phonetic point of view, characteristically fortis and voiceless (compared with such lenis, voiced sounds as /b/ or /d/); bilabial (compared with the places of articulation of such sounds as /t/ or /k/); oral (as compared with /m/ or /n/); a stop or plosive (compared with /l/ or /r/ or /f/). The /p/ phoneme may, therefore, be identified positively by stating the combination of features which are significant within the English system : fortis, voiceless, bilabial, oral stop. This is a label which will be applicable to the phoneme in most of its realizations ('most', because in such a word as cup-full the /p/ may well be realized as a labio-dental stop. Such a case is covered if the term 'labial' is used rather than 'bilabial'). It is possible, by extracting from the phonemes of a language the distinctive features which combine to form such phonemes, to account more economically for the sound system in operation in terms of fundamental phonological elements.

No two realizations of a phoneme (its allophones) are the same. This is true even when the same word is repeated; thus, when the word cat is said twice, there are likely to be slight phonetic variations in the two realizations of the phoneme sequence /k + æ + t/. Nevertheless, the phonetic similarities between the utterances will probably be more striking than the differences. Allophones of the same phoneme occurring in different words on in different situations in a word will, however, frequently show considerable differences. It is possible to predict in a given language which allophones of a phoneme will occur in any particular context or situation: they are said to have a complementary distribution, different phonetic quality occuring in the same situation. Such a generalization does not take into account those variant realizations of the same pohneme in the same situation which may constitute the difference between two utterances of the same word. When the same speaker produces slightly different pronunciations of the word cat, the different realizations of the phonemes are said to be 'free variants'. But, if both [l] and [ł] occurred in the same situation or context and had the function of distinguishing words, the two sounds would have to be treated are realizations (allophones) of different phonemes.

It is usually the case that there remains some phonetic similarity between the allophones of a phoneme: both the [l] sounds as well as the voiceless fricative variety which follows /p/ or /k/ in words such as please and clean, are lateral articulations. But the Cockney realization of dark [l] is often [o] (as in little [lɪ?o]), in which case, the distribution of the sounds still being complementary, we have to envisage the possibility of allophones belonging to the vocalic and consonantal types or are obliged to reorganize our phonemic analysis. Again, it sometimes happens that two sounds occur in complementary distribution, but are not treated as allophones of the same phoneme because of their total phonetic dissimilarity. This is the case of [h] and [ŋ] in English; they are never significantly opposed, since [h] occurs typically in initial positions in the syllable or word, and [ŋ] in final positions.A purely logical arrangement might include these two sounds within the same phoneme, so that hung might be transcribed phonemically as either /hʌh/ or /ŋʌŋ/; but such a solution would ignore the total lack of phonetic similarity and also the feeling of native speakers. The ordinary native speaker is, in fact, often unaware of the allophonic variations of his phonemes and will, for instance, say that the various [l] allophones are the 'same' sound; [h] and [ŋ], however, he will always consider to be 'different' sounds. When he makes a statement of this kind, he is usually referring to the function of the sounds in the language system and can thereby offer helpful, intuitive information regarding the phonemic organization of his language, especially when it is a question of the first phonemic analysis of a language which has no written form. In the case of a language such as English, which already has an alphabetic orthography (however inconsistent), prejudices induced by the existence of such a written form have naturally to be taken into account in evaluating the native speaker's reaction.

It sometimes happens that a sound may be assigned to either of two phonemes with equal validity. In English, examples of this kind are to be found in the plosive series. The main contrastive feature between the pairs pin/bin, team/deem, come/gun resides in the presence of aspiration in /p, t, k/ and its absence in /b, d, g/, presence or absence of voice being usually irrelevant in this initial, accented position, where /b, d, g/ are largely or totally devoiced. When /p, t, k/ follow an initial /s/, however, they are realized with no aspiration even when stressed. Thus, in the case of such words as spin, steam, scum, we have three plosive phonemes which lack the aspiration often characteristic of /p, t, k/, but which do not have the voice which sometimes accompanies /b, d, g/. Since /p, t, k/ are never opposed to /d, d, g/ following /s/ in this position, the words might, therefore, be transcribed phonemically either as /spɪn, sti:m, skʌm/ or as /sbɪn, sdi:m, sgʌm/ without ambiguity. Experimental investigations suggest that perceptually and, the same extent, acoustically /p, t, k/ following /s/ have more in common with initial / b, d, g/ than with intial /p, t, k,/.

Another case concerns the allophones of /m/ and /n/ before /f/ or /v/, in words like symphony and infant. The nasal consonant in each case is likely to be [ɱ] in rapid speech, *i.e.* a labio-dental sound anticipating the labio-dental [f]. Here again, /m/ and /n/ are not opposed, so that the sound could be allocated to either the /m/ or the /n/ phoneme. In practice, since in a slow pronunciation of the [m] sound would tend to be used in symphony and the [n] sound in infant, a phonemic differentiation is usally made..

Prosodic Features

Such features may extend in time beyond the limits of the phoneme and embrace much higher units of the utterance. Indeed, in the case of the pitch variation characteristic of an intonation pattern, analysis may involve the whole of a lengthy utterance. In this sense, such features are prosodic, or supra-segmental. All three features may be measured physiologically or acoustically; length, as duration; pitch, as the frequency of the fundamental; and stress, as a measure of intensity, muscular activity, or air-pressure. Once again, as with qualities, the absolute measurements are less useful than an assessment of relative function. It is, for instance, irrelevant to attempt to measure the precise duration of a sound, unless the language in question makes some use of length variation as a distinctive feature.

If, in a language, there appears to be a significant opposition between a long and short [a], then it may be worth determining what the distinction is in absolute terms; or, if the length of sounds appears to vary considerably according to the context in which they occur, it is worth establishing the facts by measurement. But, in a phonemic notation, it is not normally necessary to take into account more than two (or sometimes three) significant degrees of length. Similarly, the absolute pitches used in speech are less important linguistically than the pitch relationships which a native speaker distinguishes as significant. And again, stress, which in the strict sense the listener hears as loudness, rarely requires more than two or three degrees to be shown, although the speaker's intensity will show an infinite number of degrees of variation. Thus, as with qualities, a preliminary transcription may indicate as many shades of duration, pitch, and loudness as possible, but the ultimate notation will present functional categories, abstracted from the concrete expression. Pitch will be described linguistically in terms of an intonation or tone system and duration in terms of contrastive oppositions of quantity; as far as stress is concerned, it will have to be established whether it has a linguistic reality independent of the other three features of quality, quantity and pitch, and, if it has, whether it is necessary to take into account more degrees than its simple presence or absence.

Paralinguistic Features

In addition to the prosodic features concerned with pitch, rhythm, tempo, loudness, etc., there are other characteristics of the utterance which are involved in the speech communication process and which are categorized as paralinguistic. In the first place, an identification of the speaker relies largely on our recognition of his own peculiar voice quality (or 'voice set') which itself is the result of the antomical structure of his vocal organs and of his articulatory habits. Secondly, he may make special modifications of his voice quality for a particular effect: *e.g.*, he may use a whisper or a breathy or creaky voice or again, he may be stimulated to accompany his utterance with a laughing or sobbing or whining features. This second category differs from the first in that the features involved are ones which are universally used in his own language (and in most others) as signals denoting particular mental or emotional states and which are therefore capable of classification to the extent that such mental or emotional states can be categorized.

CONDITIONS OF PHONEMIC ANALYSIS

Statement concerning phonemic categories and allophonic variants can usually be made in respect of only one variety of one language. It does not follow, because, of instance, [l] and [l] are not contrastive in English and belong to the same phoneme, that this is so in other languages—in some kinds of Polish [l] and [l] constitute separate phonemes Or again, although [ŋ] is a phoneme in English, in Italian the velar nasal [ŋ] is an allophone of /n/ which occurs before /k/ and /g/. Indeed, [ŋ] might be considered an allophone of /n/ before /k/ and /g/, as in sink and finger, were it not for the fact that the /g/ in words such as sing was lost about 400 years ago; once this situation had arisen, a phonemic opposition existed between sin and sing.

It should also be noted that the number of phonemes may differ as between various types of the same language. Thus, in present-day Southern British, the words cat, half, cart contain the phonemes /æ/, /a:/, and /a:/ respectively. But another type of English may have only one vowel phoneme for all three words, the words being phonemically /kat, haf, kart/ (the post-vocalic [r] being pronounced). Such a dialect of English would have one phoneme less than Southern British English, since the opposition Sam/psalm is lost. On the other hand, this deficiency in number might be made up by the regular opposition of the first elements of such a pair as witch/which, which would establish a phonemic contrast between /w/ and /ʍ/.

It should not, however, be assumed that the phonemic systems of two dialects are different merely because the phonetic realizations of the phonemes are dissimilar. The sound sequence [sɛt], *i.e.* with a vowel in the region of cardinal 3, may be a realization of sat in one dialect and of set in another; the phonemic categories commonly represented as of set in another; the phonemic categories commonly represented as /i:, ɪ, ɛ, æ, a:/, etc., may nevertheless be present in both dialects, the vowel system in the first dialect being somewhat more 'closed' than that of the second. Or again, the diphthong [əʊ] is a realization of the phoneme of boat in educated Southern British, but is frequently a realization of the vowel in boot in a type of London popular speech; the same number of vowel phonemes occurs in both kinds of English. Moreover, two speakers of the same dialect may distribute the same number of phonemes differently among the words they use. In Southern British English, some will say off, cloth, cross with /ɔ:/, others with /ɐ/; some will say elastic with /æ/ in the second syllable, others /a:/; some will say /'ju:nɪzn/ for unison, other '/ jun:nɪsn/, etc. Ideally, phonemic analysis should be applied to the speech of one person (to one idiolect). Individuals are, however, inconsistent; in certain situations, they may change the number of their phonemes, *e.g.* the occasional use of /ʍ/; they may not always use the same phoneme in a particular word or group of words, *e.g.* the erratic use, in the some phoneme in a particular word or group of words, *e.g.* the erratic use, in the same person's speech, of /ɐ/ or /ɔ:/ in words of the off group.

To sum up, we may conclude that a phonemic analysis of a number of varieties of one language is likely to reveal: different coexistent phonemic systems; considerable phonetic discrepancies in the realizations of the phonemes of systems which have an equal number of phonemic categories, variation in the distribution of phonemes in words, even within a community using the same phonemic system; and variation of phoneme distribution, even within the speech of one individual, according to the situation. It is important to remember this likelihood of complication in both the system and its realization, not only in the present situation but also when it is a question of investigating past states of the language.

The Word as Basis for phonemic Analysis

It frequently happens that a phonemic analysis is based on a unit not larger than the word. If any larger section of the utterance is used, the analysis becomes a great deal more complicated. As Daniel Jones has pointed out, the two phrases plum pie and plump eye exemplify the sort of complication which will arise. The two phrases differ principally in the aspiration which accompanies the /p/ of pie but which is absent from the final /p/ of plump. A phonemic analysis which is based on such an extensive sound sequence would require the establishment of two /p/ phonemes, one with, one without aspiration. The difficulty is avoided if the word is treated as a complex phonetic and phonemic entity, special consideration being given to word boundaries in the utterance. If, however, the linguistic analysis is based on a sequence more extensive than the word, a mark of contrast has to be established in order to deal with the behaviour of phoneme sequences at word or morpheme boundaries.

The Syllable

The concept of a unit at a higher level than that of the phoneme or sound segment, yet distinct from that of the word or morpheme, has existed since ancient times. It is significant that most alphabets, such as our own, which have as their basis the representation of phonemes by letters (however approximately), have reached this state by way of a form of writing which symbolized a group of sounds—a syllabary. Indeed, the basis of the writing of many languages, *e.g.* that of the Semitic in this sense. The notion that there exists at this higher level a unit known as the syllable has led to many attempts in recent times to define the term. These attempts fall into two main categories: those which seek a universal definition in phonetic terms and those which look for a specific functional definition in terms of a particular language. Some of the many approaches are outlined here under:

The Phonetic Approach

(1) **The Prominence Theory.** In any utterance some sounds are said to be more 'prominent' or 'sonorous' than others, *i.e.* they are felt by listeners to stand out from their neighbours. In the word sonority /sə'/ such 'peaks' of

prominence are carried by /ə,ɐ, ɪ, ɪ/. The number of syllables being determined by the number of peaks of prominence, there are in this case four syllables. Syllable boundaries occur at the points of relatively weak prominence ('valleys'), *i.e.* at /s, n, r, t/. This theory, which is based mainly on auditory judgments, does not determine to which syllable the weak sound, constituting the boundary between two syllables, is to be attributed. Moreover, difficulties are encountered in the case of languages such as English which permit consonant clusters. The word extra, for instance, transcribed as /'ekstrə/, would show by the same procedure three peaks of prominence on /e, s, ə/, thus forming three syllables. Such a solution is at variance with the native feeling for a division at a higher level than the phoneme, which tends to be interpreted as /ek/strə/ or /eks-trə/.

(2) **The Pulse Theory.** A more fundamental approach to the syllable is concerned with the muscular activity controlling lung movement which takes place during speech and which is capable of being investigated by experimental methods. It is claimed that in any utterance there are a number of chest pulses, accompanied by increases in air pressure, which determine the number of syllables uttered. Such a theory suggests that the syllable rather than the sound is the basic unit of speech, consonantal sounds acting typically as the onset (releasing factor) and closure (arresting factor) of the syllable, while vowel sounds are nuclear to the syllable and render the chest pulse audible. Again, such a unit on the speech level may prove to be irrelevant or misleading on the linguistic level. Particularly when it is a question of the juxtaposition of two vowel sounds, the second being weakly stressed as in the position of two vowel sounds, the second being weakly stressed as in the case of seeing /si:ɪŋ/, it is doubtful whether a double

chest pluse will be evident, although it is clear that the word is to be divided linguistically into two units.

The Linguistic Approach

A unit of greater magnitude than the phoneme or sound segment is more usefully defined in linguistic terms, *i.e.* with reference to the structure of one particular language rather than in general, phonetic terms with universal application. It may be found appropriate to divide a similar sound sequence differently in different languages; *e.g.* such an utterance as [ŋga:] might be found to consist of three units in one language -/ŋ-ga-a/, two in another /ŋ-ga:/, and even one in another -/ŋga:/. The divisions to be made might be indicated by the extent of the sequence covered by different tones or stress, in which case the syllable would correspond to a unit of tone or stress. Alternatively, a statement concerning the syllables of a language may refer to the particular way in which phonemes are found to combine in that language (the earliest meaning of the term), so that certain phonemes are shown to have a typically central situation in the permissible groups, whereas others are more typically marginal in their position. Such a procedure would not, however, decide in the case of the English word /'ekstrə/ the point at which the syllabic division is to be made, since /k/ is a possible final phoneme and /str/ a permissible initial cluster, and yet /ks/ is also possible finally and /tr/ initially; both solutions would be valid in the light of the English distributional system.

If, however, the syllable is defined linguistically, *i.e.* from the point of view of distribution of phonemes, a solution can be given to most of these problems. It will be found that the phonemes of a language usually fall into two classes, those which are typically central (or nuclear) in the syllable and those which are non-central (or marginal). The term 'vowel' can then be applied to those phonemes having the former function and 'consonant' to those having the latter. The frictionless English sounds /j, w, r/, for instance, which according to most phonetic descriptions are of a vowel-like (vocoid) type, function in the language as consonants, *i.e.* are marginal in the syllable. The English voiced lateral and nasal sounds are commonly classed phonetically as of the consonantal (contoid) type because of the complete or partial mouth closure with which they are articulated. From a functional viewpoint, too, they behave as consonants, since they are usually marginal in the syllable. Nevertheless, they sometimes seem to fulfil a syllabic function without the presence of a vowel, *e.g.* in middle, botton ['mid], ['bʌtn̩]. These /l/ and /n/ phonemes can be said to be syllabic here in terms of the prominence and pulse theories; they also function as separate units in the intonation structure of English. Yet there is some difficulty in establishing their such word endings as /-dz/ and /-ts/, in which /z/ and /s/ are not times avoided by equating [l̩ , n̩] with /əl, en/ both on logical grounds and also because /'mɪdəl/, for instance, is a possible pronunciation of middle. However, if the equation with /ə/ + /l, n/ is not admitted, the cases of consonant + /s/ or /z/ are not strictly parallel even on distributional grounds. Both /l/ and /n/ pattern in such a final situation very much as vowels in that they may follow the great majority of consonants; /s/ and /z/, on the other hand, have a much more restricted occurrence in this position and are, therefore, less vowel-like.

A further illustration of the consonantal function of /j/ and /w/ is provided by the behaviour of the English articles when they combine with words beginning with these phonemes. The is pronounced /ðɪ:/ or /ðɪ/ before a vowel and /ðə/ a consonant, whenever it precedes the other English phonemes; we also have the forms a or an according to whether a consonant of vowel follows. Since it is normal to pronounce the yacht, the watch with /ðə/ and to prefix to yacht and watch rather than an, /j/ and /w/ may be said to behave as if they belong to the consonant class of phonemes, despite their vocalic quality.

It is clear that if the elements of the utterance are divided in two categories, some units which are assigned to one class according to speech (phonetic) criteria may fall into the other class when it is a question of linguistic (functional) analysis.

The symbolization of an utterance (analysed in terms of a linear sequence of sounds) will naturally differ according to whether the aim is to indicate detailed sound values—an allophonic (or 'narrow') transcription—or the sequence of significant functional elements—a phonemic (or 'broad') transcription.

(1) In the former, allophonic, type of notation, an attempt is made to include a considerable amount of information concerning our knowledge of articulatory activity or our auditory perception of allophonic features. The alphabet of the International Phonetic Association provides numerous diacritics for a purpose such as this; *e.g.* the word titles might have its phonetic features transcribed as ['t^{sh}ä·ëtl̥ːz̥]. Such a notation would show the affrication and aspiration of the initial [t], the fact that the first element of the diphthong is retracted from cardinal 4 and is long compared with the second element, which is a retracted cardinal 2 vowel, that the [ł] has a back vowel resonance and is partly devoiced in its first stage, and that the final [z] is completely devoiced in its first stage, and that the final [z] is completely devoiced. Such a notation is relatively explict and detailed, but gives no more than an impression of the complexity of the utterance as revealed by the various methods of physiological and acoustic investigation. Nevertheless, an allophonic transcription of this kind can be useful for comparative purposes, *e.g.* for the comparison of different types of pronunciation, and is a necessary first step in the notation of a language for which no phonological system has been worked out.

(2) In the sound type of notation—the phonemic, symbols are allocated only to the strictly contrastive sound categories of the language; a phonemic transcription is highly sophisticated, since a number of conventions are implicit in each symbols. The word titles, for instance, would be written /'taɪtlz/, it being assumed that the phonemes

occurring in such a context would have the predictable phonetic realizations noted in the preceding paragraph. The number and type of symbols used will, of course, depend upon the kind of phonemic solution which has been arrived at for the language. As far as English is concerned, and notably the English vowel system, several phonemic solutions are current and a corresponding number of notation systems exist, all of which are justifiable, although the choice of symbols and the conventions attached to them differ. The striking discrepancies to be found among present-day phonemic transcriptions of British English are often due to the varying significance which is attached to vowel quantity and to the degree to which the symbols are made to coincide with the ordinary Latin alphabet. Thus, in the various phonemic transcriptions of Southern British English, the vowels of cot and caught are symbolized as /ɐ, ɔ/ or /ɐ, ɔ:/ or /ɔ, ɔ:/ or /o, o:/ or /o, oo/, the last three solutions emphasizing the quantitative contrast.

A phonemic transcription, with its implicit conventtions, is the most common and least cumbersome method of indicating unambiguously the spoken realization of a language. It may happen that it has a form which is close to that of the language's orthography, *e.g.* Spanish or Serbo-Croat; it is particularly useful as a corrective instrument in the case of a language such as English where the orthography fails to mirror consistently the present-day pronunciation. a phonemic notation may also be used as a basis for teaching the pronunciation of a foreign language, the allophonic conventions to be related to a phonemic symbols being easily learnt. Sometimes, however, it may be helpful, at least in the early stages, to include symbols representing allophones in order to emphasize a particular features of the language, *e.g.* in teaching English, it is often necessary to insist upon the variety of [l] sounds by using not only [l] but also [ɫ].

INTONATION

The meaning of an English utterance, *i.e.* the information it conveys to a listener, derives not only from its changing sound pattern and the contrastive, accentual prominences already referred to, but also from associated variations of pitch. Such rises and falls in pitch level, or patterns of intonation, have two main functions:

(1) **Accentual.** Intonation changes are the most efficient means of rendering prominent for a listener those parts of an utterance on which the speaker wishes to concentrate attention; pitch change is especially significant as a cue for signalling the word or words carrying primary (nuclear) accent. It should be remembered, however, that the accentual pattern of a response is often largely conditioned by constraints imposed by the context.

(2) **Non-accentual.** In addition, intonation is used as a means for distinguishing different types of sentence, *e.g.* the same sequence of words may, with a falling intonation, be interpreted as a statement or, with a rising intonation, as a question. Moreover, a listener derives from a speaker's intonation information as to the latter's emotional attitude (to the listener or to the topic of a conversation) or personality, *e.g.* his intonation might reveal a patronizing attitude to the listener, and incredulous attitude to the topic or a querulous disposition.

In so far as a listener interprets correctly those parts of an utterance upon which the speaker wishes to concentrate attention, or is aware of the speaker's attitude to him, or makes judgments upon the personality of the speaker, the pattern of intonation used may be said to constitute a linguistic system which has a communicative function within a particular community. There seems no doubt that intonation in its accentual function and in that non-accentual function concerned with the distinction of sentence types, does constitute a linguistic reality of this kind. Since, however, we sometimes misinterpret the emotional attitude as conveyed by intonation, it may be said that non-accentual intonation patterns of this kind are less perfectly systematized, or that such linguistic systems are more numerous and applicable to smaller communities (regional or social) than phonological systems, sot hat a faulty judgment of emotional attitudes conveyed by intonation cues may derive from an interpretation of these cues in terms of our own, different, intonation usage in showing such attitudes (cf. the interpretative adjustments needed on the phonolgical level between speakers of two different types of English).

The various degress of accentuation in an utterance may be signalled by means of intonation in the following way:

(a) **Primary (Nuclear) Accent**—by means of a change of pitch direction initiated by the syllable receiving the accent (marked ˎ, ˋ, ˏˏ ˊ, ˇ,^).

(b) **Secondary (Pitch Prominent Accent)**—by means of a change of pitch level (higher or lower) on the accented syllable (marked ').

(c) **Secondary Accent Without Pitch Prominence**—secondary accent on some words may be manifested by qualitative, quantitative, or rhythmic prominence, without pitch prominence (marked ˌ).

(d) **Unaccented Syllables**—do not normally have pitch or other prominence and are unmarked.

DIFFERENCE BETWEEN PHONETICS AND PHONOLOGY

The difference between phonetics and phonology is that of generality and particularity. Whereas phonetics is the science of speech sounds, their production, transmission and reception and the signs to represent them in general with no particular reference to any one language, phonology is the study of vocal sounds and sound changes, phonemes and their variants in a particular language. If phonetics can be likened to a world, phonology is a country. Phonetics is one and the same for all the languages of the world, but the phonology of one language will differ from the phonology of another. According to John Lyons, "Phonetics differs from phonology... in that it considers speech sounds independently of their paradigmatic opposition and syntagmatic combinations in particular languages," and that phonology is the level at which the linguist describes the sounds of a particular language.

The subject-matter of phonology is the selected phonetic material from the total resources available to human beings from phonetics.The human vocal system can produce a very large number of different speech sounds. Members of a particular speech community speaking that particular language, however, use only a limited number of these sounds. Every language makes its own selection of sounds and organizes them into characteristic patterns. This selection of sounds and their arrangement into patterns constitute the phonology of the language.

To quote Robins, "Phonetics and phonology are both concerned with the same subject-matter or aspect of language,speech sounds, as the audible result of articulation, but they are concerned with them from different points of view. Phonetics is general (that is, concerned with speech sounds as such without reference to their function in a particular language), descriptive and classificatory : phonology is particular (having a particular language or languages in view) and functional (concerned with working or functioning of speech in a language or languages). Phonology has in fact been called functional phonetics."

SOME MAJOR CONCEPTS OF PHONOLOGY

1. **Phoneme.** Most linguists, until recently at least, have regarded the phoneme as one of the basic units of language. But they have not all defined the phonemes in the same

way. Some linguists like Bloomfield and Daniel Jones have described phonemes in purely physical terms. Others like Sapir have preferred psychological definitions. Some regard the phoneme only as abstractional fictitious unity and argue that in a language it is not phonemes but allophones that exist in reality. Furthermore, linguists of the Copenhagen School treat the phonemes as glassemes and regard them as algebraical units.

The term phoneme was first used in the late 1870's notably by Kruszewski. Saussure too worked on the phonemes. But the most notable work in this field was done by Sapir in 1927. Most phoneticians such as Louis Jhelmslev, Bloomfield, Trubetzkoy, Daniel Jones, Roman Jakobson, and Pike have thrown light on the phoneme.

The phoneme, according to Bloomfield, is the minimal unit of distinctive sound-feature. In Webster's Third New International, the phoneme is defined as the smallest unit of speech distinguishing one unit form another, in all the variations it displays in the speech of one person or in one dialect as a result of modifying influences, such as neighbouring sounds or stress. In Dorfman's opinion a phoneme is a single speech sound or group of similar or related speech sounds functioning analogously in a language, and usually represented in writing by the same letter, with or without diacritic marks.

According to most contemporary linguists, however, the phoneme is the minimal bundle of relevant sound features. A phoneme is not a sound; it can be realized only through one of its allophones : it is a class of sounds, actualized or realised in a different way in any given position by its representative, the allophone: it is an ideal towards which the speaker strives, while the allophone is the performance he achieves; it occupies an area within which the various allophones move and operate; its outer limits may approach but not overlap those of other phonemes, and it cannot invade the territory of another phoneme without loss of phonemic distinction.

Thus the precise definition of a phoneme has been the subject of much discussion among linguists and there are two major points of view. The first is the 'classification' theory developed by Daniel Jones whch considers the phoneme to be a group or family of related sounds, *e.g.* /p/ in English consisting of [p], [p^h], etc. or /u/ consisting of (u:), (u) etc. The second or 'distinctive feature' theory developed by N.S. Turbetzkoy and the Prague School considers a phoneme to be a bundle of distinctive features, *e.g.* /p/ in English is considered to be made up of bilabial + stop + voiceless.

Depending on the point of view taken a phoneme can be defined as "a unit, a rubric, a bundle of sound-features", or "the smallest contrastive linguistic unit which may bring about a change of meaning." Hence it is a minimum distinct functional unit. Phonemes of a language may be discovered by forming minimal pairs, *i.e.* pairs of words are different in respect of only one sound segment. The series of words pat, bat, cat, hat, sat, that, mat, supplies us with seven words which are distinguished simply by a change in the first (consonantal) element of the sound sequence. These elements of contrastive significance are phonemes and be symbolized as /p,b,k,h,s,o,m/. Similarly, in the series of words hat, hit, heat, hot, heart, the elements of contrastive significance are a,e, i,i:, o,a/

2. **Phone.** Any objective speech sound, considered as a physical event, and without regard as to how it fits into the structure of any given language, is a phone. Hence a phone in phonology is 'the smallest possible segment of sound abstracted from the continuum of speech.'

3. **Allophone.** Some sounds, the native speaker thinks are the same, while others are different. The linguist has to figure out what sounds are grouped together as the same, what it is that they all have in common among themselves and how dissimilar are they to other groups of sound in the informant's speech and what criteria the native speaker uses to tell sounds apart. We said earlier that by substituting other segments, the linguist can arrive at a list of these significant, contrastive classes of sounds called 'phonemes'. But we do not always find minimal pairs to help us figure out the list of phonemes. There must be other criteria too, which we will have to incorporate into the definition of a phoneme. The k-sound in keel, calm and cool differs. In keel it is at the front in the mouth, in calm it is a little in the centre and in cool further back in the mouth. The absence of the above mentioned features do not distort the message for the native speaker. He does not differentiate these sounds in every day speech in the sense that he is not aware of the physical differences. He thinks these sounds are members of the k-class or are all k. In other words for the phoneme /k/, central-k, retracted-k, fronted-k are all allophones.

Hence an allophone is a speech sound which is one of a number of variants of a phoneme. Such a variant can be either in complementary variation or in free variation. The occurrence of a particular allophone may be determined by its environment, or it may be in free variation. Allophones determined by environment, for example, are front or clear [l] as in lamp or light occurring before vowels and the so-called 'back' or 'dark' [l] as in old and table occurring before consonants and at the end of words. They are in complementary distribution, that is where the dark [l] appears in English, there cannot occur the clear [l]. An example of allophones occurring in free variation in the

Southern British English (R.P.) is the /r/ between vowels, as in very, which can occur either as a flap, or as a fricative. Thus allophones are phonetic variants; they are positional or contextual, or conditional variants (alternants) of phoneme.

According to Trager and Smith (An Outline of English Structure), a linguist identifies these allophones in the following way:

(a) The sounds should be phonetically similar.

(b) They should be in complementary distribution.

(c) They should exhibit pattern congruity with other groups of sounds.

4. **Diaphone.** Sometimes a sound is used by a particular speaker or group of speakers of a language, but is substituted by another sound by some other speaker or group of speakers of the same language. For example, the sound of the diphthong /ou/, as in the word 'loan' may be substituted by the vowel-sound /e/c:, or the sound of the consonants dark 'l' as in 'little' may be substituted by the sound of clear 'l' by some speaker. The bilabial plosive consonant-sounds /p/ and /b/ may often by replaced by the aspirated sound /p^h/ and /b^h/. In Hindi word ओर (meaning 'towards), the sound 'ओ' is replaced by औ and the word is spoken as और (meaning 'and'). Similarly, the consonant 'श' is replaced by 'स' /s/, and the word शीशा is pronounced as सीसा. Now, both the sound that is originally used by the speakers of language as well as that which is used by other speakers of that language, are said to constitute a diaphone. Daniel Jones has defined a diaphone in the following manner : "The term diaphone is suggested to denote and sound used by one group of speakers together with other sounds which replace it consistently in the pronunciation of other speaker."

Jones elucidates certain facts related to diaphones, which are stated belew:

(a) "Everyone has different styles of pronunciation. Such different styles are merely different ways of pronouncing the language. When a person consistently uses one sound in one style of speech but substitutes another for it in another style, it is as if two different people were speaking, and the two sounds must be regarded as two members of the same diaphone.".

(b) "Care must be taken to distinguish diaphones from phonemes. The different members of one phoneme are sounds used by one single person speaking in one particular style; their use is conditioned by the nature of the surrounding sounds in the sequence and of the degree of stress, sometimes also on length and intonation. The different members of one diaphone are found in comparing the speech of one person with that of another, or in comparing two styles of speech of the same person."

5. **Phonetic Similarity.** Phonetically similar sounds are sounds that share a phonetic feature. such as nasality /m, n, ŋ/ or labial quality (/p/ and /b/) or front vowel quality (/i/ and /e/). But the notion of phonetic similarity is not a reliable guide. In a sense all sounds are phonetically similar, and are produced by the same organs of speech. In another sense they are also dissimilar, which is why we can tell them apart. Hence phonetic similarity is a tricky notion.

6. **Complementary Distribution.** Having discovered sets of phonetically similar sounds, for examples /p/ and /b/ we must ask whether the variation in each set can be accounted for in terms of the phonetic environments of the members of the set. Mutually exclusive distribution is otherwise known as complementary distribution. For every phoneme

there may be positional variants-allophones. Sometimes an allophone occurs in a fixed place in a word. The English phoneme /l/, for example, has one form at the beginning of a word and another form at the end. In a word such as light, the first consonant is a 'clear' l, pronounced by placing the tip of the tongue just behind the teeth and keeping the back of the tongue fairly low. In hill, the tongue tip is in the same place, but the back of the tongue is raised resulting in a 'dark' l. These variants of /l/ are said to be in complementary distribution : each allophone occurs in its own predictable place in a word.

Another example of complementary distribution is found in the English phoneme /p/. When p occurs in initial and stressed position, it is pronounced with aspiration (a puff of breath). After s, this puff of breath disappears. This can be tested by holding a sheet of paper in front of the mouth and saying the words spot, spill, pot, pill. In the case of spot and spill, the paper remains motionless. But when pot and pill are pronounced, the accompanying puff of breath makes the paper billow out.

The notion of complementary distribution in the discovery and assignment of the allophones of a phoneme is useful in a number of cases, but fails in some other cases. For example, in English no word has the segment/ŋ/in its initial position. Nor does the segment /h/ ever occur in the final position. These two phones are in mutually exclusive distribution, but they are not phonetically very similar to each other. Therefore the linguist does not regard them as allophones of a simple phoneme, but two different phonemes in English, although there is no minimal pair establishing that these two sounds are in contrastive distribution. If two allophones are not in contrast, they are said to be in complementary distribution : that is, neither occurs in any environment in which the other is found.

7. **Criterion of Economy.** Yet another governing principle is economy. The list of phonemes should be as small as possible. It will be in accordance with the principle of economy if we recognize length /:/ as a phoneme in English. Similarly some others prefer on the basis of economy to transcribe choose as /cu:z/ rather than as /tf/ u:z/. These examples are given to show that there is no unified theory of phonemics or phonolgy and that there are some controversial questions that have not been resolved yet. Different linguists use different symbols, consider that material at different times, thus giving rise to different interpretations.

8. **Symmetrical Patterning.** A third principle of discovering allophones, besides those of phonetic similarity and complementary distribution, is that of symmetrical patterning. Languages seem to have symmetrical patterning. This patterning is also known as phonetic patterning or pattern congruity. This pattern differs from language to language. It is to a large extent unconscious and appears to be one of the means by which human memory is able to store a large number of items. In English, for example, many consonant phonemes are unconsciously paired together : /p/ is paired with /b/, /t/ is paired with /d/, /f/ is paired with /v/. In addition, /p/ and /t/ and /k/ behave in a very similer way to one another. Each of them has an aspirated form which occurs at the beginning of a word, as in pill, till, kill, and an unaspirated form after /s/, as in spill, still, skill.

   By pattern congruity we also mean that relationships are far more important than the phonetic characteristics of the sounds. For example, the allophones of /t/ in English are produced at different points of articulation in words like fountain, the allophone of /t/ is realized at the back of the mouth and in a word like little it is at the glottis. For this reason, they ought not to be considered allophones of a dental stop. They are phonetically similar to velar and glottal stops. But the linguist books at distribution and maintains there are parellel positional variants for /p/ and /k/. So, disregarding the physical characteristics and paying attention to the patterning, the assignment of the allophones to a phoneme is made.

9. **Neutralization.** Lack of contrast between two phonemes in one particular environment is referred to as neutralization of the contrast in the environment. This so-called neutralization of the distincition between two phonemes is a more common phenomenon than free variation between phonemes in phonology. In languages like German, Russian, Turkish, there is a phonemic distinction between voiced and voiceless consonants in most positions of the word, but in the final positions voiced consonants do not occur.

❐

6

Phonetics Alphabet

The International Phonetic Alphabet usually known as I.P.A., has been invented on the principle of one symbol for one sound and the same sound should be always represented by the same symbol. The alphabet runs to hundreds of symbols, and with it we can transcribe phonetically almost any language on the earth. Fortunately, for the purposes of English Phonetics, we need only a small part of the alphebet. Further, it will be noticed that a good number of symbols in Phonetic Alphabet are the same as the symbols in conventional English alphabet. This, perhaps, will make it easier to the student to learn the symbols and value of the sounds they stand for. Now, here is a list of English sounds and the relevant symbols from the Phonetic alphabet. Each Phonetic symbol is given on the left, and against the symbol, the sound it represents is given in familiar words, in italics.

CONSONANTS

1. p as in *park*, ap*p*le, ho*p*e
2. b ,, *b*ark, ri*bb*on, cu*b*
3. t ,, *t*en, pe*tt*y, cu*t*
4. d ,, *d*ark, pu*dd*ing, mu*d*
5. k ,, *k*in, chic*k*en, doc*k*
6. g ,, *g*od, ru*gg*ed, do*g*
7. m ,, *m*en, si*m*ple, co*m*e
8. n as in *n*eck, mea*n*ing, soo*n*

9. ŋ ,, ring, hanger, sing
10. f ,, *f*eet, laug*h*ing roo*f*
11. v ,, *v*ery, ri*v*er li*v*e
12. θ ,, *th*umb, no*th*ing, tru*th*
13. ð ,, *th*en, lea*th*er, smoo*th*
14. r ,, *r*ead, bo*rr*ow, fa*r* away
15. s ,, *s*ee, de*c*ide, mi*ss*
16. z ,, *z*ink, bu*s*y, doe*s*
17. ʃ ,, *sh*oe, fa*sh*ion, ru*sh*
18. ʒ ,, occa*s*ion, rou*ge*
19. l ,, *l*eave, be*l*ive, bi*ll*
20. w ,, *w*ood, re*w*ard
21. j ,, *y*ard, be*y*ond
22. tʃ ,, *ch*in, kit*ch*en, cat*ch*
23. dʒ ,, *j*am, magic, lod*ge*
24. h ,, *h*ave, per*h*aps

VOVELS

1. i: as in s*ee*, pl*ea*se, sl*ee*p
2. i ,, c*i*ty, g*i*ve, l*i*p
3. e ,, d*e*sk, g*e*t, b*e*st
* ξ ,, me*a*sure, th*e*re, ch*air*
4. æ ,, m*a*n, b*a*g, h*a*ppy
5. *a*: ,, ask, hard, pass
6. ɔ ,, j*o*b, d*o*g, c*o*st

7. ɔ: ,, st*or*m, c*au*se, fo*l*k

8. u ,, f*oo*t, f*u*ll, t*oo*k

9. u: ,, r*u*de, c*oo*l, fr*ui*t

10. Λ ,, *u*nder, c*u*p, s*u*ng

11. ə: ,, f*u*r, c*u*rl, h*u*rt

12. ə ,, *a*bout, fo*r*get, moth*er*

DIPHTHONGS

13. ei as in s*a*y, w*a*ste, w*eigh*t

14. ou ,, t*o*ne, g*o*es, g*oa*t

15. ai as in fl*y*, *eye*, like

16. au ,, c*o*w, ab*ou*t, dr*ough*t

17. əi ,, b*o*y, b*oi*l, b*uoy*

18. iə ,, n*ea*r, h*ere*, f*ier*ce

19. εə ,, ch*air*, c*are*, th*eir*

20. εə ,, f*our*, fl*oor*, sh*ore*

21. uə ,, p*oor*, s*ure*, t*our*

Now, to transcribe an English word or a sentence into the International Phonetic Script, the student is advised to forget the usual spelling conventions for a while. He should watch the sounds in each words carefully, and then each sound should be transcribed into the Phonetic Script, using the right symbol. The student has to guard himself against the influence of his ordinary spelling habits. He must proceed with the transcription of a word, examining carefully what sounds join to make that word. The for example, the word *book*. Though there are four letters in spelling, there are only three sounds in pronunciation *b*, *u* and *k*. So the Phonetic transcription of the word is *buk*. In *busy*, we have the sounds *b*, *i*, *z* and *i*, and it is phonetically represented by *bizi*. Here are some more examples of phonetic transcription of some words:

tin	...	tin	alive	...	əlaiv
been	...	bi:n	bird	...	bə:d
will	...	wil	girl	...	gə:l
Wheel	...	wi:l	do	...	du:
ship	...	ʃip	who	...	hu:
sheep	...	ʃi:p	through	...	θru
met	...	mek	go	...	gou
mate	...	meit	cold	...	kould
look	...	luk	both	...	bouθ
luck	...	lʌk	loud	...	laud
lock	...	lck	town	...	taun
lack	...	læk	shout	...	ʃaut
race	...	reis	boy	...	bəi
raise	...	reiz	joy	...	dʒə
rice	...	rais	pair	...	pɛə
rise	...	raiz	there	...	ðɛə
about	...	əbaut	care	...	kɛə
arrive	...	əraiv	chair	...	tʃɛə
beer	...	biə	moor	...	muə
real	...	riəl	tower	...	tauə
sure	...	ʃuə	flower	...	flauə

The student can acquire correct pronunciation only when he has a thorough knowledge of the symbols and their phonetic values. He must be able no only to transcribe a given word or passage into phonetic script but also to pronounce words and read a passage from phonetic transcription. Both can be achieved by consulting a good dictionary like the English Pronouncing Dictionary of Daniel Jones.

While it is quite easy to pronounce, or to transcribe individual words, it demands some effort to pronounce or to transcribe correctly a continuous piece of speech. The difficulty arises because, a number of structure words in English have two or more forms in pronunciation according to whether they are unstressed, as is usual, or stressed in special situations or when said in isolation. Here are some of such words and their pronunciation in unstressed and stressed positions.

Word		*Unstressed*		*Stressed*
a	...	ə	...	ei
am	...	m, əm	...	æm
an	...	n, ən	...	æn
and	...	ənd, nd	...	ænd
are	...	ə	...	a:
as	...	əz	...	æz
been	...	bin	...	bi:n
but	...	bət	...	bʌt
can	...	hən, kn	...	kæn
could	...	kəd, kd	...	kud
from	...	frəm	...	from
have	...	kəv, əv	...	hæv
has	...	həz, əz	...	hæz

had	...	həd, əd	...	hæd
must	...	məstm məs	...	mʌst
shall	...	ʃəl	...	ʃæl
should	...	ʃed	...	ʃud
some	...	səm	...	sΛm
will	...	əl, l	...	wil
would	...	wəd, əd, d	...	wud
them	...	ðəm, əm	...	ðem
was	...	wəz,	...	wΛz
were	...	wə,	...	wə:
to	...	kə, t	...	tu

Certain contracted forms in English add to the difficulty of pronouncing English. In most of the forms of spoken English the Personal Pronouns are joined on to shortened forms of the Finite Verbs, *am, is, are, has, have, had, shall, will, should* and *would*. In negative constructions employing any one of the twenty-four anomalous finites, and contracted form of the word *not* is joined on to the finite, resulting in apparently single words which have their own pronunciation. Here is the example for each case.

Uncontracted form	*Contracted form*		
	Written		*Spoken*
I am	I'm	...	aim
He is	He's	...	hi:z
She is	She's	...	ʃi:z
It is	It's	...	its
We are	We'are	...	wiə
You are	You're	...	juə

They are	They're	...	ðeə
I have	I've	...	aiv
He has	He's	...	hi:z
She has	She's	..	ʃi:z
It has	It's	...	its
We have	We've	...	wi:v
You have	You've	...	ju:v
They have	They've	...	ðeiv
I had	I'd	...	aid
He had	He'd	...	hi:d
She had	She'd	...	ʃi:d
It had	It'd	...	itəd
We had	We'd	...	wi:d
You had	You'd	...	ju:d
They had	They'd	...	ðeid
I shall	I'll	...	ail
He will	He'll	...	hi:l
She will	She'll	...	ʃi:l
It will	It'll	...	itəl
We shall	we'll	...	wi:l
You will	You'll	...	ju:l
They will	They'll	...	ðeil

N.B.—The contracted forms do not distinguish between shall and will.

I should	I'ld	...	aid
He would	He'ld	...	hi:d
She would	She'ld	...	ʃi:d
It would	It'ld	...	itəd
We should	We'ld	...	wi:d
You would	You'ld	...	ju:d
They would	They'ld	...	ðeid

N.B.—The contracted forms do not distinguish between should and would. The written contracted form sometimes. omits the *l : I'd, He'd* etc.

Negative forms with the 24 anomalous finites

am not	I'm not	...	aim nət
is not	I's not	...	iznt
are not	aren't	...	a:nt
was not	wasn't	...	wəznt
were not	weren't	...	wə:nt
have not	haven't	...	hævnt
has not	hasn't	...	hæznt
had not	hadn't	...	hædnt
do not	don't	...	dount
does not	doesn't	...	dΛznt
did not	didn't	...	didnt
shall not	shan't	...	ʃa:nt
should not	should'nt	...	ʃudnt

will not	won't	...	wount
would not	wouldn't	...	wudnt
cannot	can't	...	ka:nt
could not	couldn't	...	kudnt
may not	mayn't	...	meint
might not	mightn't	...	maitnt
must not	mustn't	...	mʌsnt
ought not	oughtn't	...	ə:tnt
need not	needn't	...	ni:dnt
dare not	daren't	...	deənt
used not	usedn't	...	ju:snt

Other subjects, besides personal pronouns, are often contraced with the same finite verbs, particularly in fairly rapid, colloquial speech. A few eamples follow:

There's nothing here.

That's enough.

The woman's gone.

The men've gone.

The weather'll change.

Now, with the help of what has been explained in this chapter, the student should be able to attempt transcription of the following passages. While transcribing, he must assume the standard English pronunication usually called, Received, Pronunciation.

No. I.—To explain simply the working of the telegraph is a puzzle for the philosopher; and no wonder simple folks come to grief over the task. The following is the explanation given to his fellow by an Italian peasant:

'Do you see those poles and wires that run along by the side of the railway?'

"I know that is the telegraph. But how does it work?"

'Nothing more simple. You have only to touch one end of the wire, and click—the other end writes it down just the same as a pen.'

'Still I don't quite see how it is done.'

'Let me try to make it plain, have you got a dog?'

'Yes.'

'What does he do if you pinch his tail?'

'Why, bark, to be sure.'

'Well then supposing your dog was long enough to reach in body from Florence here to the capital.'

'Well?"

'It's clear, then, that if you pinch his tail in Florence, he will bark in Rome. And that's exactly how the electric telegraph works.'

No. II.—'At what time are you going to the exhibition? I thought I heard you tell your brother this morning that you expected to meet him there at about two.

Yes. Would you like to join us there?

I would, with pleasure, but I am not sure whether I can. In any case I must leave early to catch the four train. I do not live here now; I live in the suburbs and I want to get home before it is dark.

Are you really in such a hurry to get home? Must you? If it is solely on the account, we can take you back in our car.

Can you? That will splendid! All right.

CLASSIFICATION OF CONSONANTS

The consonants are the sounds formed either by stopping the mouth-passage completely, for a moment, or by sufficiently restricting the mouth-passage to produce a perceptible friction. Some of them are articulated by the lips, some by the teeth and yet some by the palate and so on. So, consonants can be classified according to the manner of articulation. If we classify consonants according to the organs which articulate them, we find seven main classsies of consonants. They are:

I. *Liabial* consonants are also called lip-consonants and they are subdivided into two classes.

   (a) *Bi-labial,* namely consonants which are articulated by the combined activity of the two lips. Examples, *p, b, m.*

   (b) *Labio-dental,* namely sound formed by setting the lower lip against the upper teeth. Example, *f, u.*

II. *Dentals* are sounds articulated by the lower lip set against the upper teeth. Examples are, θ, ð.

III. *Alveolar* consonants are sounds formed by the tip or blade of the tongue touching the teeth-ridge. Examples are, *t, d, l, r, s, z.*

(IV). Palato-Alveolar consonants are articulated like alveolars. But there is also a simultaneous activity of raising of the main body of the tongue towards the hard palate. Examples are ʃ, 3, tʃ, *d3.*

V. *Palatal,* namely sounds formed by the front of the tongue raising towards the hard palate. Example J.

VI. *Velar* consonants are articulated by the back of the tongue touching the velum or the soft palate. Examples are, *k,g.η.*

VII. Glottal sounds are articulated in the glottis, Example, *h.*

It we classify English consonants according to the manner of articulation, we distinguish six main classes. They are:

1. *Plosive* consonants, namely, sounds formed by completely blocking the air-stream and again suddenly releasing it, so that the air escapes with an explosive sound. Examples are *p, b, t, d, k, g.*

2. Affricate consonants resemble plosives to a large extent. But in the case of these consonants, the air-passage is released not so suddenly as in the case of plosive, but less quickly. Further it can be observed that the main body of the tongue touches a large area of the hard palate. Eamples are *tʃ, d3.*

3. *Nasal* consonants are made by closing the mouth at some point, and by lowering the soft palate so that the air-stream is compelled to pass out through the nasal cavity. Examples are m, n, ŋ.

4. *Lateral* sounds are articulated by obstructing the air-stream in the middle of the mouth so that the air is made to escape through one or both sides example, *l.*

5. *Fricative* consonants are formed by restricting and narrowing the air-passage at some point so that the escping air makes a sort of hissing sound caused by friction. Examples are *f, v, θ, ə, s, z, ʃ,* 3

6. Semi-vowel sounds are otherwise called gliding consonants. They start in one vowel position and imperceptibly move away to the position of some other vowel. Examples w, *j.*

The classification may be very conveniently shown by the following table:

Table of English Consonant Sounds

Manner of articulation	*Place of articulations in the mouth*							
	Labial							
	Bi-labial	*Labio dental*	*Dental*	*Alveolar*	*P a l a t o - Alveolar*	*Palatal*	*Velar*	*Glottal*
Plosive	*p, b*			*t, d*			*k, g*	
Affricate					*tʃ, d3.*			
Nasal	*m*	...		*n*			*n*	
Lateral								
Fricative		*f, v*		*s,z, r*	ʃ, 3			*h*
Semi-Vowel	w					J		

Of these consonants some are voiced and some are voiceless.

Voiced : *b, d, g, d3, n, n, l, r, v, ð, z, 3, w, j.*

Voiceless : *p, t, k, tʃ, f, s,ʃ.*

Indian students can easily pronounce, with intelligibility, consonants like p, t, k, b, d, g, m, n, h, j. But they need some efforts to familiarise themselves with the rest of the consonants, and to use them intelligibly in their own speech. It is hoped that the following description of each of the difficult consonants will be of some help to our students.

ŋ as in *song* (səŋ), *ink* (iŋk). This is called voiced velar nasal. In making this sound the soft palate is lowered so as to touch the back of the toungue and close the mouthpassage. The air is thus forced to pass out through the nasal cavity. The place of articulation is generally at the velum, though there may be a degree of variation as to which part of the velum is used. This sound occurs sometimes in the company of g sound as in finger (fiŋgə), anger (æŋgə), youngest (Jaŋgist) and so on. It also occurs without being followed by g, as in singer (siŋə) longing and so on. In some parts of England the latter type of the sound is becoming obsolete.

f as in *foot* (fut), safe (seif) and offer (cfə). This is a voiceless labio-dental fricative. In producing this sound the lower lip is brought against the upper teeth. The air passage is thus restricted and a slight friction is caused. Some Indian students find it difficult to distinguish between p and f. In making the sound p, both lips touch each other and the air passage is completely blocked. But in the formation of f sound the upper lip is almost idle. The lower lip and upper teeth join to produce this sound by narrowing the air passage.

In careless speech f is dropped in expressions-like *half-past* twelve which is pronounced h a : p ə s tw ȩ̄ lve for ha : f pa:s tw ȩ̄ lv.

v as in *van* (væn), *move* (mu:v) and so on. This is a voiced counterpart of f. Like f, it is a labio-dental fricative. The mechanism of producing this sound is the same as that of f. The difference is simply that f is voiceles and v is voiced.

In rapid speech v of *of* and *have* are dropped before another consonant, especially when they are followed by the word *the*. For example, *out of the way* is pronounced aut ə ðə wei and "*you shouldn't have been so silly*" is pronounced ju: ʃudnt ð bin sou sili.

θ as in *thin* (θin) *method* (mȩ̄ θəd). This is a voiceless dental fricative. This is one of the difficult sounds for Indian students. In pronouncing this sound the tip of the tongue is set against the upper teeth. The tongue-tip tends to touch the upper teeth, but does not actually touch them. If the tongue is made to touch the upper teeth, it blocks the air passage resulting in production of a plosive consonant which exists in many Indian languages. We should understand that English θ is not the same as our त, though the place of production of these two sounds is almost the same. But the manner of production of production is different. त is plosive and θ is fricative.

ð as in them (ðem) and *this* (ðis). This is a voiced counterpart of *θ*. The tongue position and the manner of production are the same as for *θ*. But this is a voiced sound, while *θ* is a voiceless consonant. Just as *θ* is mistaken of त this sound is mistaken for द. The difference between ð and द is the same as the difference between *θ* and त.

Sometimes *θ* and ð are interchangeable in English. For example, in compounds, words like *withdraw, withhold,* the medial sound is pronounced *θ* by some people and ð by others.

s as in *see* (si :) *acid* (æsid). This is a voiceless alveolar fricative. This is generally articulated with the tip of the tongue tending to touch the teethridge. The resulting restriction of the air-passage causes friction which produces hissing sound. This is almost equivalent to the sound स in our languages. Some however pronounce the sound with the blade of the tongue raised towards the teeth ridge, while keeping the tip of the tongue down near the lower teeth. The resulting sound is not very much exactly s, but close to श sound of Indian languages. The s sound would not present any difficulty if we could distinguish स from श and श from ष.

z as in *zeal* (zi: 1) and *choose* (tʃu:z). This is a voiced alveolar fricative. The manner and place of production of this sound are the same as those of s. The difference is that this is voiced. By our students, this is often mistaken for ज sound. They must watch the tongue position in each case. In the case of च (d_3) sound the tongue is made to touch the teethridge. But in producing z sound, the tongue tends to touch the teeth ridge, but leaves some passage to the escaping airstream.

ʃ as in *ship* (ʃip) *nation* (neiʃn). This is called voiceless palato-alveolar fricative. This is one of the frequently mispronouced sounds. Some of us cannot distinguish between s *and* ʃ. It should be noted that s is a hissing sound and ʃ is a sort of whistling sound. Try to whistle without protruding your lips, that is, keeping them in neutral position, and you get the ʃ sound. This is produced by the combined activity of the blade of the tongue and the front part of the hard palate. By many of us it is pronounced very like our स or English z. This should not be difficult if we could pronounce our ष sound correctly. The author notices, with pain, that many of us can not precisely distinguish between स, श, ष.

Z as in *measure* (me$_3$ȩ̄), *pleasure* (ple3ȩ̄) *rouge*, (ru :3). This is a voiced palato-alveolar fricative, that is, a voiced counterpart of ʃ. The tongue position is the same as in the case of ʃ. The blade of the tongue is raised towards the front part of the hard palate to narrow the air-stream. To the resulting whistling sound (ʃ), voice is added by making the voical cords vibrate.

j as in *yard*, (j a : d), *young* (jʌŋ), issue (issue:). This is one of the two semi-vowels; the other is w which we will discuss presently. j is a voiced palatal consonant. ʃt is called a semi-vowel because sometime it is difficult to notice where precisely the vowel i: ends and the consonant j begins. i: is the vowel sould nearest to j. i: is pronounced by raising the front part (just behind the blade) of the tongue towards he hard palate. If slightly frontier part of the tongue is raised, the resutl is j sound, a consonant.

w as in *win* (win), *wait* (weit) wc:k). This is a voiced bi-labial consonant, but, paradoxically called semi-vowel. The vowel sound nearest to this is u:. The affinity between the vowel u: sound and the consonant w is due to the lip position in their pronunciation. In both cases the lips are brought into activity ; they are rounded. But in the case of the vowel the rounding lasts for sometime till the lips take up a new position to pronounce the following sound as in *music* (mju:zik), use (ju:z), tune (tju:n). But in the case of w, the lips are slightly rounded and again soon spread before they take up a new position to produce the following sound. Many of our students find it difficult to distinguish w from v. It should be noted that in pronoucing v, the lower lip is raised towards the upper teeth to cause friction, by narrowing the air-stream. In the case of w, the teeth remain idle.

Again in the case of v, a sort of buzzing should is produced, but w does not give any such buzz.

Words written with *wh* are commonly pronounced with w, and h is silent. Examples, *which* (witʃ), *when* (wȩ̄ n) *what* (wət) *why* (wai). But there are some exceptions in which the reverse process takes place; in words like *who, whom, whose, whole,* the w sound is silent and the h is pronounced, hu: hu:m hu:z, houl, Tendency to pronounce hw should be avoided in all thse examples.

tʃ as in *church* (tʃd:tʃ), fetch (fȩ̄ tʃ). This is considered to be a single sound, although for the sake of convenience it is phonetically represented by two symbols, a plosive t followed by a fricative ʃ. This is called a palato-alveolar affricate. In making this the blade of the tongue is made to touch the front part of the hard palate making complete contact. Then the blocked airstream is released and the result is the sound tʃ. In some Indian languages there are two or more varieties of this sound. Our students should learn to pronounce this by correctly placing the tongue against the front part of the hard palate. If, instead of the blade of tongue touching the front part of the hard palate, the tip of the tongue touches the teeth-ride, the resultant sound is a variety of tʃ found in some Indian languages. For instance, Telugu has three varieties of tʃ which can be phonetically represented by ts, $tʃ^h$. The first of these sounds is made by the action of the tip of the tongue against the teeth ridge. The second of them roughly corresponds to the English sound. The third is only as aspirated form of the second and this occurs in English in initial syllables as in charter, ($tʃ^h$a:tə). So, those students whose native language his ts, should distinguish this sound from tʃ.

It has been mentioned that this should be treated as one sound and it must be distinguished from the sequence t+ʃ which occurs in compound words like *courtship* (kc:t-ʃip), *hat-shop* (hætʃcp) *nut-shell* (nΛt-ʃel).

d_3 as in *judge*, ($d_3\Lambda d_3$) *page* (peid_3) *major* (meid_3ə) *charge* (tʃa: d_3). This again must be treated as one sound though two symbols are used for the sake of convenience. This is called a voiced palato-alveolar affricate. The articulation and tongue position are similar to those tʃ. Some Indian language have two more varieties of this sound. One of those varieties is the aspirated from of d_3, but this sound is not usually aspirated in English. One of the varieties of this sound in Indian languages, is dz which is produced by the tip of the tongue touching the teeth ridge. But in making d_3 the blade of the tongue is made to come into contact with the front part of the palate. Our students should make some efforts to find to which of the varieties of d_3 in their own languages this sound corresponds, and to distinguish this sound from other varieties. Again, care must be taken to distinguish this sound from 3. Many of our students are in the habit of substituting d_3 for 3.

l as in *leave* (li:v), laugh (la:f), bill (bil). This is called a voiced alveolar lateral. It is articulated by the the tip of the tongue against the teeth-ridge. The tip of the tongue touches the centre of the teeth ridge and an aperture is made on either side through which the air passes out. As the air passes through the aperature, the contact between the tip of the tongue and the teeth ridge is released.

This is not, by itself, a difficult sound for Indian students. The sound occurs in many of our languages. But speakers of some of our languages, especially South Indians, articulate l sound by curling the tip of the tongue backwards and then bringing the lower surface of the tip of the tongue into contact with the front part of the hard palate. The sound produced by this activity does not exist in English, and care must be taken to avoid it while speaking English.

It has been said that l is not a difficult sound for our students. But there are two cheif varieties of this sound in Received Pronunciation. Both of them have the same primary articulation of the tip of the tongue against the teeth ridge But they differ in the quantity of the sound called resonance. The two chief varieties are 'clear'. l as in *leave* (li:v) *lucky*, (lΛki), *lose* (lu:z), *value* (vælju) and dark 'l' are in *feel* (fi:l), *people* (pi:pl) and so on. Clear varieties of 'l' are used when 'l' is followed by a vowel or j sound, as in *list* (list), *lot* (lot) *value* (vælju). But when it is followed by a back-vowel the 'l' used is less clear. Dark varieties of 'l' are used in final position and before consonants as *shall* (ʃę̄), *cool* (ku:l) *field* (fi:ld), *alter* (c:ltə) and so on.

r as in *red* (rę̄ d), *hearing* (hiəriŋ) *print* (print) *try* (trai), far away (fa:r əwei). This is one of the very difficult sounds for Indian students. The difficulty is chiefly due to apparent arbitrariness in choosing to pronounce it or to make it silent. Wherever it is pronounced the r sound is made by causing the tongue tip to virbrate against the teeth ridge, when *r* or *re* takes the final position in a word or when *r* is followed by a consonant, it does not have any consonantal value. Thus, *farm* is pronounced fa:m, as if it had no *r*, because it is followed by a consonant. Similarly in words ending with *r* or *re*, it is generally silent as for example in *poor* (puə), *fire* faiə) and pure (pjuə).

Where r is pronounced, three cheif varieties of it are distinguished. They are as follows:

(a) *Fricative r:*—This is the usual sound given to the written r when it is followed by a vowel in a word. Examples : *red* (rę̄ d), *arrive* (əraiv) and so on. This is not a difficult sound to pronounce. Bu it should be borne in mind that r is always pronouced when it is followed by a vowel, unless it is followed by *e* in final position.

(b) *Linking r :*—When a word ending with written r is followed in the sentence or phrase, by a word beginning with a vowel, usually r has a consonantal value. But where such words are pronounced by themselves r sound is silent. Here are some words ending with r uttered in isolation and in the company of words beginning with vowel sounds.

here (hiə) but here it is (hiər itiz)

far (fa:) but far away (fa:r əwei)

never (nę̄ və) but never again (nę̄ vər əgę̄ n)

four (fɔ:) but four of them. (fd:r dv ðę̄ m)

(c) *Intrusive r* : This is a r sound which does not exist in spelling, but intrudes when the word is pronounced in the company of certain other words. This r is generally inserted when words spelt with final -a are followed by words beginning with a vowel. Many people in the South of England prononce for instance :—

India and Ghana as (indiər ən ga:nə)

China and Japan (tʃainər ən d_3əpæn

the idea of it (ði aidiər əv it)

Some regard this sort of intrusive r as bad pronunciation on the ground that it does not correspond to spelling. In Modern times there has been a tedency to avoid it.

CLASSIFICATION OF VOWELS

The main difference between consonants and vowels is, that in consonants, the air-stream is either altogether trapped for an instant or, so far narrowed that a certain amount of friction is caused, but, in vowels, the mouth-passage is not sufficiently closed to produce friction. In fact, the distinction between consonants and vowels depends upon the degree of narrowing of the mouthpassage through which the air has to escape. A sound in which there is either an audible friction or a short but complete stoppage of the air, is called consonant; sounds in which there is an uninterrupted flow of the air-stream, are called vowels. Before we turn to the problem of classification of vowels, it should be borne in mind that, among consonants, some are voiced and some are voiceless or breathed; but, all vowels are voiced sounds.

Classification of vowels largely depends upon *(a)* the part of the tongue which is raised *(b)* the hight to which it is raised and *(c)* the position of the lips. Now, let us consider briefly each of these three aspects of classification of vowels in English.

(a) The Part of the Tongue. In the production of some English vowels, the front part of the tongue is raised to the closest position to the teethridge. Vowels produced in this manner are called *front vowels*. Examples are i: as in key (ki:) and *feed* (fi:d); i as in *bid*; e as in *bed*; æasin *man* (mæn). There are some vowels in English which are produced by the back of the tongue raising towards the soft palate. Such vowels are called *back vowels*. They are a: as in *calm* (ka:m), c: as in fall (fc:1—), u as in *look* (luk); u : as in fool (fu:l).

Then, there are some vowels which are produced in the middle of the mouth with the middle part of the tongue. They are intermediate between front and back vowels, and are called *central vowels*. Examples: Λ as in done (dΛn); as in word (wə:d); ə as in *age* (əgou).

(b) Height of the Tongue. There are some vowels in the production of which the tongue is held as high as possible consistently with not producing and frictional noise, and such vowels are called *close vowels*. Examples are i: as in feed (fi:d) and u: as in food (fu:d). Then there are *open vowels*, in the production of which the tongue is held as low as possible. They are, a: as in father (fa:ðə) and æ as in man (mæn).

It is convenient to distinguish two more classes. They are intermediate between close and open vowels and are called half-close and *half-open* vowels. Sound e as in *men* can be taken as an example of half close class of vowels and æ as in man (mæn) can be taken to represent the half-open group of vowels.

(c) The Position of the Lips. The lips are made to hold different positions in pronouncing different vowels. In the production of certain vowels, the lips are drawn together and slightly rounded and protruded Vowels produced with the lips in that position are called rounded vowels. Again, there are two types of liprounding, called *close-lip-rounding* and *open-lip-rounding*. In the case of close lip-rounding the lips are drawn very close, protruded, and a narrow opening is made. An example of vowel produced with the lips in this position, is u: as in food (fu:d). In open lip-rounding lips are kept quie apart and rounding also is not so complete and the opening is fairly wide. Examples of vowels produced with lips in this position are ɔ as *hop* (hɔp) and c: as in *fall* (fɔ:l). Vowels produced with the lips in neutral or natural position are called unrounded vowels. Examples a: as in father (fa:ðə) and i: as in feed (fi:d).

ENGLSIH VOWELS IN DETAIL

Let us now consider each vowel in turn.

No. 1. i:, as in *sea* (si), *meet* (mi:t) *key* ki:) *field* (fi:ld), *seize* (si:z), *these* (ði:z). The diagram shows that this is a close, front, unrounded vowel. In final position, some people use the diphthongal variety of this sound. The diphthong may be phonetically represented by ij, as for instance, in see (sij), key (kij).

No. 2. i, as in words like *sit* (sit), *city* (siti), *busy* (bizi), *bit* (bi), *fill* (fill), *basket* (ba:skit). This is a front unrounded vowel less closed than the vowel discussed above.

No. 3. e, as in words like *ten* (ten), *tmen* (men), *bread* (bred), any (eni), bury (beri). This is a front, unrounded vowel between half close and half-open positions.

*ę̄ as in measure, (mę̄ 3ə), there (ðcə), chair (ðʃę̄ ę̄). This is a front unronunded vowel more open than No. 3. Its exact position is between No. 3 and 4. It has not been given any number, perhaps because some people use it as a variant of No. 3. However, this sound ocurs quite frequently sometimes as in independent word and sometimes as a component of a diphthong.

No. 4. æ as in words like man (mæn), sat (sæt), that (ðæt), pack (pæl), flat (flæt). This is a front unrounded vowel, more open than the vowels discussed above. This is often phonetically represented by the symbol *x*. Different people use different shades of this vowel.

If the vowel is given slightly fronter articulation it ceases to be a vowel and becomes the consonant ja. Care must be taken to avoid this. In America and some parts of England this sound is preferred to a fully back a:. Thus they pronounce *dance* as dæns instead of da:ns, *past* as pæst instead of pa:st, *grass* as *græs* instead of *gra:s*, *path* as *pæθ* instead of *pa:θ*.

No. 5. a:, as in words like *calm* (ka:m) *father* (fa:ðə), and *farther* (fa:ðə), *laugh* (la:f), *clerk* (cla:k), star (sta:) This is an open back unrounded vowel. This should not be cunfused with No 4. In pronouncing this sound some people open the mouth widely as if they were yawning. But neutral position of the lips would be preferrable.

No. 6. ɔ as in words like *not* (nɔt), *doll* (dɔl), *hop* (hɔp), *fault* (fɔlt), *false* (fɔls), *long* (lɔŋ). This is a back vowel produced with the mouth almost open and the lips slightly rounded. In careless speech, sometimes it is likely to be replaced by sort of a:. For instance, Americans usually pronounce hot, office, operate with a:.

No. 7. ɔ: as in words like *or* (ɔ:) *saw* (sɔ:); *thought* (θɔ:t)' *horse* (hɔ:s); *fall* (fɔ:l); *flaw* (flɔ:); *water* (wɔ:tə). This is a back vowel with the mouth position more or less as that in the case of No. 6. In fact, this is a lengthened variety of No. 6. Many words spelt with *of*, *as*, have an alterantive pronunciation with No. 6. They are *off* (ɔf, ɔ:f); *often* (ɔfən, ɔ:fn); *cross* (krɔs, krɔs); *lost* (lɔst, lə:st).

No. 8. u, as in words like *push* (puʃ); *could* (kud); *look* (luk), *full* (ful). This is a back vowel with the mouth almost closed and the lips slightly rounded.

No. 9. u:, as in words like moon (mu:n) rude (ru:d), choose (t;ʃu:z) fool (fu:l), tomb (tu:mb). This is a back, rounded, nearly close vowel. This can be said to be a lengthended variety of No 8. Different shades of this vowel are found among different people. Some pronounce it with slight diphthongal colour and some distinguish this from No. 8. However, this is not a difficult sound for Indian students.

No. 10. ʌ as in words like *fun* (fʌn); *done* (dʌɔn); *blood* (blʌd); *mutton* (mʌtn); *London* (lʌndən). This is a half open-unrounded vowel. In rapid speech some people exchange this sound with a: or ə. Care must be taken to avoid this.

No. 11. ə: as in words like *fur* (fə:); search (sə:tʃ); *word* (wə:d); *heard* (hə:d); *kernel* and *colonel* (kə;nl); *bird* (bə:d). This is a half close and half-open variety of central unround vowel. Various shades of this sound are heard among the speakers of Received Pronunciation. In place of this sound, a lengthened variety of No. 10 (ʌ:) is often heard. This is a difficult sound for Indian students. The student is advised to find out a few more words where this vowel occurs.

No. 12. ə as in words like *age* (əgou); *children* (tʃildrən); *nature* (neitʃə); *china* (tʃainə); *suppose* (səpouz); *silent* (sailənt); *attack* (ətælk); *sirprise* (səpraiz). This is a very short sound and therefore it is difficult to describe it with precision. This is called a 'neutral' vowel and it never occurs in accented syllables. It takes the place of most other vowels when we utter them in rapid speech, without stress. It is a central, unrounded vowel pronounced with the mouth held between half close and half open position, and the lips taking neutral position. Several distinguishable varieties of this sound are heard from speakers of Received Pronunciation. The student is advised to see Chapter 3 and notice the difference in pronunciation of this sound in stressed and unstressed forms.

DIPHTHONGS

The vowels that have just been described are called pure vowels, since each sound consists of a single vowel. We shall now describe sounds which are a combination of two or three vowel sounds. Such sounds are called diphthongs. Each diphthong starts with a vowel sound and almost imperceptily glides to another with which it ends. In pronouncing a diphthong, the first component of it must be gven greater value than the second. Diphthongs are generally classified into two *(i)* closing diphthongs and *(ii)* Centering diphthongs. Closing diphthongs are those in which the second component is one of the close or half-close vowels. Centering diphthongs are so claled because, each of them ends with ə, which is a central vowel.

Closing Diphthongs:

No. 13. ei, as in words like *nay* (nei), *tape* (teip), *day* (dei), *ale* and *ail* (eil), *daisy* (deizi), *railway* (reilwei). The usual mistake done by in pronouncing this diphthong is that they flatten it till it becomes e (No. 2).

No. 14. ou, as in words like *go* (gou), *road* (roud), *so* (sou), *foe* (fou), *toe* (tou), *hope* (houp), *soul* (soul), *noble* (noubəl), *don't* (dount). This is a difficult sound for many of our students. The usual mistake about this sound is that it is often pronounced as long O. Daniel Jones suggests that it is a useful exercise for students of speech to practise saying repeatedly a sentence like *Oh no, I don't know*.

No. 15. ai, as in *time* (taim), *try* (trai), *by* and *buy* (bai), *bite* (bait), *child* (tʃaild) *resign* (rizain). This starts with the mouth well open. When ai is followed by ə the sequence is sometimes treated as triphthong, as for instance in *fire* (faiə), *umpire* (ʌmpaiə), *irony* (aiərəni). This is a difficult sound and needs some special efforts to master it.

No. 16. au, as in words like *how* (hau), *town* (taun), *out* (aut), *bough* (bau), *house* (haus), *plough* (plau), *loud* (laud). The mouth position in starting of this sound is as that of No. 15. But this ends in u (No. 8). In some words it is followed by ə, Examples, *flower* and *flour*, (flauə), *hours* (auəz), *power* (pauə).

No. 17. ɔi as in words like *boy* (bɔi); *voice* (vɔis); *toy* (tɔi) ; *buoy* (bɔi); *loyal* (lɔil). It starts at the vowel No. 6 and ends with No. 2.

CENTERING DIPHTHONGS

No. 18. iə as in words like *deer* and *dear* (diə); *mere* (miə); *hero* (hiərə); *sere* (siə); *clear* (kliə); *idea* (aidiə); *pierce* (piəs). This begins at i (No. 2) and glides to the central vowel (ə). Between the two components of the diphthong j sound should not be allowed to intrude.

No. 19. ɛ̄ ə as in words like *care* (kɛ̄ ə); *chair* (tʃɛ̄ ə); *mare* (mɛ̄ ə); *fare* (fɛ̄ ə); *there* (ðɛ̄ ə) and *their* (ðɛ̄ ə). This starts with ɛ̄ which is placed between Nos. 3 and 4, and glides to the central vowel ə. Care must be taken not to ignore the second element in the diphthong.

No. 20. ɔə as as in words like *more* (mɔə), *floor* (flɔə); *sword* and *soared* (sɔəd); *nor* (nɔə); *your* (jɔə); *shore* (fɔə); *pour* (pɔə). This is a very difficult sound for non-native speakers of English. Many people reduce it to a shortend form of No. 14 so that *floor* is often heard as flow. However, this diphthong alternates with pure vowel No. 7. Intelligibility does not suffer much by substituting one for the other, in this case.

No. 21. uə as in words like *tour* (tuə), *moors* (muəz), *poor* (puə); *sure* (fuə); *truer* (truə).

It is obvious that this diphthong starts with No. 8 and ends with No. 12. The only difficulty with this sound is that it is often flattened to simple u: (No. 9) by Indian students so that *poor* is often heard as pu:

We have completed description of vowels and diphthongs. Now, the complete vowel list is given below, with their numbers, symbols and examples.

PURE VOWELS

Front	No. 1	No.2	No.3	No.4	
	i: (sea)	i (sit)	e (ten)	æ (man)	
Back	No. 5	No.6	No.7	No.8	No. 9
	a: (hard)	ɔ (not)	ɔ: (or)	u (good)	u : (pool)
Centre	No. 10	No. 11	No. 12		
	ʌ (come	ə : (fur)	ə (ago).		

DIPHTHONGS

Closing Diphthongs:

No. 13	No. 14	No. 15	No. 16	No. 17
ei	ou	ai	au	ɔi
(day)	(so)	(my)	(now)	(boy)

Centering Diphthongs:

No. 18	No. 19	No. 20	No. 21
iə	ę̄ ə	ɔə	uə
(dear)	(chair)	(four)	(poor).

PHONEMIC CONTRAST

Distribution of Consonants. The phonemic contrasts have been worked out in syllable initial and syllable final positions, using minimal and sub-minimal pairs by keeping the tone constant. The canonical shape of morphemes, in Thadou, is monosyllabic, hence, there are no medial consonants excepts the intra-morphemic ones. The medial contrasts have been worked out only at morpheme boundaries.

SYLLABLE INITIAL

p/ɐh/b/m	pón	=	'cloth'
	phón	=	'bubble'
	bón	=	'mud'
	mól	=	'(to) fade'
,/b	vū	=	'to bore a hole'
	bū	=	'nest'
	vŭi	=	'to bury (a thing)'

	bŭi	=	'wild rat'
t/th/d/n	túl	=	'Spike'
	thúl	=	'a particular type for basket'
	dúl	=	'bright (esp. used for black)'
	nún	=	'to admit (one's fault)'
	nál	=	'to slip (lose footing)'
th/l/h/	thá	=	'energy'
	hlá	=	'moon, month'
	lá	=	'song'
k/g/η/x	kóη	=	'hips'
	góη	=	'thin'
	xóη	=	'wearing'
	ηóη	=	'neck'
	kúη	=	'to burn'
	kúη	=	'form, shap'
	xúη	=	'drum'
m/n/η	mÀt	=	'bug'
	nÀt	=	'illness'
	ηÀt	=	'to face, facing'
	mêi	=	'cloud'
	nêi	=	'possess' to own
	ηêi	=	'inelody'
h/x	hái	=	'to stop' (trans.)

	xái	=	'to hang'
	hài	=	'breeding'
	xài	=	'balance'
c/z/s	căη	=	'to paw (observe a hunt)'
	zăη	=	'light (in weight)'
	săη	=	'high, thousand'
	cùl	=	'faded colour'
	zùl	=	'wet, abortion (of animal)'
	sùl	=	'u' terus'
p/t/c/k	pè?	=	'kick'
	tè?	=	'beat'
	cè?	=	'scatter'
	kè?	=	'broken'
ph/th/hl/x	pbÀt	=	'goodness'
	thÀt	=	'to kill'
	thlÀt	=	'deliver'
	xÀt	=	'one'
b/d/z/g	bóη	=	'cow'
	dóη	=	'young'
	zóη	=	'monkey'
	góη	=	'thin'
s/x/h	sil	=	'wash'
	xit	=	'tie'
	hil	=	'teach'

Medial (at morpheme boundary)

There is no medial consonant except on the morpheme boundary, therefore, the morphas combined can be free or bound form. Morpheme boundaries are indicated by hyphens.

p/ph/b/v/m	phÀ-pá	=	'overtake'
	À-phá	=	'good'
	À-bá	=	'car-ring'
	À-vá	=	'leakage'
	À-má	=	'he'
t/th/d/n	ki-t-im	=	'to abstain (doing work)'
	À-thim	=	'dark'
	À-dim	=	'full'
	À-niŋ	=	'corner'
	À-nim	=	'low'
	À-tâ?	=	'hard'
	À-thâ?	=	'to itch'
	À-dâ?	=	'wide'
	À-nâ?	=	'spring'
th/l/hl	ki-thÀt	=	'to commit suicide'
	ki-lèt	=	'to float'
	sÀ-hèl?	=	'to feel'
	ki-thō	=	'to wake up'
	ki-lò	=	'to resemble'
k/g/x/ŋ	ki-kói	=	'to go in accompany with hands on shoulder'

	ki-xái	=	'to hand oneself'
	À-gó	=	'dry'
	ki-ηái	=	'to lean (against something)'
	ki-kin	=	'to spit'
	À-ki-xit	=	'to tie'
	ki-gin	=	'to prepare'
	mÀ-sÀη-in	=	'before'
m/n/η	À-mÀn	=	'to be in time'
	À-nÀt	=	'his illness'
	ki-ηái	=	'to long for'
c/z/s	ki-cát	=	'fear'
	ki-záp	=	'to fan'
	ki-sát	=	'to fight (to cut each other)'
h/x/?	ki-hù	=	'to defend (self)'
	À-ki-xù	=	'to put on (head gear)'
	sù?-hlóm	=	'to decrease'

SYLLABLE FINAL

Voiced, aspirated stops, fricatives and affricates, do not occur finally. In rapid speech, the voiceless stops in the syllabes baring sharp falling tone are realised as giottal stops. Only the following consonant phonemes occur finally: p, t, ?, m, n, η, l, hm, hn, hη. (cf. Firth : 1936, 63-64 for the pre-aspiration and syllable final elements).

p/m	dÀp	=	'cold'
	dÀm	=	'well, healthy'
	hlèp	=	'to tempt'

	hlèm	=	'unreal'
p/t	nÀt	=	'pain'
	nÀp	=	'mucus'
	hát	=	'strong'
	háp	=	'to bark'
t/n	mÀn	=	'price'
	mÀt	=	'bed bug'
	mit	=	'eve'
m/n/η	tÀm	=	'to rebuke'
	tÀn	=	'to cut'
	tÀη	=	'to roll'
	kim	=	'complete'
	kin	=	'duty'
	kiη	=	'concertrated smoke sticken on wall'
m/hm[1]	kùhm	=	'year'
	kùm	=	'to alight, step down'
n/hn	káhn	=	'to bind'
	kán	=	'to step over'
η/hη	ciη	=	'to memorise'
	cibη	=	'wise'
	bùη	=	'chapter, portion'
	bùbη	=	'to bend (oneself)'

The /?/ and /l/, though occur finally, but they do not form minimal pair with any other phoneme, that is why no example is being given here.

ALLOPHONIC DISTRIBUTION OF CONSONANTS

/p/	[p7]	Bilabial voiceless unreleased stop; occurs finally and in close syllable.		
		[zÀp7]	=	'swim'
		[zúÀp7]	=	'six'
		[gÀp7-hlÀη]	=	'steaks'
	[p]	Bilabial voiceless stop; occurs elsewhere.		
		[pÀt7]	=	'cotton'
		[pū]	=	'grand-father'
/ph/	[ph]	Bilabial voiceless aspirated stops occurs initially and medially but not in the final position.		
		[phíe]	=	'flesh'
		[phú]	=	'to fall a tree'
/b/	['b]	Bilabial voiced protruded stop; occurs initially while followed by a high falling tone on the back vowel only.		
		['bui]	=	'food'
	[b]	Bilabial voiced stop; does not occur finally.		
		[bá?]	=	'branch'
		[bíem]	=	'round, circular'
/t/	[t7]	Aveolar voiceless unreleased stop; occurs finally or in a close syllable.		

[lù·t^{7}] = 'to enter'

[sùt^{7}] = 'pestle'

[t] Aveolar·voiceless stop; occurs elsewhere.

[tòη] = 'to work'

[ti·η] = 'cane'

/th/ [th] Alveolar voiceless aspirated stop; does not occur finally.

[thá·o̥̭] = 'grease'

[thÌm] = 'calm, quite'

/d/ [d] Alveolar voiced stop; does not occur finally.

[dèi] = 'to like'

[dí Al] = 'sea'

/bl/ [bl] Pre-aspirated lateral which does not occur finally.

[hlèp^{7}] = 'to fold (cloth, rope etc.'

[hlài] = 'to run'

/c/ [c] Voiceless alveo-palatal affricate; occurs while followed by central and back low vowels, *i.e.*, /A, a/ and preceded by pause.

[cAÌ·-pá.η] = 'fore-head'

[ċá.] = 'smell'

[ċǍup] = 'lung'

[c] Voiceless palatal affricate; occurs elsewhere, but not finally.

[lî.] = 'to shut (mouth)'

[cùł] = 'faded colour'

/k/ [ḳ] Viceless post velar stop; occurs before the back vowels.

[kù?] = 'exceptionally old'

[k] Voiceless velar stop; occurs elsewhere.

[klèn] = 'to take along'

[kī.l] = 'curl (of hair)'

/g/ [g] the voiced velar stop; has two allophones.

[g̣] whose distribution is parallel to the viceless varietires *i.e.*, [g̣], [g]

[glél] = 'to think'

[gÌl] = 'guts (intestines)'

[g̣á.ɨ] = 'pregnant'

[g̣ó.t⁷] = 'to rub'

/?/ [?] Glottal stop; does not occur inicially.

[né?] = 'to push'

[pà?-cā] = 'flower'

/v/ [v] Labiodental voiced frictive; does not occur finally.

[vùt⁷] = 'to dig (a hole)'

[và?] = 'light'

/x/ [x] Voiceless velar fricative; does not occur finally.

[xè?] = 'to spin'

[xÀt⁷] = 'one'

/h/ [h] Voiceless glottal fricative; occurs initially, but finelly it is not articulated.

[hé.u] = 'needle'

/s/ [s] [š] Voiceless palatal fricative has two allophones [s] and [š] whose distribution is not clearly demarcated. [š], in the speech of some people occurs only while followed by a high vowel but same of the others have only [s]. In the speech of the people of a particular village I could only secord [š] and no [s] at all. The allophonic distribution can be considered as the regional variation between South and North. In this study both the allophones are considered as free variants. The phoneme does not occur in the final position.

/z/ [z] [ž] Voiced counterpart of */s/* has the same distribution as above and does not occur in the final position.

/m/ [m] Bilabial voiced nasal; occurs in all the positions.

[mái] = 'face'

[mú.o] = 'bud'

/n/ [n] Alveolar voiced nasal; occurs in all positions.

[né.] = 'to eat'

[mó.ł] = 'breast'

The voiced velar nasal has a wide range of occurrence in all the positions.

[ŋÀl] = 'aggressive'

[pÁŋ] = 'round granary made of bamboo.'

/l/ [ł] The phone occurs while preceded by a back vowel carrying a sharp falling tone and followed by pause.

[mÀł] = 'thigh'

[cúł] = 'faded colour'

[l] Alveolar voiced lateral; occurs in all other positions.

[Ió.] = 'earning, earn'

[lê.i] = 'earth'

/hm/, /hn/, /hŋ/

The initially aspirated nasals are posited as monophones in the study, though with scanty examples. On the basis of criteria laid down by various scholars for the test of mono-and bi-phonematics (Srivastava: 1968). It should be made clear here that Martinetian theory is not possible for this language because of the lack of consonant clusters in the language. The test was possible on the basis of different tones, which has been arried out. However, the question is still open for the discussion of the monophonemes.

CONSONANT CLUSTERS

Consonant clusters for the tone and monosyllabic languages can be divided into two different categories, (i) intra-morphemic consonant clusters and (ii) inter-morphemic consonant clusters. The intramorphemic clusters cover he geminates and consonant clusters within a morpheme while intermorphemic consonant clusters are interpreted as the clusters on morpheme boundaries.

Consonant clusters of the first category are not found in the language except that the glottal stop /?/ is sometimes followed by a stop while the syllable is affected by a sharp falling tone. This, as a matter of fact, I have not considered as glottal stop plus consonant but as the overlapping of the tone in the boundary of glottal stop. One more point should be made clear here that one can be tempted to posit a geminate in the situation while a particular morpheme affected with rising tone is preceded by a third person marker boundmorpheme /À/ (with falling tone), the initial consonant of the following morpheme gets lengthened or fortis. The point will become clear in the following examples:

/À	+	móhl/	[Àmmóhi]	=	'(it) blunt'
/À	+	sáη/	[Àssáη]	=	'(it) high'
/À	+	nién/	[ÀunĬen]	=	'(he) dirty'

In such cases the consonants are considered as fortis and not geminates.

The intermorphemic consonant clusters are considered as medial clusters and can be divided into two broad categories.

(i) Liquid + C²

(ii) Stop + C.

The chart below will made the situation clear and is supported by the examples on the following pages. Consonants which do not occur as first member of the clusters are restricted to occur in the final position also.

	p	t	c	k	ph	th	b	d	g	hl	v	x	h	s	z	m	n	η	I
p	+	+	+	+	+	+		+	+	+	+	+	+	+		+	+	+	+
t	+	+	+	+	+	+	+	+	+	+	+	+	+		+	+	+	+	+
?	+	+	+	+	+	+	+	+	+	+	+	+	+	+		+	+	+	+
m	+	+	+	+	+	+	+	+	+	+	+	+	+	+	+	+	+	+	+
n	+	+	+	+	+	+	+	+	+	+	+	+	+	+	+	+	+	+	+
η	+	+	+	+	+	+	+	+	+	+	+	+	+	+	+	+	+	+	+
I	+	+	+	+	+	+	+	+	+	+	+	+	+	+	+	+	+	+	+
hn												+							

/pp/	kivȯppī	'to be friendly with'
/pt/	cėptÀn	'to circumcise'
/pc/	nÀpcā	'dare, desire for'
/pk/	xu̇pkáη	'patella'

/pph/	ȯpphėŋ	'chest' (flat)
/pth/	sȯpthí en	'wash (clean'
/pd/	đòpdȯ?	'to lift'
/pg/	túopgin	'sound of cannon'
/pth/	gÀphlėŋ	'the stick on which meat is suspended on the fire'.
/pv/	gủpvėi	'six-times'
/px/	hòpyÀt	'one part (portion)'
/ph/	céphÀm	'are (you) smoking'
/ps/	sÀpsėt	'to call names, curse'
/pm/	zòpmÀt	'to join'
/pn/	thlėpnā̄	'temptation'
/pŋ/	kápŋủl	'fainted (by injection), proper name'
/pl/	kȧplī	'kill, dead'
/tp/	kòtpī	'gate'
/tt/	hittủi	'louse (egg)'
/tc/	kicắt	'afraid'
/tk/	bòtkė?	'to tear (cloth)'
/tph/	xủtpháŋ	'palm'
/tth/	phÀttLėi	'prosperity'
/tb/	kȯtbil	'handle of the door'
/td/	xủtdiò?	'to beg'
/tg/	xủtgiò?	'empty handed'

/thl/	kȯthlá	'window'
/tv/	vủtvȧ	'dust'
/tb/	vủthȯm	'to bore a hole'
/tx/	kȯtxủm	'side pillars of the door'
/tz/	xủtzėm	'ring'
/tm/	bitzmē	'small louse'
/tn/	hlėtṃȯŋ	'to change money'
/tŋ/	xủtŋȯŋ	'wrist'
/tl/	pa᷄tl͡ei	'marsh'
/?p/	ȧ?pī	'hen'
/?t/	ȧ?tủi	'egg'
/?c/	ȧ?cȯ	'beard of cock'
/?k/	vȯ?kủŋ	'plate for pig'
/?ph/	sủ?thȯn	'to bubble'
/?th/	sủ?ptȯn	'to call (attention)'
/?b/	ȧ?bȯm	'foul case'
/?d/	dȧ?dủl	'brinjal'
/?g/	cȧŋtė?á	'dragon fly'
/?hl/	sủ?hlȯm	'decrease'
/?v/	pȧ?vuɨ	'garland'
/?x/	sủ?xaȯ	'rope'
/?h/	nȧ?gȧɨ	'snore'
/?s/	ȧ?sī	'star'
/?m/	jủo?m`δŋ	'to sell away'

/ʔn/	ȧʔnȯu	'chicken'
/ʔl/	bu̇ʔlu̇t	'dirt particle'
/mp/	kėmpu̇m	'porch'
/mt/	pu̇mtōn	'guava'
/mc/	sÁmcī	'hair thread'
/mk/	cėmkȯn	'scimitar'
/mph/	tȯmphá́ɨ	'reed'
/mth/	sÀmthi	'comb'
/mb/	sÀmbá́ʔ	'plate of hair'
/md/	kėmdȯʔ	'resting place (in the way)'
/mhl/	hlimblȧ	'to foresake'
/mv/	lÀmvȧɨ	'bewildered'
/mx/	thí́emxÀt	'some'
/mb/	cėmhȧ	'sharp edge'
/ms/	kȧmsÀn	'fire' (old term)
/mz/	cėmzā m	'sword'
/mm/	gÀmmȧŋ	'jungle, woods'
/mn/	tėmnȧʔ	'invitation'
/mŋ/	zėmŋȧt	'club (in cards)'
/ml/	tòmlÀŋ	'back part of the house'
/np/	hlėapí́e	'to select a present'
/nt/	su̇ŋmÁntÀm	'diamond'
/nc/	incu̇ŋ	'roof'
/nph/	tÀnphé́	'calves'

/nth/ zùntphȧ? 'to urinate'

/nb/ dȯabu̇t 'answer'

/ng/ vā̄ngiη 'thunder'

/nhl/ inthliηnĭ 'day before yesterday'

/nv/ lí́envál 'too big'

/nx/ dȯ xȯ 'melon'

/ηb/ nÀηhȯ 'you (pl.)'

/ns/ insùn 'refter'

/nz/ pu̇azėn 'embroidered cloth'

/nin/ hlānmȯl 'graveyard'

/nn/ zānnī 'yesterday'

/nη/ gí́ennaɨ 'zealous'

/nl/ zȧnlė 'at night'

/ηp/ kėηpī 'toe'

/ηt/ kėηrȯ 'sole'

/ηc/ kėηcȯη 'ankle'

/ηk/ kėηkȯ? 'shoe'

/ηph/ kėηphȧη 'foot'

/ηph/ tȯηthim 'a particular tree'

/ηb/ bùηbùt 'to turn over' (trans.)

/ηd/ núηdėl 'to chase'

/ηg/ kȯηgà? 'belt'

/ηhl/ hùηkùη 'to arrrive'

/ŋv/	kȯŋvÀŋ	'a small basket hanging on the waist'
/ŋx/	tȯŋxÀm	'seat (to hide)'
/ŋs/	cá̄ŋsȧl	'granary'
/ŋz/	sȧŋzā	'lakh'
/ŋm/	giŋmő	'to suspect'
/ŋn/	mÀŋnōm	'to enjoy'
/ŋŋ/	thiŋŋȯt	'worm eaten tree'
/ŋl/	cu̇ŋlĀm	'upon'
/lp/	pí̄ Alpā	'sparrow'
/lt/	kÀltcu̇	'to climb up'
/lc/	kí̄ elcÀl	'he goat'
/lk/	tilkīlcát	'castrate'
/lph/	kȯlphḗ	'lightening'
/lb/	kÀlbī	'rungs'
/ld/	nėAldi	'sand'
/lg/	lȯlgu̇ɨ	'neck'
/lthl/	gu̇lthlȧ	'winged snake'
/lv/	gȯlvȧ	'to celebrate'
/lx/	zȧlxu̇n	'cot'
/lh/	lȯlhőm	'throat'
/ls/	gu̇lsȯ?	'cobra'
/lz/	xúlzin	'traveller'

/lm/	gí elmÀl	'pen (writing)'
/ln/	sí elnóu	'calf (of mithun)'
/lŋ/	kí elŋùi	'sheep'
/ll/	bȯkllóu	'to refute (order)'
/hnx/	sihnxùp	'a small box for precious things'

VOWELS

Vowels in all the positions except a few restrictions which will be dealt while giving the details of phonemic contrasts and allophonic distribution. The phonemic contrast is shown in all possible environments on the basis of minimal and sub-minimal pairs as below:

(1) Initial

A/a	Àn	'meal, food'
	ān	'triumphen'
	Ā m	'interrogative particle'
	ām	'ambers'
i/e	īn	'to conceal (the truth)'
	ēm	'to glitter'
	in	'house'
	ėn	'greedy to get'
o/u	ȯp	'chest'
	u̇m	'to surround'
	ō	'vocie'
	ū	'elder sibling'

(2) Medial

A/a	ȯÀm	'well'
	bÀŋ	'whiteness'
	bȧŋ	'to hang'
i/e	hit	'louse'
	hėt	'to load'
	A-lin	'big'
	A-lėn	'flight'
o/u	pu̇on	'cloth'
	pȯn	'grassy land'
	ku̇oŋ	'plate'
	kȯŋ	'waist'

(3) Final

The phoneme /A/ does not occur finally if alone and, therefore, it is difficult to show the final contrast of the two phonemes /A an a/.

i/e	ki	'horn'
	kė	'to split'
	cí	'variety'
	cė	'wet'
u/o	kixȯ	'to thrwo'
	kixu̇	'to cover'
	pȯ	'to comb'
	pu̇	'elderly (male)'

(4) Allophonic Distribution of Vowels

Each of the six phonemic vowels has a range of allophones which occur in different environments infinanced by (i) tone and (ii) contiguous vowels. These factors take precedence inthe conditioning of allophones resulting a variety of length and quality.

One more point which requires charification is that the /e/ and /o/ in Thadou are lower than the present position and should be transcribed as /ɛ/ and /ɔ/ but for the convenience of typing the earlier symbols are used.

The closed vowels /i/ and /u/ become a bit open and the position is lowered in certain environments especially while affected by a slow rising tone. In such an environment there emerges two archiphonemes /U/ and /I/ by neutralizing the contrast between /ɔ/ and /u/- and /ɛ/ and /i/ respectively. The examples in this section will clerify the point.

/i/ The high front unrounded vowel has five allophones occurring in different environments.

[I] Front unrounded lower high vowel; occurs in monosyllables while affected by the sharp falling tone.

[cÌŋ]	'to presserve'
[ŋÌm]	'clean'

[i̯] Non-syllabic high unrounded vowel; occurs as first member of thw vowel clusters when the second vowel is an /e/.

[ci̯e]	'go'
[bî̯e]	'to slap'

[ɨ] Central unrounded high vowel; occurs as second member of vowel cluster while the first members is a back vowel.

[k̩ɔ̀ɨ]	'to place, put'
[tùɨ]	'water'

[i.] High front unrounded long vowel; occurs while affected by the level tone.

[ī.m]	'to hide'
[xī.]	'bead'

[i] High front unrounded vowel; occurs elsewhere.

[xî]	'to tie'
[phí t⁷]	'to remove the roof'

/e/ Mid-front unrounded vowel has two allophones with their occurrences as follows :

[e] Higher mid front unrounded variety; occurs while forming a cluster with /i/ and before the glottal stop with a sharp falling tone. The second condition is restricted to certain dialects only.

[kėi]	'I'
[pį̂e]	'to give'

[s] Lower mid front unrounded vowel; occrs elsewhere.

[bέl]	'kettle'
[lέŋ]	'king'

/A/ Mid back unrounded vowel has two allophones occurring in complementation with each other as :

[ə] the mean-mid unrounded central vowel; occurs in the initial position and in vowel clusters.

[∂ŋ̀]	'food'
[dí ∂l]	'sea'

[Λ] Lower-mid back unrounded vowel; occurs elsewhere.

[dΛ̀m]	'healthy'
[sΛ̀m]	'hair'

/a/ Lower back unrounded vowel has a long variety also conditioned by the pitch.

[a.] Occurs while affected by a slow rising tone in an open syllable.

[kǎ.]	'to cry'
[lǎɪ]	'dance'

[a] Occurs elsewhere.

[lȧ?]	'among'
[thāl]	'to fill (liquid)'

/o/ The mid back roundd vowel, has a number of allophones occurring in different environments:

[U] As stated above, the allophone takes the shape of an archiphoneme between /o/ and /u/ while affected by a rising tone.

[o̯] The non-syllabic variety occurs as second member of vowel cluster in an open syllable while preceded by /a/.

[thāo̯]	'grease'
[pāo̯]	'language'

[o.] The lengthened allophone occurs while affected by a level tone in all the environments and a slow rising tone preceded by a pause.

[lō.]	'earning'
[ǒ.m]	'to boil'

[ɔ] Occurs elsewhere.

[ḳɔ̀ɨ]	'retain, keep'
[zɔ̀ŋ]	'monkey'

/u/ High back rounded vowel has the following allophones.

[U] Lower high rounded back vowel occurs while affected by sharp falling and sharp rising tones.

[Ùm]	'remain'
[zÙn]	'melt'
[gÙ]	'bamboo'

[u̯] Non syllabic high rounded vowel occurs as a member of the vowel cluster while other member of the cluster is affected by the tone and not the phone under discussion.

[ḳȯ.u̯]	'hole'
[tu̯ȧ]	'now'

[u.] High back rounded long vowel; occurs while affected by a level tone.

[cū.n]	'to bundle'
[bù.?]	'nest'

[u] Occurs in all other positions.

[hʉ́i]	'wind'
[xùt[7]]	'hand'

(5) Vowel Clusters

Thadou has a number of two vowel sequences in the medial and final positions but no initial vowel sequence is found. In certain cases, where /A/ forms a sequence with any other vowel, it will be more appropriate to call it a diphthong instead of vowel sequence. /A/ as a second member of the sequence is sometimes the outcome of slow rising tone, however, here it is placed in the list of vowel sequences and not as diphthong. In all the vowel sequences only one member forms the syllable peak, while other works as one onset or coda depending on the tone. A table of vowel sequences is given below followed by supporting examples.

Second Member.	**i**	**e**	**A**		**o**	
First Member						
i		+	+ (m)			+
e	+		+			+
A	+		+	+ (m)		
a	+			+	+	+
o	+		+ (m)			+
u	+		+ (m)		+	

FORM CLASSES (VERB) DIAGRAM

The hierarchical structure of the position classes in the predicate is given below which gives the complete picture of the predicative construction. Examples for the constructions are given in the following pages. See relevant sections for negation and interrogation.

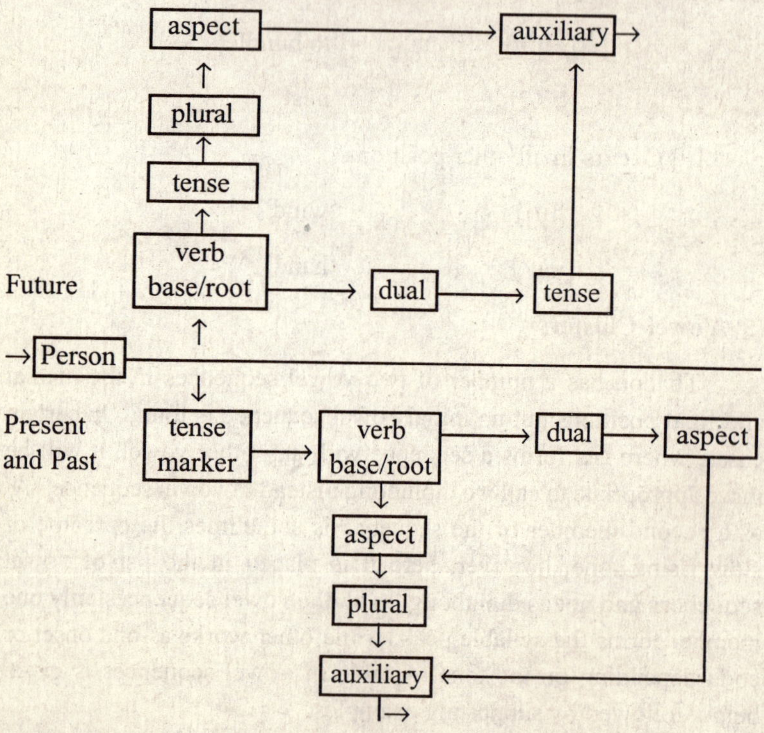

Note:

1. Present tense does not take any marker, hence the tense marker is irrelevant for it.
2. All the stages between verb-base/root and auxiliary are optional for the purpose of a minimum construction.

Verbs

Verbs can be classified in two different categories, full verbs and auxiliaries. Further sub-classification of both the categories is possible, the auxiliary being divided into obligatory and optional or secondary.

(a) Obligatory auxiliaries : è, Ahī

(b) Optional or secondary auxiliaries:

Full verbs are those which can take:

(i) tense, aspect, mood and number affixes.

(ii) negative and interrogative suffixes.

Further sub-classification of full verb provides us with two types of verbs, *i.e.*, basic and derived.

(1) Basic Verbs

Are those which are formed from non-derivative stems and are both transitive and intransitive.

(2) Derived Verbs

While deriving the verbs fromt he nouns following morphological processes are used. The derived verb forms enter into further constructions of verb bases.

(a) Prefixation. A bound morpheme *ki-*, also used as neuter marker (2.4.3.1) is prefixed to the noun base or a bound form. These roots are always transitive.

lŏ́i	=	‘friend’	kīlói	=	‘to accompany with’
vȯp	=	‘lap’	kīvȯp	=	‘to carry (in lap)’
thÀt	=	‘killinġ’	kīthÀt	=	‘to commit suicide’
tėm	=	‘request’	kītim	=	‘to request’
-çắt	=	‘fear’	kīcắt	=	‘to fear’

(bound form).

(b) Internal Change. The suprasegmental feature of the morpheme, *i.e.*, tone, is changed to get a verb from the noun base. These forms contribute the maximum number of the derivative verbs.

Cò?	=	‘purchase’	cŏ́?	=	‘to buy’
lĕ́	=	‘licking’	lė	=	‘to lick’
pe	=	‘denotion’	pĕ́	=	‘to give’

(c) Deletion. In this class of derivation final consonant of the noun-base in deleted to get the verb form. One more morphological process is also applied in some of the cases. If the noun base has /A/ as medial vowel it is changed to /a/ after deleting the final consonant. /A/ never occur finally in the language.

xŭ́t	=	‘cough’	xŭ́	=	‘to cough’
vĕ́t	=	‘sight’	vĕ́	=	‘to see, look at’
kÀp	=	‘cry’	kȧ	=	‘to cry’
nÀt	=	‘pain’	nȧ	=	‘to ache’

Person Markers

Person markers are the possessive prefixes in Thadou, which express the three persons (first, second, third). Number, which is not separated by these markers, is expressed by adding some other suffixes to the verb (-hlȯn-for dual and -ū- for plural). It has already been discussed that these suffixes are also used with the nouns, adjectives, etc., and cannot be adopted as a criterion to define the verb. Frist person exclusives and inclusives are also marked:

	Singular	*Dual*		*Plural*	
1st	kĀ-	KĀ-	(exclusive)	KĀ-	(exclusive)
		ī-	(inclusive)	ėi-	(inclusive)
2nd	nĀ-	nĀ-		nĀ-	
3rd	Ā-	A-		A-	

First person exclusives always take the dual and plural suffix *-hlȯn* and -ū- respectively but for the dueal inclusives it is optional.

kĀnēi	=	'I eat'
kĀnē-hlȯn-ė	=	'We two eat (excl.)'
īnē-hlȯ-ė/ī-nēi	=	'we two eat (incl.)'
kĀnē-ū-wè	=	'we eat (excl.)'
ėinē-ū-wé	=	'we eat (incl.)'
nĀnē-yé	=	'you eat'
nĀnē-hlȯn-è	=	'you two eat'
nĀnē-ū-wé	=	'you (pl) eat'
Ānē-yé	=	'he eats'
Ānē-hlȯn-è	=	'they two eat'
Ānē-ū-wè	=	'they (pl) eat'

Verb Bases

In addicion to the basic and derivative verbs Thadou has another class of verb basis which are formed from the first two classes or from some nouns by means of some formational techniques of affixation and juxtaposition. Such bases, once formed, function as the bare-roots for grammatical constructions and the meanings to carry out. Follwing four main types are found in the language :

1. Causative base
2. Interative base
3. Compound base
4. Neuter base

The last class of bases can further be divided into two sub-classes on the basis of their construction :

(a) Passive base.

(b) Reciprocal base.

We can further group the first three bases into one group termed as active bases.

(1) Causative Base is built by the process of suffixation. A morph *-sà?* 'to allow', 'to compel', is suffixed to the verb root (both full and derivative) and in some cases to a neuter base.

tā́n	=	'stop'	tānsȧ?	=	'to cause to stop'
pu̇n	=	'increase'	pùnsȧ?	=	'to cause to increase'
sėi	=	'speak'	sėisȧ?	=	'to cause to speak'
nḗ	=	'eat'	nėsȧ?	=	'to cause to eat'
vḗt	=	'sight'	vḗtsȧ?	=	'to cause to see'
cíe	=	'go'	ciesȧ?	=	'to cause to go'
hu̇η	=	'come'	hu̇ηsa?	=	'to send'
mū́	=	'see'	mū́sȧ?	=	'to show'

kāp	=	'shoot'	kāpsȧ?	=	'to cause to shoot'
tủ?	=	'hold'	tủ?sȧ?	=	'to make to hold'
kīzȀp	=	'swim'	kīzȀpsȧ?	=	'to cause to swim'
kīcắt	=	'afraid'	kīcắtsȧ?	=	'to frighten'
kinḗl	=	'argue'	kīnḗlsȧ?	=	'to cause to argue'

(2) Iterative Base is formed by completely reduplicating the verb root of the basic verbs. In case of derivative verbs of *ki*-suffix the derivative suffix is dropped in the second syllable of reduplication. The base gives the sense of prolongness, repetition of the action and putting stress on the action.

dȯn	=	'to drink'	dòn-dòn	=	'drink and drink'
hlắi	=	'to run'	hlắi-hlắi	=	'run and run'
cṓm	=	'to jump'	cȯm-cȯm	=	'jump and jump'
kivȯ	=	'to beat'	kīvȯ? vȯ?	=	'beat and beat'
kilṓː	=	'to accompany'	kīlṓi lṓi	=	'accompany on'

(3) Compound Base is formed by juxtaposing two verb roots or a bound from (gĀ- 'go, walk') and a root. On the basis of this rule iterative bases also form a part of the compound base.

cȯm = 'jump' + kắi = 'cross' =

cȯm-kȧi = 'jump acros'

vȯ = 'beat' + kė? = 'break' =

vȯkė? = 'break open'

hủŋ = 'come' + kīlė = 'return'

hủŋ kīlė = 'return back'

gĀ = 'go' + kȯu = 'call' =

gĀ kȯu = 'go and call'

(4) Neuter Base is formed by prefixing kī- to the basic verb roots or nouns. These can be called passive and reciprocal.

(a) Passive Base:

thÀt	=	'kill'	kīthÀt	=	'be killed'
dȯp	=	'to life'	kīdȯp	=	'be lifted'
tÀn	=	'to cut'	kītÀn	=	'be cut'

(b) Reciprocal Base is built by prefixing *i-* to the derivative verbs and to the passive bases.

kīhlėp	=	'deceive'	īkīhlėp	=	'decieve each other'
kīmú	=	'see'	īkīmú	=	'see each other'
kīpȯm	=	'embrace'	īkīpȯm	=	'embrace each other'
kītÀn	=	'be cut'	īkītÀn	=	'cut each other'
kīthu̇?	=	'revenge'	īkīthu̇?	=	'to tak revenge on each other'

In some cases the noun suffix *-tò?* is also used with the reciprocal bases while conjugated. In such cases *i-* is optionally dropped.

sil	=	'wash'	kīsil	=	'to take bath'
(ī) kīsiltȯ?	=	'to wash each other'			
(ī) kīzȧptȯ?	=	'to fan each other'			

Auxiliary Verbs

The two obligatory auxiliary verbs *-è*, -Abí selectionally occur at the end of the verb pharase or noun phrase (shown below). The distribution can be presented as :

-Ahi which becomes -A-or-hÀ- before the interrogative marker -m occurs afterward :

(a) all the nouns and nominalized verbs

Rām Ahi	=	'(he) is Ram'
lēxĀbu̇ Ahi	=	'(it) is (a) book'
bȯη Ahi	=	'(this) is (a) cow'

(b) any form talking *-di*

Ācie diη Ahi	=	'he will go'
nĀpie diη nAhi	=	'you will give'

(c) continuous markers láitȧ?/ *pèttȧ*?

Ānié-lȧitȧ?-Ahi	=	'he is eating'
nĀ-cie-pėttȧ? nĀhi	=	'you are going'

(d) in case of interrogatives

ból hÀm	=	'is doing'?
cie hÀm	=	'is going'?

-è: becomes

(a) *-i* after vowel sequence /ie/ and perfect marker *-tá*,

(b) *-yè* while preceded by / i- /

(c) *-wè* while preceded by / u-, o- /.

But remains unchanged in all other cases. It occurs after all the forms where -Āhì does not occur.

Certain other changes in respect of *-è* take place while occurring in a phrase.

(a) If the auxiliary occurs afte rany of the final consonant p, t, m, n, η, it takes the nasal counterpart of the preceding consonant.

kĀvȯp-mė	=	'I carry (in lap)'
nĀbȯt-mė	=	'you tear'

tȯm-mė	=	'covers'
tÀn-nė	=	'cuts'
teŋ-ŋė	=	'flies'

(b) If a derivative verb of deletion type ends in / -u / it becomes /-iye /:

phʊ́t	=	'beating of heart'
phʊ́	=	'to beat (heart or pulse)'
lu̇ŋ-Āphʊ́iyė	=	'heart beats'
Amȧ Axʊ́iyė	=	'he coughs'

❐

7

Morpheme and Morphology

Morphology is the science and study of the smallest grammatical units of language, and of their formation into words, including inflection, derivation and composition. According to Dorfman, morphology is the study of the ways and methods of grouping sounds into sound-complexes or words, of definite, distinct, conventional meaning. Bloomfield calls it the study of the constructions in which sound forms appear among the constituents. Broadly speaking, morphology is the study of the patterns of word-forms. It studies how the words are formed, where they originate from, what their grammatical forms are, what the functions of prefixes and suffixes in the formation of words are, on what basis the parts of speech of a particular language are formed, how the systems of gender, number, plural etc. function, and how and why the word-forms change.

Morphology is "a level of structure between the phonological and the syntactic." It is complementary to syntax. **Morphology** is the grammer of words; **syntax** the grammer of sentences. One accounts for the internal structure, or 'form' of words (typically as sequences of morphemes), the other describes how these words are put together in sentences. A discussion of how plurals are formed, for example, would belong to morphology, while a discussion of prepositional phrases would belong to syntax. The way morphemes combine to form words is known as the morphology of a language. Morphology, therefore, refers to the form of words themselves in a language system, whereas **syntax** refers to the form of the arrangement of words in phrases and sentences. Agreement, for example, is a morphological feature and word-order is a syntactic feature of a language system.

Morphology is not only the synchronic study of word-forms but is also the study of the history and development of word-forms. So it is both a synchronic **(in a given time)** and a diachronic **(across time)** study of the word-forms. When it is only synchronic, it is called **morphemics.**

The **morphological analysis** is the observation and description of the grammatical elements in a language by studying their form and function, their phonological variants, and their distribution and mutual relationships within larger stretches of speech. It may be either synchronic or diachronic, or may be both synchronic and diachronic.

Accordingly, languages differ more in morphology. The variety is so great that no simple scheme will classify languages as to their morphology. One such scheme distinguishes analytic languages, which use few bound forms, from synthetic which use many. Another scheme of this sort divided languages into four morphologic types, *isolating*, *agglutinative*, *polysynthetic* and *inflecting*. Since the speaker cannot isolate bound forms by speaking them alone, he is usually unable to describe the structure of words. The statement of morphology requires systematic study. The ancient Greeks made some progress in this direction, but, in the main, our technique was developed by the Hindu grammarians. No matter how refined our method, the in clusive nature of meanings will always cause difficulty, especially when doubtful relations of meaning are accompanied by formal irregularities. In describing the modulations and modifications which occur in syntax, we naturally take the absolute form of a word or phrase as our starting point, but a bound form which occurs in several shades will lead to several entierly different forms of description, according to our choice of a basic alternant. Very often there are further difficulties. Sometimes a grammatical feature, such as a phonetic modification, appears to express a meaning which is usually expressed by a linguistic form, as in man: men, where modification of the vowel takes the place of the plural suffix. The principle of immediate constitutents leads us, at the outset, to distinguish certain classes of words, according to the immediate constituents:

A. Scondary words:

1. *Compound words,* containing more than one free form.
2. *Derived secondary words* containing one free form.

B. Primary words, not containing a free form.

1. *Derived primary words,* Containing more than one bound form.
2. *Morpheme-words,* consisting of a single (free) morpheme.

As examples of relatively simple morphologic arrangements we may take the constructions of secondary derivation that appear in English plural nouns (glass-es) and past-tense verbs (land-ed). Regular alternations play a great part in the morphology of most languages. No all regular alternations are phonetic or automatic. In German, for instance, the singular nouns are divided, by certain syntactic features, into three forms-classes which are known as genders now, German plural nouns are derived from singulars by the addition of bound forms which differ according to the gender. We have not yet described in terms of phonetic modification, the kinship of the *three alternants* (–iz, –x,–s) of the form that appears in *English plural nouns*, Since in this case the absolute form is necessarily serves s the starting point of description, we reach the simplest formula if we take (iz) as the basic alternant also of the bound form.

A survey of English *plural nouns* will soon show that the statement we have made holds good for an indefinitely larger number of forms, but not for a certain limited number of exceptions. In some instances the constituent form in the plural differs phonetically from the underlying singular noun. Where the two treatments occur side by side, there is usually some slight difference of connotation between the variants.

The bound forms which is *secondary derivation* are added to the underlying form, are called *affixes*. *Affixes* which precede the underlying form are prefixes, as be-in be-head-those which follow the underlying form are called suffixes, as (–iz) in glasses or Rish in boyish. Affixes added within the underlying form are called *inflixes*. Modulation of secondary phonemes often plays a part in morphologic constructions. In some languages modulation has greater scope. In Sanskrit with some suffixes the derivative form keeps the accent of the underlying from. In languages with auxiliary phonemes of pitch, these may play a part in morphology. In all observation of word-structure it is very important to observe the principle of immediate constituents.

In languages of complex morphology we can thus observe a ranking of constructions: a complex word can be described only as though the various compoundings, affixations, modifications and so on, were added in a certain order to the basic form. In languages of this type then we can distinguish several ranks of morphologic structure.

In many languages these ranks fall into classes: the structure of a complex word reveals first, as to the more immediate constituents, an outer layer of inflectional constructions and then an inner layer of constructions of word-formation. This distinction cannot always be carried out. It is based on several features. The constructions of inflection usually cause closure or partial closure, so that a word which contains an inflectional construction (an inflected word) can figure as a constituent in an morphologic constructions or else only in certain inflectional constructions.

Another peculiarity of inflection, in contrast with word-formation, is the rigid parallelism of underlying and resultant forms. Thus, nearly all English singular nouns underlie a derived plural noun and, vice versa, nearly all English plural nouns are derived form a singular noun.

The parallelism of inflected forms goes hand in hand with a further characteristic: the different inflections differ in syntactic function. If there are several ranks of inflection we get compound paradigms, the inflections of the English noun, for instance, consist of an outer construction, the derivation of the possessive adjective, and an inner one, the drivation of the plural.

	Singular	*Plural*
Nominative-accusative	man	men
Possessive adjective	man's	men's

We come, finally to an important characteristics of inflection, akin to those we have mentioned, the derivational unity of paradigms. The inflectional forms of a paradigm do not enter into composition and derivation, but the paradigm as a whole is represented by some one form. An English paradigm consists of an underlying word (itself a member of the paradigm) and some secondary derivatives containing this underlying word, as a constituent in further derivation and composition, the paradigm, as a whole, is represented by the underlying form, the English language, accordingly may be served to have word-inflection, word-derivation and word-composition.

In many languages, especially in those which have a more complex morphology, none of the forms in a paradigm can conveniently be viewed as underlying the others. In some languages of this type, the common element of the paradigm differs from the stem which represents the paradigm in derivatives and compounds.

The possessive-adjective form in the English compounds like bull'eye the plural form in long legs are due, as we shall see, to the phrasal structure of these compounds. Real exception do, however, occur. If a language contained too many cases of this sort, we should simply say that it did not distinguish such morphologic layers as are denoted by the terms inflection and word-formation.

MORPHEMES

Minimal units of grammatical structure, such as the four components of **un + faith + fulness,** are called morphemes.

Telephones has three morphemes {tele}, phone, and {-s} while **telephone** has two and **phone** just one. Morphemes are customarily described as minimal units of grammatical analysis–the units of 'lowest' rank out of which words, the units of next 'highest' rank are composed. So morphemes are those distinct, minimal syntactical units which form words. They can also be defined as the minimal units of meaning out of which meaningful words are composed in various ways.

A morpheme thus is a distinct linguistic form. It is a minimal unit of speech that is recurrent. It has a grammatical function. It is semantically different from other phonemically similar or identical linguistic forms, and is not divisible or analyzable into smaller forms. If we try to break or analyze a morpheme into its constituents, it loses its identity, and we end up with a sequence of meaningless noises, *e.g.* **nation** (na+tion, or nati-on). Analyzling the morphemes leads us straight into the realm of phonology.

Morphemes may or may not have meaning, may or may not have a phonological representation. [un-] has a negative meaning in **unfriendly, unhealthy, unable, unemployed** and many other words, but is meaningless in **under.** {-er} has a constant meaning in **teacher, heater, reader, writer, speaker, pointer, leader,** etc. But it would be difficult to pin down any constant meaning for **spect in respect, inspect, circumspect,** for **pro** in **protest, professor, prospective, process,** etc. In plural words like **sheep, fish** we have two morphemes in each words; the first morpheme in each case has a phonological representation but the second one has no phonological representation and is called **zero morpheme.** Morphologically the plural noun sheep is [sheep]+ { }, that is to say that the word **'sheep'** is made up of two morphemes sheep plus a **plural morpheme** which is present in the meaning but is not physically present in spelling or pronunciation.

Morphemes sometimes vary in their phonological manifestations. **Pro,** for instance, is pronounced differently in **profess** and the noun **progress.** The plural morpheme is pronounced (s) in words like **cats,**

maps and **snacks;** [z] in **dogs, hands,** and **ideas;** (iz) in words like **churches, judges, classes;** but it has no phonetic form at all in the plural nouns such as **sheep, fish**, etc. Then there are completely idiosyncratic forms such as **oxen, children, brethern.** It is not always clear whether or not a given sound sequence should be considered a morpheme. For instance, should **animal** be said to consist of two morphemes **anima** (a) and (b) l, or just one? Consider **natural:** It has two morphemes (nature) and {-al}. Shouldn't we then regard **woman** as a word having two morphemes {wo-} and {man} ? A sound sequence is a morpheme in some words; it is not in some others. **Un** clearly is a morpheme in **unnatural** and **unfaithful** but it is not a morpheme in **under** or **sun.**

A morpheme may be monosyllabic as {man} and {a/an/the} or polysyllabic as {happy} and {nature}.

CLASSIFICATION OF MORPHEMES

We can classify the morphemes in the following way:

(1) Lexical and Grammatical Morphemes. Ronald W. Langacker in his book, Language and Its Structure, has divided morphemes into two classes: lexical and grammatical. Lexical morphemes are forms like boy, write, paper and pen. Grammatical morphemes are forms like some, with, a, an, the , to, and from. Lexical morphemes are nouns, verbs, adjectives, and adverbs. They have more or less independent meaning, so that one or a series of lexical forms in isolation can be fairly meaningful. Pen suggests something quite definite to us, as do boy, paper and write. Lexical morphemes are very large in a language; the number may go up to ten millions as in English. Grammatical morphemes are elements like prepositions, articles, conjunctions, forms indicating number, gender or tense, and so on. Grammatical morphemes, by and large, do not change frequenty: new members in their family in any language are added rather infrequently. But lexical morphemes go on changing frequently; new members are added to the lexicon quite often.

However, the distinction between lexical and grammatical morphemes is artificial and inadequate. "Hood' is lexical morpheme in **she wears a hood, but is** not so in **boyhood**. Prepositions are classed as grammatical morphemes, yet they are not all empty of semantic content. Even small grammatical morphemes such as the **{-ly} in rapidly** the [un-] in **unemployment** and the [er] in **teacher** have definite semantic content. Hence the necessity of a more rationalistic division of morphemes.

(2) Free and Bound Morphemes. A more acceptable and more satisfactory classification than the one mentioned above classifies morphemes into free and bound forms. The whole classification can be represented in the following manner–

Morphemes

- Free
- Bound
  - Prefix (initial position)
  - Infix (middle position)
    - Derivational
      - Class-maintaining
      - Class-changing
    - Inflectional
    - Bound bases
  - Suffix (final position)

These will be defined and illustrated in the following discussion. Morphemes, as defined earlier, are the minimum grammatical forms of language. Some of them can occur alone, others cannot. Forms which do not occur alone are bound morphemes and those which occur alone are free morphemes. **Rat, cat, go, black, the, yet, but, and** are free morphemes. Affixes to the words such as **-ness, -less, pre, up-, up-, de-, con-, -er, ment** are all bound morphemes.

(a) Roots and Affixes. The root morpheme is that part of the word which is left when all the affixes have been removed. Root morphemes may be bound or free, and are potentially unlimited in a language because languages go on creating new words or borrowing 'loan-words' from other languages. In a word like **unfaithful, faith** is the-root, the **-un** and the **-ful** are affixes; the **un-** is a prefix, whereas the **-ful** is a suffix.

All affixes are bound morphemes, for they cannot occur alone. A word which consists of only free root morpheme is called **monomorphemic,** *e.g.* **cat, rat.** The words containing more than one root are called **polymorphemic** *e.g.* air-craft; they can co-occur or without affixes; they are often called **compunds words.**

Root and affixes may be of any structure and length, though-affixes generally tend to be shorter than roots. The criterion of determining the root is its indivisibility into constituent morphemes by matching its parts with the parts of other words in the language.

The affixe is the recurrent formative morpheme of words other than roots. Affixes are of three types– **prefix, infix** and **suffix.** In the English words such as **receive, remove, deceive perform, unfaithful, unemployment, re-, de-, per, un-,** are all prefixes. The prefixes are affixed before the roots, and cannot occur independently, they are bound morphemes. The plural formative **-s, -en;** the verb paradigm affixes **-ing,-d-ed,** etc. The comparative and superlative ending of the adjective **(er,** and **-est)** and so many other final position formatives such as -**ness, -less, -ment** are called suffixes. The suffixes are affixes after the roots or after the root-suffix.Infixes are less commonly found in English apart from one mode of analysis of plurals like **gees, men.** Infixes are found in Cambodian, in Sudanese and in Sanskrit too.

(b) **Inflection and Derivation.** Both inflectional and derivational morphemes are suffixes; they are bound morphemes following a root. Inflection and derivation are therefore, the sub-categories of suffixes. But they differ from each other. If one kind of suffix is affixed to a root we cannot affix any other. Suffix *e.g.*, in **agreed** and **agrees, -d** and **-s** are suffixes and do not therefore allow any further affixation of a suffix. Such affixes which do not allow further affixation called inflections, or inflectional morphemes. The suffixes which may be followed by other suffixes are called **derivational** suffixes. For example, **-ment,-ble** are derivational suffixes in **agreement** and **agreeable**, because both can be followed by other suffixes and can, for instance, become **agreements** and **agreeableness** after the addition of the suffix-s and **-ness** to **agree+ment** and **agree+able** respectively.

Inflectional suffixes have a very wide distribution; that is that words which they mark have a great many members. Inflectional suffixes are always final in the morpheme groups to which they belong. They are of wide occurrence; they make large words. Their distribution is regular. Derivational suffixes, on the other hand, may be final in the group to which they belong, or they may be followed by other derivational suffixes or by inflectional suffixes. They are of relatively limited occurrence, and their distribution tends to be arbitrary. (Prefixes are always derivationals).

Inflectional suffixes are 'terminal', and their termination never changes the class (part of speech) of the root, for example, in **sweeter** and **sweetest,** the termination of -er -by -est does not change the part of speech; both the forms remain adjectives; come in a verb in **They come late**, and if we add an inflectional suffix **-ing** we get the form **coming** (as in **They are coming)** which is still a verb. An inflected form can be replaced by another inflected form only, *e.g.*

He [drink-s / steal-s / play-s

but not

He steal/drink/play, etc.

An inflectional suffix occurs at the end position of a form; no further affixation in a from is possible after an inflection. We can say

develop+s

root (-) inflectional suffix

develop+ment

root+derivational suffix + s Inflectional suffix

but not

develop	**s**	**ment**
root	inflectional suffix	derivational suffix

So an inflectional suffix is essentially terminal, whereas a derivational suffix is not essentially terminal. Derivational suffixes can occur medially and/or finally, but inflectional suffixes occur only finally.

(c) **Class-maintaining and Class Changing Derivational Suffixes.** Derivational suffixes can be subclassfied into two types: *(i)* Class-maintaining derivational suffix and *(ii)* Class-changing derivational suffix. The class-maintaining derivational suffixes are those which produce a derived form of the same class as the underlying form; they do not change the class of a part of speech. In **boyhood, childhood, kinship, principalship, hood** and **-ship** are class-maintaining derivational suffixes. In these examples they produce nouns out of nouns after suffixation. The class-changing derivation are those that produce a derived form of another class. In **teacher, boyish, development, national, -er -ish, -ment, -al** are class-changing derivational suffixes. In **teacher,** a verb teach has become a noun after suffixing the -er. In boyish, a noun boy has become an adjective after suffixing the **-ish.**

We can further review the example of morphemes in the following manner–

		Bound Morphemes			
			Suffix		
Words	*Free Morpheme (root)*	*Prefix*	*Derivational suffix*		*Inflectional Suffix*
			Class maintaining	*Class Changing*	
(1)	*(2)*	*(3)*	*(4)*	*(5)*	*(6)*
Pre-establishment	[establish]	[pre-]		[-ment ment	

Contd.

(1)	*(2)*	*(3)*	*(4)*	*(5)*	*(6)*
Establishmen-tarianism.	[establish]			-arian -ism]	
Penominalizations	[nominal]	[pre]		[-iz -ation]	[-s]
Principalships	[principal]		[ship]		[-s]

(d) Bound Bases. Bound bases are those morphemes which serve as roots for derivational forms but which never appear as free forms. In words such as **conclude, preclude, include, exclude,** the **clude** is a bound base; and so is the **-ceive in receive, perceive, deceive.**

(3) Compounds. A compound is a lexical unit in which two or more lexical morphemes (free roots) are juxtaposed, **e.g. aircraft, textbook, white-cap, slow-down, bed-side, fingerprint.**

(4) Idioms. An idiom is a phrase the meaning of which cannot be predicted from the individual meanings of the morphemes it comprises. Idioms are complex lexical items, it is difficult to translate them from one language into another; they have culturally determined meanings. Most idioms are 'frozen metaphors', their meanings must be learnt as a whole, *e.g.* give way, in order to.

MORPHS

Any phonetic shape or representation of a phoneme is a morph (Hockett). Each morph, like each phone, or each person or each day, happens only once and then it is gone. To quote John Lyons, "When the word can be segmented into parts, these segments are referred to as morphs." Thus the words shorter is analyzable in two morphs, which can be written orthographically as short and **er,** and in phonological transcription /fǝt/ and /ǝ/. Each morph represents a particular morpheme, but each morpheme does not have a morph. For example, the plural noun **sheep** has one morph, but it has two morphemes [sheep] and [ ] **went** has one morph, but two morpheme [go] and [ed.]

ALLOMORPHS

It frequently happens that a particular morpheme is not represented everywhere by the same morph, but by different morphs in different environments. The alternative phonological manifestation or representations of such a morpheme are called **allomorphs** or 'morpheme alternants' and 'morpheme variants'. An allomorph. therefore, is a non-distinctive variant of a morpheme. Or, it may be called a family or class of morphs which are phonemically and semantically identical, that is an allomorph is "a family of morphs which are alike in two ways: *(i)* in the allophones of which they are composed and, *(ii)* in the meaning which they have" (Nelson Francis).

The allomorphs are phonologically conditioned. Their forms are dependent on the adjacent phonemes. Or else, they are morphologically conditioned. That is, when morphemes are affected by their phonological environment 'sandhi', they become allomorphs. For example, /-z/, /-s/, /-iz/ and /θ/ are the various allomorphs of the plural morpheme {-z} in English.

The study of different shapes of allomorphs is half-way between phonology and morphology, and is sometimes referred to as **morphophonology** or **morphonology**. In America where phonology is considered as part of descriptive linguistics synchronic linguistics has relied on phonemic analysis, the term **morphophonemics** is used for this aspect of grammer.

PHONOLOGICAL CONDITIONING

The English plural morpheme provides very good examples of both phonologically and morphologically conditioned allomorphs. /-s/ , /-z/, and /iz/ are all phonologically conditioned allomorphs of the English plural morpheme.

1. /-s/ appears with morphs ending in /p, tk, f, θ/.
2. /-z/ appears with morphs ending in /b,d, g, v, ðm, n, ŋ, l, r, y, w,/
3. /-iz/ appears with morphs ending in /z.ʃ, tʃ, dʒ/

These generalizations can be exemplified in the following manner:

form taking /s/	**forms taking** /z/	**forms taking** /iz/
cups/kʌps/	hubs/hʌbz/	classes /kla: siz/
hats/ hæts/	hands/hændz/	mazes/meiziz/
thanks/θæŋks/	dogs/dɔgz/	dishes/diʃ iz/
coughs /kɔfs/	gloves/glʌvz/	garages/gæraʒiz/
hycinths/haiəsinsθs/	rims/rimz/	churches/tʃʌvʃ iz/.

If we study these data to find a principle governing this distribution we will discover that these generalizations can be restated in even more general and precise terms, as given below:

1. /-s/ appears after morphs ending in voiceless morphemes, except the sibilants and affricates.
2. /-z/ appears after morphs ending in voiced morphemes except the sibilants and affricates.
3. /-z/ appears after morphs ending in sibilants and affricates.

That is, the linguist has stated the conditions or explained what factors are responsible for the particular physical form of the plural. Since the factors in this case are the preceding sound segments, he classifies this as phonological conditioning.

Another example of this phonologial conditioning is the past tense morpheme of English [-ed]. It is also regularly represented by three phonologically conditioned allomorphs /t/, /d/ and /-id/. The rule governing their distribution is as follows:

1. /id/ occurs after morphs ending in alveolar stops /t/ and /d/ as in wanted/w: ntid/and wedded/wedid.

2. /d/ occurs after voiced phonemes except /d/ as in **loved** / l^vd/ **called/k: ld./.**

3. /t/ occurs after voiceless phonemes except /t/ as in **helped**/ helpt.

MORPHOLOGICAL CONDITIONING

In pairs such as **man-men, child-children,** and **deer-deer,** in which second item can be said to contain the "plural" morpheme, we cannot state the variation, if any, between the two forms in terms of phonetic evnironments. Instead we must refer to each morpheme separately or, alternatively to their phonemic shapes, and specify the allomorph of the 'plural morpheme' separately for each. This kind of variation among allomorphs is called morphological conditioning. The morphologically conditioned allomorphs of a morpheme are regarded as irregular in contrast with the phonologically conditioned allomorphs, which are regarded as regular. **Men, children** and **deer** are therefore irregular English plurals, just as are **alumni, criteria, mice, women** and **oxen.** The 'past tense' morpheme also has its irregular allomorphs, as in **drank, brought, swam, was, had, put, took, fled, built,** and so on likewise, the "past participle" morpheme has irregular alomorphs, as in **drunk, brought, sum, been broken, stood, put** and **on.**

Let us analyze some of the words stated above:

Oxen-oz+/- n/

Deer-+/θ/

We noticed in the earlier section on "phonological conditioning" that the linguist was making some very useful generalization. But in cases of 'oxen' and 'deer' his prediction went wrong: we did not have "oxes" and "deers.' On the other hand we found the sense of plural was retained in "oxen" and "deer." Though the sense is retained, yet the form is puzzling. So he concludes that the morpheme ox itself is perhaps the condition factor and not the sound sequences of which it is composed for this new plural marker. So he calls this **morphological conditioning.**

ZERO SUFFIX

There are certain forms which have the same singular and plural forms such as sheep, deer, cattle. Such forms in the singular and the plural are not different. They are homophonous. However, the linguist, for the sake of uniformity assumes that the plural morpheme is present but its phonetic manifestation or representation is zero. It has no visible marker in the environment of **sheep, deer, or cattle.** He would therefore, analyze these in the following manner:

sheep+/θ/

deer+/θ/

cattle+/θ/

AFFIXES

Affixes are bound morphemes. Depending upon the position of the affixes in relation to the base, affixes can be classified into prefixes (those that precede the base) and suffixes (those that follow the base). For example, in 'untimely', 'un-' is a prefix, 'time' is the base and '-ly' is a suffix. Infixes are inserted inside the base (*e.g.*, Latin 'linguo' has n as the infix); in Arabic 'qariba' (be near) becomes 'iqtaraba' (to cause oneself to come near). Suprasegmentals like words-stress, tone, etc., that are relevant to the description of words, are superfixes.

Affixes that are used to derive words (*i.e.*, changing words from one type to another) are derivational affixes. Affixes that are used to inflect words are inflectional affixes. Derivational prefixes occur before the base. In the position after the base, the derivational suffixes are added first and then the inflectional suffixes. Inflectional suffixes occur at the end. For example, in 'disagreements', 'dis-' is a derivational prefix, '-ment' is a derivational suffix and '-s' an inflectional suffix. In inflected languages three are inflections for number, gender, person, case, tense, etc.

The base which functions as the nuclues is also called the root; it may be bound or free. The addition of a derivational affix makes it a stem and inflections are added to the stem. For example, 'agree' is the base; if 'dis-is' added, it becomes a stem; 'disagree' is a stem and the third person singular present tense inflection can be added to the stem: 'He disagrees'; 'disagreement' is a stem and a plural inflectional suffix can be added to that.

MORPHOPHONEMICS

The study of the phonemic structure of morphemes (*i.e.*, the changes that morphemes undergo in certain positions) is called morphophonemics. In generative phonology, the changes that take place in the values of phonological features are stated in terms of various types of rules.

(1) Zero modification [as in sheep (sing.)–Shee (pl.); cut (present)–cut (past)] and process morphemes [*i.e.*, change of vowel in pairs like 'take–took', 'man–men'] were pointed out earlier.

(2) Suppletion is the replacement of the entire form. In English the forms 'am', 'is' 'are', 'was', 'were' are the suppletive variants of the form 'be'.

(3) Syncretism is the use of a single, non-divisible unit to manifest more than one component of meaning.

Examples: English: He runs. ('s' marks the present tense and third person singular)

Hindi: kərta:he ('a:' marks both number and gender)

(4) Assimilation refers to the change of one sound into another sound because of the influence of neighbouring sounds.

Assimilation may be progressive, regressive, reciprocal or distant.

(5) Dissimilation is the opposite of assimilation in that one or more consonants or vowels of one morpheme become unlike those of another morpheme whenever these morphemes combine.

(6) Syncope is the elumination of medial vowels or consonants.

(7) Apocope is the loss of a final sounds or syllable.

(8) Reduplication is the repetition of identical forms.

(9) Metathesis is a change in the order of the elements of a morpheme.

Example: Anglo-Saxon; wœps, bren → Mordern English: wasp, burn

(10) Epenthesis is the addition of elements (phoneme or phonemes or a syllable) whenever two or more morphemes combine.

(11) Demination is the reduction of long or double consonants or vowels into short ones.

Example: Kannada: ibb(a) ru 'two people' → ibru

(12) Gemination is the doubling of consonants or vowels.

Example: Hindi: bhul^kkar

(13) Complex or unusual clusters may be simplified by inserting a vowel between the consonants or prefixing a vowel or through assimilation or by dropping one.

VOWELS

The vowels of English are all voiced because they are formed by the voiced air passing through different mouth-shapes. They are made by the different positions of the tongue and the lips. It is, therefore, convenient to classify the vowels according to the positions of the main parts of the tongue.

In the production of most vowels the tongue is convex to the palate. Vowel, therefore, be conveniently arranged according to the position of the highest point of the tongue. There are front vowels, in the production of which the front of the tongue is raised in the direction of the hard palate as in | i: | in | fi:d|.

Then, there are back vowels in the production of which the back of the tongue is raised in the direction of the soft palate as in saying in | u: | in | fu:d|. Again, there are vowels intermediate between front and back. We call them central vowels. Examples of central vowels are:

There are in R.P. (Educated Southern British English) twenty distinctive vowel sounds. Twelve of them are pure vowels called monophthongs and the remaining eight are called diphthongs. Pure vowels can again be divided into short and long vowels. Examples of short vowels are | I, ∪ ∂ | while long vowels are | i:, a:, ⊃: u: |

A DETAILED DESCRIPTION OF VOWELS

A Front Vowels | i:, i, e, æ |. In articulating | i: | the front of the tongue is raised in the direction of the hard palate to a position almost near close. The lips are spread while the tongue is tense. So | 1: | can be described as a Front close unrounded vowel. Examples are | Si:t, mi:t, gri:t, stri:t | etc. | i: | is always longer in the final position as also before voiced consonant as in |bi:d, si:z, li:g | etc.. as also in | bi:, si: | etc. Vowel | 1 | - | 1 | is a short pure vowels. In articulating it, the near part of the front of the tongue is raised towards the hard palate a little above the half close position. The tongue is more or less relaxed and lips are loosely spread. As it is near the central part of the tongue we can call it a centralised front unround vowel. Examples: | sit, bit, It, hit | etc.

| 1 | is longer before voiced consonant and shorter before the voiceless one. Examples: | b i d | an and | bit | respectively.

Short pure vowel | e |. In articulating | e | the front of the tongue is raised towards the hard palate to a height between half close and half open. Lips are spread loosely and the tongue is tense. Thus | e | is called a front unrounded vowel between half-close and half-open.

| e | does not occur as a sound in a word finally. It occurs only initially and medially. Examples are | *e.g.* | and˙| beg | respectively. Also | e| is longer before voiced consonants and shorter before voiceless consonants. Examples are | bed | and | bet | respectively.

Pure Vowel æ. In forming | æ | the front part of the tongue is raised towards the hard palate a little below the half open position. Lips are open and neutral. So | æ | is a Front unrounded vowel just below the half open position.

| æ | does not occur in the final position; it occurs only in the intial and medial positions. Examples are | æ | and | m æ n | respectively.

| æ | is longer before a voiced consonant and shorter before a voiceless one. Examples are | læg | and | læk | respectively.

Back Vowels. The back vowels of R. P. | ∪, u: d, ⊃:, a: | | a: | is Back, Open and Unrounded vowel. In forming this the part of the tongue between the centre and the back, (nearer the back rather than the centre) is in the fully open position. The jaws are wide and the lips are neutrally open. | a: | is thus a back open uprounded vowel

| a: | can occur initially, medially and finally a word as in a:sk, ba:sk, ka: |

| a: | is longer in the final position and before voiced consonants but shorter before voiceless consonants. Examples are | ka:, a:m, a:t | respectively.

The Back Vowel | ¬D |. Manner of articulation: the back of the tongue is just above the fully open position. The jaws are wide open and the lips are slightly rounded. | ¬D | is, therefore, a Back, Rounded Vowel just above the open position. It occurs only initially and medially in words. Examples are | Dks | and | bDks | respectively | ¬D | become slightly longer before voiced consonants than before voiceless ones. Examples are | hDg | and | hDt | respectively.

The Back Vowels | ⊃: |. This vowel is relatively longer than | D |. In forming this sound the back of the tongue is raised towards the soft palate between the half open and half close positions. The lips are rounded. | ⊃: | is, therefore, described as a Back Rounded Vowel between half open and half-close positions. | ⊃: | can occur in any position, initially, medially or finally.

Examples are | ⊃: t |, br⊃:t | respectively. Also, | ⊃: | is longer before the voiced consonants than before voiceless consonants. Examples are | b⊃:l | and | b⊃ ks | respectively.

The Back Vowel | ∪ |: In the articulation of this vowel the front part of the back of the tongue is raised towards the soft palate to a height just above half close. The tongue is lax and the lips are rounded. | ∪ | is thus a Back Rounded Vowel just above half close. | ∪ | does not occur initially; it occurs only medially and finally as in words it occurs initially and finally as in word | p∪t, p∪l, p∪ | medially and in | t∪| finally.

The Back vowel | u: |. This vowel sound is relatively longer than that of | ∪ |. In the articulation of | u: | the back of the tongue is raised in the direction of the soft palate as high as very near the close position. The lips are closely rounded and the tongue is tense. So | u: | is called a Back, Close, Rounded Vowel. | u: | can occur in any position, initially, medially and finally. Examples are | u:z |, | bu:t | and | zu:t | respectively.

Again, like other vowels | u: | is longer before voiced consonants and shorter before the voiceless ones. Examples are | ru:d | and | ru:t | respectively.

The Central Vowels are | ^ 3:, ∂ |

| ^ | - In the articulation of this central vowel, the centre of the tongue is raised towards that part of the palate which is between the hard palate and the soft palate. The central part is raised to a height just above the open position. The jaws are wide and the lips are neutral and open. The vowel occurs initially and medially. Examples are | ^P | and k^p | respectively | 3 |. In articulating this central vowel too the tongue is raised in the direction of that part of the palate

which is between the hard and the soft palates. The tongue goes to a height between half close and half open. The lips are spread. | 3: | is called a Central unrounded vowel between half-close and half-open; |3: | occurs in any position, initially, medially or finally. Examples are | 3:li | |, | b3:d | and | b3: | respectively when followed by a voiced consonant | 3: | is longer than when it is followed by a voiceless consonant as in | h3:d | and | h3:t|

Central vowel | ∂ |. This vowel can be in two positions:

When it is non-final, it has the same manner articulation as vowel | 3: | has. The only difference between the two is that length. So | ∂ | is a central unrounded vowel just above half open. Final | ∂ | is seen in words like | ple3∂, me3∂ | tre3∂ | etc.

| ∂ | is the most frequently used vowel in English pronunciations. It can occur in any position, initially, medially and finally. Examples are | ∂baut, p3:m∂n∂nt, | din∂ | etc.

Also, | ∂ | is used frequently in the weak forms of many words. Examples are | ∂, ∂n Ò∂, t∂, h∂, f∂ | etc. | ∂ | does not occur in accented syllables.

DIPTHONGS

From the point of view of their quality, vowel sounds are of two types: monopthong and dipthong. Monopthongs are pure vowels and dipthongs are gliding vowels. 'A vowel that does not change in quality' may be called a monopthong; and a vowel sound with a continually changing quality may be called a dipthong.

A pure vowel is one for which the ograns of speech remain in a given position for an appreciable period of time. A dipthong is a vowel sound consisting of a deliberate, *i.e.* intentional glide, the organs of speech starting in the position of one vowel and immediately moving in the direction of another vowel. A dipthong, moreover, consists of a single syllable–that is, the vowel-glide must be performed with a single impulse of the breath; if there is more than one impulse of breath, the ear perceives two separate syllables.

A dipthong, thus, always occupies one syllable. If two adjacent vowels form the nuclei of two successive syllables, they are not a dipthong. For example the vowels in **bay, boy,** and **buy** are diphthongs, but the vowels in **doing** are two different vowels since they belong to two different syllables.

One end of the dipthong is generally more prominent than the other. Dipthongs are termed 'decrescendo' or Falling if the first element is louder or more prominent than the second, and 'crescendo' or Rising if the second element is louder or more prominent than the first. All the English dipthongs are falling dipthongs, because in them the first element is louder or more prominent than the second element.

Dipthongs are represented in phonetic transcription by a sequence of two letters, the first showing the position of the organs of speech at the beginning of the glide, the second their position at the end. In the case of the 'closing' dipthongs the second letter indicates the point **toward which** glide (movement) is made.

In English, for example, there are two kinds of diphthongs: the closing dipthongs and the centring dipthongs. Dipthongs are described by indicating the position of the tongue and the lips in the beginning and at the end of the glide. For example, /ai/ in the English word buy can be described as a glide or movement from front, open, unrounded to front, half-close, unrounded. The descriptions of the dipthongs of R.P. are given below:

/ou/as in **boat:** closing dipthong, beginning at a central position below half-close and moving in the direction of /u/. The lips are neutral in the beginning and rounded towards the end.

/ei/ as in **pay:** closing dipthong, beginning at a slightly below half-close position and moving towards R.P. /i/. The lips are spread.

/ i/ as in **boy:** closing dipthong, the glide begins near the back half-open position and moves in the direction of /i/.

The lips are open rounded at the beginning and neutral at the end.

/ai/ as in **buy:** closing dipthong glides from the front open position towards /i/. The lips change from a neutral to a loosely spread position.

/au/ as in **how:** closing dipthong, glides from /ạ/ towards /u/. The lips are neutral in the beginning and weakly rounded in the end.

/i/ as in **peer:** centring dipthong, the glide begins at /i/ and moves towards /∂ /. The lips are neutral.

/e / as in **air:** centring dipthong, the glide begins between half-close and half-open position and moves towards/∂/. The lips are neutral.

/u / as in **poor:** the centring dipthong, the glide begins at /u/ and moves to /e/. The lips are weakly rounded at the beginning and neutral at the end.

To summarise the description of vowel sound should include information about the position of the soft palate, the position of the lips, the part of the tongue raised and the degree of raising. It is difficult to judge the exact tongue positions for a vowel.

A system of eight primary cardinal vowels enables us to describe any vowel sound in relation to them. These cardinal vowels are represented by the symbols [i, e, ɛ,a æ, c, o, u,]. Some languages have nasalized vowels also. Some vowels are relatively 'pure'; others have glides and are called diphthongs. Vowels are classified according to the part of the tongue raised into front, central, and back vowels. Vowels are classified into close, half close, half-open vowels according to the height of the tongue.

PHONETIC TRANSCRIPTION

Phonetic transcription is a device in which we use several symbols in such a way that one symbol always represents one sound. It is also known as phonetic notation, it is an 'attempt on paper, a record of the sounds that speakers make.' By looking at an English word in its written form one cannot be sure of its pronunciation, whereas by looking at it in phonetic transcription one can be. Most of our phonetic transcriptions are **phonemic** transcriptions, that is, each symbol represents a phoneme, a distinct sound unit in language. A pair of square brackets [ ] indicates a phonetic transcription. Phonemic transcriptions are enclosed within slant bars / /.

(1) **The Narrow and Broad Transcription.** A broad phonetic transcription, that is the phonemic transcription is the transcription of the phonemes of a langauge, *e.g.* the English words **peak** and **speak** can be transcribed as /pi: k/ and /spi: k/ respectively, although there occurs the aspirated **variety** of phoneme /p/ in the first word **(peak)** and the unaspirated variety in the second. But the narrow transcription, also called **the allophonic transcription,** indicates the precise phonetic quality of each segment. In this type of transcription the aspirated variety of /p/ as in the word **peak** can be indicated by transcribing the words [p^hi: k]

(2) **The Usefulness of the International Phonetic Alphabet.** The I P A gives us a uniform international medium of studying and transcribing the sounds of all the languages of the world. Many languages in the world have no orthographic (written) form at all. It has been made possible to study such languages with this alphabet. In other words, the IPA is 'a precise and universal' means (*i.e.* valid for all languages) of writing down the spoken forms of utterances as they are spoken without reference to their orthographic representation, grammatical status, or meaning.

As regards English, the IPA helps us in establishing and maintaining international intelligibility and uniformity in the pronunciation of English. With the help of the IPA we can easily teach the pronunciation of English or of any other language. The IPA has contributed a lot in the teaching and description of language. The teachers and learners of English can improve, and standardize their pronunciation and can overcome the confusion created by the spellings with the help of the international phonetic alphabet.

English is a notorious example as one of those languages in which the pronunciation of words in most cases do not go by the spellings of words because there is no one-to-one correspondence between the letters of the alphabet and the sounds they represent. Take for example the vowel 'a'. Its sound differs so widely from word to word as given below:

1. 'a' is | a: | as in 'ask', 'bask', 'task', etc.
2. 'a' is | el | as in 'pay', 'may', 'say', etc.
3. 'a' is | ¬D | as in 'was', 'wasp', etc.
4. 'a' is | ⊃: | as in 'ball', 'tall', 'hall', etc.
5. 'a' is | l | in 'village', 'damage', etc.
6. 'a' is | æ | in 'man', 'pan', 'ran', etc.

Similarly, there are more-than-one sounds of other vowels 'e', 'i' 'o' and | u |'

Naturally, for correct pronunciations we resort to the use of phonetic Alphabet in which one phonetic letter stands for one and only one sound only.

Again, in English 'Ch' has three different sounds to confuse the learners of English sounds. For Example 'Ch' is |ʃ | sounds in 'machine', Chauffeur', Chagrin as |məʃ i:n,ʃ aufə ʃægrin | But it gives the sounds of | tʃ | | as in 'choice' | t ʃ⊃ Is !, Chair' | t ʃeə | and 'choose' | tʃu:z |. Lastly 'Ch' gives the sound of | K | as in character | kəræktə |, chord | k⊃:d| and chemistry | kemistri |.

Similar is the case with some other letters of English alphabet, that have more than-one sounds. Examples are the cases of 'c', 'g', 'f, 'gh' etc.

This lack of one-to-one relationship between spelling and pronunciation is found in several languages besides English. French is one of them, in which several letters become silent.

In order to remove these short comings phonetic transcription is a very useful device for the purpose of correct pronunciation as IPA (International Phonetic Alphabt) has symbols to represent all the sounds that exist in the languages of the world. Researches and improvements are consistently made in IPA. Till now the list of symbols stands corrected upto 1979.

The International Phonetic Alphabet with symbols and diacritics makes it possible for us to write words as they are produced. Such writing is called phonetic transcription. The phonetic transcription provides pronunciation of words in dictionaries. It is with the help of phonetic transcription that the sound systems of different languages or those of the varieties of the same language can be compared to one an other.

THE SYLLABLE STRUCTURE

A syllable is one of the units into which a word may be divided. Usually it consists of a vowel sound with a consonant before or after it, but in English a syllable may consist of a single vowel *e.g.* | ∂ | or it may be a single consonant as | n | or | i |.

A syllable corresponds to a chest pulse or a musle monement, pushing the air out of the lungs. Many words in English are mono-syllabic *i.e.* consiting of one syllable only *e.g.* | ræt, kæt, r^n, sit | etc. The number of syllables in a word corresponds to the number of vowel sounds in that word.

A syllable consists of one or more speech sounds. These sounds are vowels and consonants. If a syllable consists of just one sound, it is usually a vowel as | a: | or | ∂∪ |. But sometimes a consonant may also constitute a syllable as |ʃ | or | ! |.

If a syllable has more than one speech sounds, one of them must be a vowel.

As in |'eni". The nucleus of a syllable which is usually a vowel in symbolised as | V | and the marginal element which is usually a consonant is symbolised as | C |.

The following, therefore, are some types of the structure of a syllable composed of vowels and consonants.

Word	*Structure*	*Word*	*Structure*
I | 2I |	V	all | ⊃:l |	VC
a | ∂ |	V	no | n∂∪ |	CV
an | ∂n |	VC	So | s∂∪ |	CV
as | æ z |	VC	See | si: |	CV
Can | k æ n |	CVC	play | pleI |	CCV
live | 1Iv |	CVC	tray | trei |	CCV
leg | leg |	CVC	below | bl∂u |	CCV
Stray | streI |	CCCV	Straw | st⊃: |	CCCV
Screw |skr∪: |	CCCV	Strong |strD η |	CCCVC
Street | stri:t |	CCCVC	Stream | stri:m |	CCCVC
Sprained | spreind |	CCCVCC	Sprawled | spr⊃:ld |	CCCVCC
Strained	CCCVCC	employ	VCCCV

Contd.

Word	*Structure*	*Word*	*Structure*
| streind |		| impl⊃l |	
distory	CVCCCV	ethereal	VCVCVC
| distr⊃l |		| lθl∂rl∂l |	
evasion	VCVCC	eve | l:V |	VC
|ivel3n |			
evaporate	VCVCVCVC	European	CVCVCVC
| ivæp∂relt		| j∪∂r∂ pl∂n |	
evasive IVESIV	VCVCVC		

FRICATIVES

A fricative is articulated with a stricture of close approximation: that is, the two articulators are brought so close to each other that the gap between them is very narrow. The air that is compressed by pressure from the lungs escapes through the narrow gap with audible friction.

In English there are 9 fricative consonants. These are:

/f/ and /v/ : labiodental fricatives

/θ/ and /ð/ : dental fricatives

/s/ and /z/ : alveolar fricatives

/ʃ/ and /z/ : palato-alveolar fricatives

/h/ : glottal fricative

of these. /f/. /θ/, /s/, / /ʃ/ and /h/ are voiceless and /v/, /ð/ /z/ and /ʒ/ are voiced.

/f/

1. During the articulation of /f/, the lower lip is brouht very close to the upper front teeth so that the gap between them is

extremely narrow. The soft palate is raised and thus the passage of air is blocked completely. The air escapes through the narrow gap between the lower lip and the upper front teeth with audible friction. The vocal cords are held wide apart and they do not vibrate. /f/ is thus a voiceless labio-dental fricative.

Spellings: /f/ is represented by

(i) the letter f as in five, fool

(ii) the letters ff as in coffee, affair

(ii) the letters ph as in physics, photograph

(iv) the letters gh as in cough, rough.

Distribution:

/f/ can occur initially, medially and finally as in five (initial) offer (medial) and roof (final).

(v)

2. /v/ is articulated exactly like /f/ described above except that during the articulation of /v/ the vocal cords vibrate producing voice. /v/ is thus a voiced **Labio-dental fricative.**

Spellings: /v/ is represented by

(i) the letter v as in over,

(ii) the letter f as in of

(iii) the letters ph as in nephew.

Distribution:

/v/ occurs initially, medially and finally, as in vine (initial) cover, (medial) and love (final).

/θ/

3. The tip of the tongue makes a light contact with the edge of the upper front teeth. The soft palate is raised so as to shut off the

nasal passage of air. The air escapes through the narrow space between the tip of the tongue and the front teeth, causing audible friction. The vocal cords do not vibrate. /θ/ is thus a **voiceless dental fricative.**

Spellings:

/θ/ is represented by the letters th as in thin, thick, path, etc.

Distribution:

/θ/ can occur initially, medially and finally in a word as in thick (initial), etheral (medial) and oath (final).

/ð/

4. /ð/as articulated exactly like /θ/ described above, except that during the articulation of /ð/ the vocal cords vibrate producing voice, /ð/ is thus a **voiced dental fricative.**

Spellings: /ð/ is represented by the letters th as in then and that.

Distribution: /ð/ occurs initially, medially and finally in a word as in then (initial), leather (medial) and soothe (final).

(s)

5. /s/ is articulated by placing the tip and blade of the tongue very near the teeth ridge so that the space between them is very narrow. The soft palate is raised, shutting off the nasal passage of air. The vocal cords do not vibrate. The air escapes through the narrow gap between the tip and blade of the tongue and teeth ridge with audible friction. /s/ is thus a **voiceless alveolar fricative.**

Spellings: /s/ is represented by

(i) the letter s as in sin.

(ii) the letters ss as in message, pass.

(iii) the letter c, (followed by the letter e or i) as in cease, cell.

(iv) Medial and final x is pronounced /ks/ as in ox, box, taxi.

(v) the letter sc as in Scene, Science

Distribution:

/s/ can occur initially, medially and finally as in seen (initial), passive (medial) and less (final).

(z)

6. /z/ is articulated exactly like /s/ described above, except that during the articulation of /z/ the vocal cords vibrate producing voice. /z/ can thus be described as a **voiced alveolar fricative.**

Spellings: /z/ is represented by

(i) the letter z as in zoo, zero, lazy

(ii) the letter (medial and final) s in poison, dogs

(iii) the letter ss as in scissors

(iv) the letters zz as in buzz.

Distribution:

/z/ occurs initially, medially and finally as in zoo (initial), puzzle (medial), and lose (final).

(ʃ)

7. The tip and blade of the tongue are brought very close to the teeth ridge. Simultaneously the front of the tongue is raised in the direction of the hard palate. The soft palate is raised, thereby completely blocking the nasal passage of air. The air escapes through the narrow passage between the tip, blade and front of the tongue and the teeth ridge and hard palate, with audible friction. The vocal cords do not vibrate. /ʃ/ is thus a **voiceless palatoalveolar fricative.**

Spellings: /ʃ/ is represented by

(i) the letters sh as in shine sheep

(ii) the letters ch as in machine

(iii) the letter s [+u] as in sugar.

(iv) the letter tio as in nation, caution.

(v) the letter c as in efficient.

(vi) the letters ss as in pressure.

(vii) the letters ci as in conscience.

Distribution:

/ʃ/ occurs initially, medially and finally as in shell [initial] pressure (medial) and fish (final).

/ʒ/

8. /ʒ/ is articulated exactly like /ʃ/ described above, except that during the articulation of /ʒ/ the vocal cords vibrate producing voice /ʒ/ is thus a **voiced palato-alveolar fricative.**

Spelling: /ʒ/ is represented by

(i) the letters si as in decision, vision.

(ii) the letters s [+u] as in pleasure, leisure.

(iii) the letters ge in French loan words like rouge, garage.

Distribution: /ʒ/ occurs only medially in English words. It occurs finally in French loan words. It does not occur initially *e.g.* pleasure [medial] and mirage (final).

/h/

9. The vocal cords are kept close together so that the glottis is very narrow. The air escapes through the narrow glottis with audible friction. /h/ is thus **voiceless glottal fricative.** In English /h/ occurs only in syllable-initial positions, always followed by a vowel. It may thus be regarded as a strong, voicelss onset of the succeeding vowel.

Spelling: /h/ is always represented by the letter h.

Between two vowels /h/ may be voiced as in behind, beehive.

Distribution: /h/ occurs only initially and medially as in hat (initial), behave (medial).

LATERAL

A lateral consonant is articulated with a complete closure in the centre of the vocal tract the air escaping along the sides of the tongue.

In English there is one lateral consonant which is /l/.

/l/ is articulated by the tip of the tongue making a firm contact against the teeth ridge. There is thus a complete closure in the middle of the mouth. The soft palate is raised so as to shut off the nasal passage of the air completely. The sides of the tongue are lowered so that the lung air is free to escape along sides of the tongue without any friction. The vocal cords vibrate, producing voice. /l/ is thus **voiced alveolar lateral.**

Spellings: /l/ is represented by the letter l as in leave and by letters ll as in villain. It should be remembered that the letter l is silent in words like calm, palm, alms, etc.

Allophonic Variants

(i) A dental [l] is used when followed by /θ/] or /Ò/-

/helθ/ (/l/ followed by /θ/)

/telðem/ (l/followed by /ð/)

(ii) in R.P. there are two varieties of /l/. One is called a 'clear' /l/ and the other of 'dark' /l/, (the phonetic symbols are [l] and [ð] respectively).

'Clear' /l/ is articulated by making a closure in the middle as described above and simultaneously raising the front of the tongue in the direction of the hard palate. In R.P. this varierty of /l/ is used before vowels and /j/, *e.g.*

live /liv/

lure /ljuə.

'Dark' /l/ is articulated by making a closure in the middle as described above and simultaneously raising the back of the tongue in the direction of the soft palate. In R.P. it is used before consonant other than /j/ and finally *e.g.*

told /tould/ (before a consonant)

tell /te l/ (finally)

(iii) In R.P. /l/ is syllabic (*i.e.* it functions as the nucleus of the syllable) in certain words like.

little /'litl/

cattle /kaetl/ (The final /l/ is syllablic in these words)

Distribution:

/l/ occurs initially, medially and finally as in leave (initial), pulley (medial) and pull (final).

FRICTIONLESS CONTINUANT

A frictionless continuant is articulated with an open approximation of the articulators, so that the air passes between the articulators without any friction. Thus the sound is vowel like, but it is included in the list of consonants because it never functions as the nuclues of a syllable.

In English there is one frictionless continuant which is symbolized by /r/. The tip of the tongue is raised in the direction of the hinder part of the teeth ridge. The soft palate is raised so as to shut off the nasal passage of the air. The air from the lungs comes out through the gap between the tip of the tongue and the post-alveolar region without any friction. The vocal cords vibrate, producing voice. /r/ is thus a voice postalveolar frictionless continuant.

Spellings: /r/ is represented by the letter /r/ but in R.P. it occurs only before a vowel sounds *e.g.* in red, run, dry, trial. /r/ is not pronounced in other positions, *e.g.*, in words like garden, larder, early, jerk, etc.

Allophonic Variants: (i) A voiced post-alveolar fricative /r/ (phonetic symbol [i] is used after /d/ as in dry, draw.

(ii) A voiceless post-alveolar fricative /r/ (phonetic symbol [r] is used after aspirated /p/, /t/ and /k/ as in pray, try, and cry).

(iii) A voiced alveolar, single flap-phonetic symbol [ ] is used when /r/ occurs between two vowels and after /θ/ as in.

very ⎤
sorry ⎦ /r/ between two vowels

three (/r/ after /θ/

Distribution: In R.P. /r/ occurs initially and medially, but only before a vowel sound. It does not occur finally. For example.

red (initial)

moderate (medial)

[Linking /r/: In R.P. /r/ does not occur finally, but in connected speech, /r/ is retained when followed by a vowel in the following words. For example, the word far is pronounced /fa:/ but in far away the final r in far is pronounced because away in isolation begins with a vowel sound. The phrase far away is pronounced /fa:r/ A few other examples are:

pepper	/pep /
pepper and salt	/pepər n'sa:lt/
here	/hiə/

here and there /'hi r ən' ðə/

father /fa: ðə/

father is at home /fa: ðə r izə t'houm/

Intrusive /r/: Some people use an /r/ at word boundaries if the first word ends in [ ] and the second begins with a vowel even if thee is no r in spelling. Thus, we often hear

/'lɔ : rən ':c də [law and order]

/'dramər n 'mju:zik/ [drama and music]

SEMI-VOWELS

A semi-vowel is a vowel glide to a more prominent sound in the same syllable. In English there are two semi-vowels, /j/ and /w/.

/j/ is a **palatal semi-vowel.**

/w/ is a **labio-velar semi-vowel.**

/j/ is a glide from /i:/ and /w/ is glide from /u:/ Though these sounds are vowel-like in their articulation, they are classified as consonants because they do not function as the nucleus of any syllable.

/j/

1. The soft palate is raised, shutting off the nasal passage of air. The front of the tongue assumes a position for a vowel between close and half-close and quickly glides to the position of the following vowel. The vocal cords vibrate, producing voice /j/ is thus a **voiced unrounded palatal semi vowel.**

The lips are normally spread or neutral during the articulation of /j/ but there may be anticipatory lip rounding if the immediately following vowel is a wounded vowel as in you, yawn etc.

Spellings: /j/ is represented by the letter y as in yes, yard, beyond, yellow. The letters u, eau, ue, ew and jew are pronounced / ju/, as in unit, beauty, due dew, view.

/w/

2. The soft palate is raised to shut off the nasal passage of air completely. The back of the tongue is raised in the direction of the soft palate to the position for a vowel between close and half-close and the lips are rounded. Then the tongue quickly glides to the position of the following vowel. The position of the lips also changes depending upon the immediately following vowel. The vocal cords vibrate, producing voice. /w/ is thus a **voiced rounded labio-velar semi-vowel.**

Spellings: /w/ is represented by

(i) the letter w as in west.

(ii) the letters wh a in why.

(iii) the letter q or g + u as in queen, language

(iv) the words, one, once, suit also have the sound of /w/.

Distribution: /w/ occurs initially as in west (initial) and queen (middle). It does not occur finally.

Most Indians do not have /w/ as a distinct phoneme in their English. Instead, they generally use a voiced labio-dental frictionless continuant phonetic symbol [b] the sound represents the Devnagari symbol (व) . Most Indians use [V] even in place of the fricative /v/. There is no distinction in their speech between minimal pairs like

wine	vine
west	vest
wail	vale
why	vie
went	vent
wile/while	vile
whale	vale

/w/ can be acquired easily by trying to say /u:/ and then quickly moving on the vowel.

LIST OF PHONETIC SYMBOLS AND SIGNS

a Cardinal Vowel no. 4 (approximately as in French **Patte**); used for first element of Eng. dipththong (ai̯)

æ front vowel between open and half-open (Eng. vowel **cat**).

ɑ Cardinal Vowel no. 5 (approximately as in French **pas**); used for first element of Eng. diphthong [aʊ], and for Eng [ɑ:] in car

D open rounded Cardinal Vowels no. 5 (Eng. vowel in **dog**)

b voiced bilabial plosive (Eng. **b in labour**)

ɓ voiced ingressive bilabial plosive

β voiced bilabial fricative

c voiceless palatal plosive

Ç voiceless palatal fricative

ɔ Cardinal Vowel no. 6 (approximately as in German **Sonne**); used for Eng. [:] in **saw**, and first element of diphthong [i]

d voiced alveolar plosive (Eng. **d** in **lady**)

ď voiced ingressive alveolar plosive

ð voiced dental fricative (Eng. **th** in **other**)

e Cardinal Vowel no. 2 (approximately as in French the); used for Eng. [e] **in bed**, and first element of diphthong [ei]

ə unrounded central vowel (Eng. initial and final vowels in **another**)

r retroflexed central vowel (American **er** in water)

ε Cardinal Vowel no. 3 (approximately as in French pere); used for first element of diphthong [ε] ɜ unrounded central vowel (Eng. vowel in **bird**)

f voiceless labio-dental fricative (Eng. *f* in **four**)

ɟ voiced palatal plosive

g voiced velar plosive (Eng. **g** in **eager**)

ɠ voiced ingressive velar plosive

h voiceless glottal fricative (Eng. h in house)

ɦ voiced glottal fricative (sometimes Eng. **h** in **behind**)

i Cardinal Vowel no. 1 (approximately as in French (**si**); used for Eng [i;] in **see**

ɨ unrounded central close vowel

ɪ centralized unrounded half-close vowel (Eng. vowel in **sit**)

j palatal unrounded semi-vowel (Eng. **y** in **you**)

ɾ linguo-alveolar tap (sometimes **r** in Eng. **very**)

k voiceless velar plosive (Eng. **c** in **car**)

l voiced alveolar lateral continuant (Eng. **l** in **lay**)

ɫ voiced alveolar lateral continuant with velarization (Eng. ll in ill)

ɬ voiceless alveolar lateral fricative (Welsh ll)

m voiced billabial nasal (Eng. **m** in **me**)

ɱ voiced labio-dental nasal (Eng. **m** in **comfort**)

ɯ unrounded Cardinal Vowel no. 8

n voiced alveolar nasal (Eng. **n** in **no**)

ŋ voiced velar nasal (Eng. **ng** in **sing**)

ɲ voiced palatal nasal (French **gn** in **vigne**)

o Cardinal Vowel no. 7 (approximately as in French **eau**)

ø rounded Cardinal Vowel no. 2 (approximately as in French **peu**)

œ open rounded Cardinal Vowel no. 3 (approximately as in French **peur**)

θ voiceless dental fricative (Eng. **th** in **thing**)

p voiceless bilabial plosive (Eng. **p** in **pea**)

r linguo-alveolar roll (Scottish, Italian r); also used for Eng. **r** in **red** voiced post-alveolar frictionless continuant (Eng. r in red)

ɹ voiced retroflex frictionless continuant

ʀ voiced uvular roll

ʁ voiced uvular fricative or frictionless continuant

S voiceless alveolar fricative (Eng. **s** in **see**)

ʃ voiceless palato-alveolar fricative (Eng. **sh** in **she**)

t voiceless alveolar plosive (Eng. **t** in **tea**)

ʇ voiceless alveolar click

u Cardinal Vowel no. 8 (approximately as in French **doux**); used for Eng. [u:] in **do**

ʉ central rounded close vowel

ʊ centralized rounded half-close vowel (Eng. **u** in **put**)

v voiced labio-dental fricative (Eng. **v** in **ever**)

ʌ unrounded Cardinal Vowel no. 6; used for Engl. vowel in **cup**

ʋ labio-dental frictionless continuant

w labio-velar semi-vowel (Eng. **w** in **we**)

ʍ voiceless labio-velar fricative (sometimes Eng. **wh** in **why**)

x voiceless velar fricative (Scottish **ch** in **loch**)

y rounded Cardinal Vowel no. 1 (approximately as in French **du**)

ʎ voiced palatal lateral continuant (Italian **gl** in **egli**)

ɣ unrounded Cardinal Vowel no. 7

z voiced alveolar fricative (Eng. **z** in **lazy**)

ʒ voiced palato-alveolar fricative (Eng. **s** in **measure**)

Φ voiceless bilabial fricative

¿ voiceless alveolar lateral click

? glottal plosive (stop)

: indicates full length of preceding vowel

. indicates half length of preceding vowel

! main accentual stress or pitch prominence on following syllable secondary accentural stress on following syllable

: high unaccented pre-neuclear syllable

; high falling pitch

; low falling pitch

: high rising pitch

: low rising pitch

; falling-rising pitch

. rising-falling pitch

. syllable carrying secondary accent

. syllable, immediately following nucleus, carrying secondary accent based on quality/ quantity

. syllable carrying primary (nuclear) accent

. unaccounted syllable

. naslization, *e.g.* [õ]

. centralization. *e.g.* [ö]

. more open quality, *e.g.*. [o]

. closer quality. *e.g.* [c]

. devoiced lenis consonant, *e.g.* [z] (above in the case of [ŋ˚, 3˚, g˚])

. syllabic consonant, *e.g.* [n] (above in the case of [ŋ])

. dental articulation, *e.g.* [t̪]

[ ] phonetic transcription

/ / phonemic transcription.

INTONATION IN ENGLISH

To read or recite well involves a perfect understanding of the construction of sentences, and ability to anlyse complex froms of composition, and to discriminate between esesential and expletive words. It also involves a nice perception of the qualities of modulation, and of their relation to expressiveness, together with ability to regulate the voice so as exactly to suit the sound to the sense. The study of the art of reading is thus valuable as a means of improvement in composition, as well as for its influence in refining the taste, and exercising all the faculties of perception, expression, and adaptation.

In good reading or recitation, the thoughts of the writer must first be taken into the reader's mind, and then delivered as the writer himself might have uttered them immediately on their conception. In silent reading, or the perusal of language for our own information, we gather the sense as we proceed, and correct misapprehensions by reflection: in reading aloud for the information of others, we must perfectly comprehend the matter before we utter it, so as to avoid misleading the hearer. A practised reader can, no doubt, exercise sufficient revision at the time of reading, but keeping his eye in advance of his utterance, to read ordinary composition farily at first sight; but for public reading this would be insufficient. Whatever is to be read in public should first be well studied in private. The reader, thus knowing definitely what he has to express, will give forth no uncertain sounds, and his manner will have the freedom of delivery from memory without the disadvantage of its constraint upon the mind. His whole attention will be concentrated on the object of his reading—the effective conveyance of the matter and spirit of the composition. The presence of the book before him will be necesssary chiefly to give confidence, and prevent the possibility of rambling. The eye, assisted by memory, will take in clauses and even sentences at a glance, so that it may be freely raised during utterance. If the eye of a reader is fixed on the book, he seems to be perusing it for his own information; but if he looks his hearers in the face, as with due preparation he should be able to do, his delivery may have all the qualities of spontaneous oratory, and he to the hearers speaking rather than reading. This effetiveness is rarely exemplified, because the requirements for public reading are so little understood, and so habitually neglected in our system of education. The tameness, monotony, and rhythmical singing so generally associated with reading, have created a prejudice against the use of 'paper' in pulpit addresses, in consequence of which, in some churches, the practice of reading sermons is discountenanced, while in others it is positively interdicted. The quality of sermons, as compositions, is seriously impaired under such circumstances: but the cure for bad reading—against which the prejudice is directed—is good reading. All men cannot be orators, but all may be taught to read oratorically.

The chief points of difference between ordinary reading and the utterance of spontaneous composition are the uniform force and time, and continuative tones of the former, as contrasted with the reflective breaks and varying modulations and emphases of the later. The speaker feels what he wishes to say, and he conveys with definiteness the felt relation of each word to the idea which is dominant in his mind. Expletive and explanatory phrases are given parenthetically; ellipses, interpolations between grammetically related words, similies, quotations, and all other elements of rhetorical style, are indicated by chaines of modulation; and the point of every sentence is made unmistakably apparent. The reader sees all the parts of a sentence level to his eye, and he is apt to deliver them with a corresponding indiscriminatives of manner; either without variety of time, tone, and stress, or with mere alternation of force and feebleness, or the equal indefiniteness of emphasis on every phrase.

The first requisite for effective reading is a clear conception of the author's intention, together such a command of the voice as may enable the reader to express that one meaning to the exclusion of all other possible meanings. For every cluster of words is like a many-sided crystal, which may be made to throw from any of fecets, accordingly as one or another of them is presented uppermost. The most prominent word in the utternance of a sentence is not necessarily the most important grammatical word, but that which is new in reference to the context; and such words as are already before the mind whether stated, inferentially included in former expressions, or otherwise implied—are pronounced with subordinateness of manner.

The tendency of the best teachers nowadays is to place little reliance on the artificial rules laid down by writer on elocution (although these rules have some values as attempts more or less successful to furnish students with a notation of vocal inflections and tones), and to instruct rather by direct imitation of nature; and undoubtedly the best way to learn the art to go to a cultured master. Still some useful practical hints may be given here. And, first, as to the management of the breath. This is alomost as important to the speaker as to the singer, for on it depend ease and fluency of utterance, artistic grouping of words, and resonance of voice.

Probably the best description even given of good articulation—on which so much of the clearness and carrying quality of speech depends—is that of Austin; 'In just articulation the words are not hurried over, nor precipitated syllable over syllable; nor, as it were, melted together into a mass of confusion; they are neither abridged, nor prolonged, nor swallowed, nor forced, and, if I may so express myself, shot from the mouth; they are not trailed nor drawled, nor let to slip out carelessly, so as to drop unfinished. They are delivered from the lips as beautiful coins newly issued from the mint, deeply and accurately impressed, perfectly finished, neatly struck by the proper organs, distinct, shape, in due succession, and of due weight.'

Good pronunciation is very important to the speaker, for nothing so disturbs the attention of an audience as a solecism in pronunciation. Association with persons of education and refinement, particularly in youth, is of course the surest way to acquire a good pronunication, though the student may do a good deal for himself by listening attentively to public speakers of acknowledged culture, and also by consulting a good pronouncing dictionary. Provincialisms of speech, which are generally to be found in the vowel sounds, and of 'accept', such as the 'Scotch accept,' as the peculiar singsong utterance heard in Scotland is called (arising mainly from a monotonous use of certain inflections of the voice), must be got rid of. The tones of the speaking voice are all more or less inflected—that is, they do not remain for any appreciable time on any one pitch. In this respect they differ essentially from singing tones, which are level, and only varied in pitch. The term 'modulation, as understood by elocutionists, has reference to the general pitch of the vocal inflections in a passage. The inflections themselves are all either rising or falling. The rising turn of voice carries on the hearer's attention to what is to follow, and is used conseqently when a statement is incomplete; the falling turn directs attention to what has gone before, and is used consequently when a statement is complete. The former asks, or appeals to the hearer; the latter affirms, or enjoins from the speaker. The former is negative; the latter is positive. Simple inflections rise or fall directly from their accentual pitch—that is, from the accented syllable of their termination; and the range of the inflection may have any extent, from less than a semitone to more than an octave, according to the nature and force of the sentiment. The strongest rising tones are expressive of interrogation, incredulity, or entreaty;

and the strongest falling tones, or affirmation, assurance, or command. In ordinary unimpassioned narrative, or description, or plain argument, the range of the inflections will be correspondingly more limited. Compound inflections unite the two vocal movements—falling before a rising termination, and rising before a falling termination—with one accentual impulse; and the effect of this opposition of tone is to add to the expressiveness to the termination of a suggestion or inference (frequently of an ironical nature) in according with the expressiveness of the commencing turn. Thus: 'Not ŏne,' with compounded rising tone, implies 'but more'. 'Even one,' with compound falling tone, implies 'and not more'.

The emphatic force of tones depends on their accentual pitch in relation to that of preceding tones, as well as on the extent and the direction of the inflection. The amount of possible variety in these degrees is exceedingly great, but the peculiar expressiveness of individual modes of inflection is definite, traceable to systematic principles, and of limited extent, depending principally on three qualities:

1. Rising or falling inflection as well as termination; as,

   Cónstánt, Cónstánt

2. Rising or falling inflection with opposite termination; as;

   Cŏnstánt Cônstánt

3. Inflection higher or lower than preceding pitch; as ;

   díe? to to drêam.

   To Sléep. sléep?

These three sources of vocal variety the student of elocution should have under ready and perfect control. The acute accent (') is used to denote the rising inflection, and the grave accent (') the falling inflecton.

To acquire a natural style of reading, the chief point to be attended to is the logical clausing of sentences, so as to present, with separate completeness to the hearer's mind, every fact and every associated 'circumstance, whether principal or subordinate. Punctuation is not a sufficient guide for this purpose; it will sometimes even mislead. Thus, in the following sentence from Macaulay's Essay on Milton, no comma occurs, but the reader will nevertheless divide the period into a least three modulative clauses: 'The blaze of truth and liberty may at first dazzle and bewilder nations which have become half blind in the house of bondage'. Here the first section contains the subject of the sentence, the second the predicate, and the third the object, with its dependent clauses. It is to be observed that the object 'nations' is separated from its govenring verb 'bewilder,' only because the former is itself the governing antecedent to a new but subordinate sentence.

Nor is any particular mode of vocal inflection necessarily associated with any of the marks of punctuation. This is particularly to be noted in connection with the sign of interrogation. The position of this mark too, at the end of a period often misleads readers into an unnatural tone. The interrogative part of the sentence may not extend beyond a single clause, and this may be followed by many clauses within the same period. The mark of interrogation would therefore be better placed at the beginning of a sentence. But, as above shown interrogative may sometimes require for its just expression any one of all the tones in the gamut of speech. Thus: 'Will you?' If pronounced with a simple rising tone, this questions asks or appeals and with an extended range of inflection, it expresses doubt or surprise. But the form of words does not necessitate the rising tone. Thus: 'Will you?' If pronounced with a simple falling turn, the question expresses desire or expectation on the part of the speaker: and with an extended range of inflection, it conveys more or less of authoritative injunction.

Nothing marks out the finished reader so clearly as his power of modulating his voice. It is by subtle changes of tone that the infinite varity of feeling is represented, and a speaker or reader who wishes to fix and continue to hold the attention of his audience must acquire acquire the power of dramatising his speech by means of modulation. His effects must, of course, be 'natural'—there must be no undue straining after effect. On this subject the student cannot do better than read and re-read Hamlet's famous speech to the players, in which they will find the whole sum and substance of the art of dramatic speaking. In addition, the following paragraphs of practical instruction will be useful:

> **The Keys of the Voice.** The voice is usually considered as capable of assuming three keys—the low, the high, and the middle. This variety is undoubtedly too limited; but for the first lesson of a student it may perhaps be sufficiently useful. A well-trained voice is capable of ranging in these with various degrees of laudness, softnes, stress, continuity, and rapidity. Before pointing out passages where the adoption of these united qualities of voice is required, it is necessary to consider the means by which the voice, as an instrument is made capable of acquiring these qualities.
>
> **Strees, Sudden and Gradual.** If the muscles of the glottis are forcibly tightened, the sounds are given out with a force which has tempted some to call it explosive power. So important is this compression of the throat to the acquistion of distinctness and power in speaking, that it is impossible to arrive at eminence in speaking without its employment. This compression may be familiarly illustrated by stating that it is nothing more than that exertion of the muscles of the breast and throat which we experience when we endeavour to raise anything exceedingly heavy, or that closing up of the throat which takes place before coughing. If the pronunciation of a learner is relaxed or feeble, he might, in the pronunciation of such a word as power, compress his lips, then exter the muscular action of the throat, then relax the lips suddenly, and the consequence will be a forcible pulsation of the voice. In doing this, it should be kept in mind that the compression of the lip must be firm, in accordance with the compression of the throat. This sudden and forcible utterance may at

first be practised on vowels, or sounds beginnning with mutes. In the syllables beginning with semi-vowels, the explosive action follows the aspiration; thus, in same, the hissing sound of s is first heard, and the muscular compression necessary to give stress to a must be made immediately after. The vowel-sound *ah* preceded by a consonant should be practised most frequently. The practice of explosion has led several speakers into a disagreeable separation of the consonant and vowel sounds; thus blame is sounded blame, and sometimes with an approximation to the aspiration the a, like bl-ame. Whatever for is given to the consonant-sounds, or to the vowel-sound on which they alight, the one should flow into the other smoothly.

Swell and Vanish of the Voice. What are termed the swell and vanish of the voice are accompanied by a gradual compression and relaxation of the muscles, and are employed together in the pronunciaton of solemn and magnificent passages.

Speaking Voice—Acquired Voice. In common conversation our tone is light, and appears to come from the lip; in serious and impressive speaking it appears to be formed farther back, and is accompanied by a greater tension of the muscles of the throat. This peculiar voice, which is adapted to the expression of what is solemn, grand, and exciting, 'is ormed in those parts of the mouth posterior to the palate, bounded blew by the root of the tongue, above by the commencement of the palate, behind by the most posterior part of the throat, and on the sides by the angles of the jaw. The tongue, in the meantime, is hollowed and drawn back, and the mouth is opened in such a manner as to favour the enlargement of the cavity described as much as possible.

Low Key. To acquire strength and distinctivness in this key, the remarks made in the last paragraph will be found useful. It is a rare accomplishment, but one which is a most valuable principle in speaking. Strengthening the low notes, after forming them, should be a great object with the student of elocution; but it too often happens that the acquisition of a screaming high note is reckoned the desideratum in declamation. The difficulty of being ditinct and audible in the low key is at first disouraging; but practice will in most cases attain the object.

Middle Kye. This is the key of common discourse. It is capable of being rendered effective for public speaking, by the sudden force and swell which have been already mentioned. Sheridan points out a simple method of acquiring loudness in this key: 'Anyone who through habit, has fallen into a weak utterance, cannot hope suddenly to change it; he must do it by degrees and constant practice. It would therefore recommend it to him, that he should daily exercise himself in reading or repeating in the hearing of his friend; and that, too, to a large room. At first, his friend should stand at such a distance only as the speaker can easily reach in his usual manner of delivering himself. Afterward, let him gradually increase his distance, and the speaker will, in the same gradual proportion, increase the force of the voice.' In doing this, the speaker still keeps on the same pitch of voice, but gives it with greater power. If his friend were to go beyond the reach of the middle key, then the speaker would employ the high bawling note which one would use in calling to another on the opposite side of a broad river. It is material notice that a broad river. It is material notice that a wellformed middle key, and even a low key, is capable of filling any room; and that the neglect of strengthening the voice in these keys leads a speaker to adopt the high shouting note which is often heard in our pulpits. Exhaustion and hoarseness ensue; and the difficulty of utterance gives a vehemence to the address of the speaker, which is often out of harmony with the sentiments which he delivers.

High Key. This key of the voice, though very uncommon in ordinary speaking or reading, ought to be practised, as it ends to give strength to the voice generally, and as it is freqently employed in public speaking. Every one can speak in a high key, but few do it pleasingly. There is as compression necessary in the high notes, as well as the middle and the low: this compression distinguishes the vocifierous passion of the peasant from that of the actor or orator. We are often struck with the height of tone assumed by the chivalrous actor; but we hear every day high and louder tones from untutored people: the difference lies in the modulation. Strength and soundness in the high notes may be acquired by inflecting vowels, and continuing them on a monotone.

Time. We noticed the principal keys of the voice, and the method by which they may be successfully attained, and also the stress or power of the voice in these keys. Modulation also includes the consideration of the time which is natural in the pronunciation of certain passages. The combinations, then, of pitch, force, and time, are extremely numerous; as low, loud, slow; low, soft, slow; low, feeble, slow; low; loud, quick, &c.: middle, loud, slow; midle, soft, slow; middle, feedle, slow, &c. Thus we have a copious natural language, adapted to the expression of every emotion and passion.

Modulation of Emotion. The application of these qualities of voice in the expression of emotion would lead us into a field of inquiry too wide for a volume such as this. A few passages, however, may be given here as fit exercises for particular combinations of these qualities. Practice in reading dramatic dialogues, particularly those in which male and female voices are represented, in the best way to acquire flexibility in modulation. It should be borne in mind that a male voice can only reproduce female voice by suggestion, and vice versa.

The effect of a transition from the major to the minor key in music is not more striking than the variety which the voice will occasionally assume. A change of key is generally necessary at the commencement of a new sentence. When in the preceding sentence the voice has sunk down towards the close, in the new sentence it sometimes recovers its elasticity, and sometimes it continues in the depressed note on which the preceding sentence terminates. This latter is generally the case when the second sentence is illustrative or expository of the first.

No blessing of life is comparable to the enjoyment of a discreet and virtiuous friend. It eases and unloads the mind, clears and improves the understanding, engenders thoughts and knowledge, animates virtue and good resolutions, soothes and allays the passions, and finds employment for most of the vacant hours of life.

Here the second sentence, beginning, It eases, assumes the low note, which terminates the preceding sentence. In the remaining clauses the voice is varied, in order to rivet the attention on each particular.

Specially, in the same sentence, has a similar effect:

The flying Mede—his shaftless, broken bow.

The fiery Greek—his red pursuing spear.

Opposition, variety, modification of the sense, interruption of the thought, whether in one sentence or in separate sentences, produce a change of key.

To die—to sleep: to sleep! perchance to dream:

Ay, there 's the rub.

In these examples the shifts of the voice take place with the sentence; and it may perhaps be thought that they do not come wihtout the rule which was laid down for commencing a new sentence or paragraph. But they are founded on he same principle—the mood of the speaker's mind. In passionate the changes of key are more frequent than in argument, as the mind is more restless; in latter case, it is principally at the beginning of sentences or paragraphs that a change is necessary. In order to keep the minds of an audience awake to an arguement, it is well that the speaker should at times use the artifices of sincerity, wonder, & c., to indicate the feelings which must fill the breast of every one who speaks with intensity.

Passion—Its Modulation. The management of passion in according to the character that is represented to labour under it, must be intuitively present to the mind of the dramatic author. The person who acts as character has, in some respects, a minuter and more delicate task to perform, as he must watch over every tone, and gesture, and keep them in consistency with the situation of the person represented. There is a smile of beningnity, of love, of contempt; there is a smile of innocence and of guilt; of dignity and of silliness; there is the smile of the peasant and that of the king. To vary the expression of passion, so as to preserve it in keeping with the character—to exhibit inferior and incidental passions, as modified by a dominant one—are the attainments of a great actor, who, in his delineations, is not always assisted by the composition of the dramatist. For, although in representations of passion the dramatist exhibits the sentiment of passion in agreement with the character represented, yet the actor has the difficult task of preserving the consistency to the functions of voice, look, and gesture, in those portions where there is little excitement, and where the familiar parts of the dialogue are apt to make one forget the idiosyncrasy of the character. The influence of passion on utterance, and that analysis of the structure of eloquent composition, must be investigated, the we may be enabled to give that reading, as it is called, which a cultivated taste prefers.

Up with my tent ! my tent ! Here will I lie to-night—

But where tomorrow: ? Well, all's one for that.

Who hath described the number of the traitors?

Richard III.

The guilty mind is full of starts, and will catch prophecies from its own inadvertent words. There is a mark pause after 'night;' the mention of 'to-night' calls his mind to the future. 'But where tomorrow?' follows in a deep, slow, reflective voice. The familiar direction and remark of 'Up with my tent! Here will lie tonight,' are spoken, not in a careless, light voice, but in a suppressed tone; the mind is oppressed with suspicion, and the fear of impending viel and and most familiar expression are tinged with a shade of the ruling passion.

The utterance of familiar, incidental remarks, then, must be in keeping with the colouring of the ruling passion. There is nothing which lends more life and reality to a picture than these trivialities; but their introduction required a delicated appreciation of character, and of the varying moods of the mind. In the lines above, we observe that Richard's habitual state of mind would lead him to speak even common things in a tone of suppression. Accordingly, in certain tragedies, the tone of the principal character, from the beginning to the end, is what may be termed passion-formed, and extends over the business of every scene. In the lines we have quoted, the familiar direction is tinged with the state of mind; in those which are to follow, the familiar remarks are strongly coloured by an incontrollable ruling passion at the moment, and courtesy is carried off in the whirl wind of rage.

Desdémona. I will not stay to offend you.

Lodovico. Truly an obedient landy:

I do beseech your lordship, call her back.

Othello. Mistress.

Desd. My lord?

Oth. What would you with her?

Lod. Who, I my lord?

Oth. Ay, you did wish that I would make her turn:

Sir, he can turn, and turn, and yet go on,

And turn again; and she can weep, sir, weep;

And she 's obedient, as you say, obedient,

Very obedient: Proceed you in your tears.

Concerning this, sir—O well-painted passion!

I am commanded home: Get you away;

I'll send for you anon. Sir, I obey the mandate,

And will return to Venice;—Hence, avaunt!

Cassio shall have my place. And, sir, to-night,

I do entereat that we may sup together.

You are welcome, sir, to Cyrpus.

Othello—**Shakespeare.**

A violent passion does not long keep possession of the mind. It has a train of feelings flowing from it, and the utterance must be varied accordingly. There is a beautiful examplification of this in the reply of Coriolanus to Aufidius, on being taunted as a boy.

Aufidius. Name not the god,

Thou boy of tears.

Coriolonus, Measureless liar, thou hast made by heart

To great for what contains it.

Boy ! Cut me to pieces, Volscians: men and lads,

Stain all your edges on me. Boy!

If you have writ your annals true, 'tis there,

That like an eagle in a dovecot, I

Fluttered your Volscians in Cordioli:

Alone I did it, Boy ! But let us part,

Lest my rash hand should do a hasty deed

My cooler thought forbids.

Coriolanus—**Shakespeare**

In this piece the word 'boy' is repeated thrice; and an inexperienced speaker might rise in intensity on each succeeding reiteration. But a little reflection will show that each succeeding 'boy' should sink in intensity, the last being merely slightly contemptuous. In the first part of the quotation astonishment and rage completely occupy the mind, and the word boy is given full and prolonged, with rising inflection. But a man in vehement commotion soon becomes ashamed of his own situation: if he is proud, his mind whispers to him that he is giving his enemy an advantage, by acknowledgeing that he has to power of moving him so much. In such situations the mind will suddenly adopt ironical and sneering language, which may argue contempt and coolness. 'Tis there, that, like an eagle in a dovecot, I fluttered your Volscians in Corioli.' After this, the mind, as if it felt that it had got satisfiaction for the insult by the taunt thrown out, acquires more calmness, and the last 'boy' is light contemptuous. So quickly has the passion exhausted itself, that, in the end, prudence has obtaind a place: 'But let us part, lest my rash hand should do a hasty deed my cooler thought forbids.'

Imitative Modulation. In all languages there is a connection between certain words and their pronunciation, naturally significant of the ideas which they represent. In those words which signify objects with which sound and motion are associated, the connection is obvious. By a natural association this imitation is extended to the qualities of roughness, smootheness, height, extension, etc., and also to the metaphysical qualities of gentleness, melancholoy, etc. To heighten this imitation in common conversation, or in plain reading, would be ridiculous; but in descriptive reading the voice enters into the imitation, and seems to endevour to give every word a natural expression. It increases the effect of a reading or recitation to give an imitation—taking care always not to 'o' erstep the modesty of nature—of the tone of the person who is represented. Some of these tones are faulty qualities, and have been divided by elocutionists into the Guttural, the Oral, the Nasal, and the Falsetto. The Guttural quality is the deep rasping sound emitted from the larynx. It expresses loathing, rage, revenge, and horrors.

How like a fawning publican he loks!

I hate him for he is a Christian.

If I can cathc him once upon the hip.

I will feed fat the ancient grudge I bear him:

Cursed by my tribe if I forgive him

Merchant of Venice—**Shakespeare.**

The Oral quality (oris, of the mouth) is the tone resulting from slovenly articulation, particularly when caused by affection or indolence.

Extempore Force. There is one species of force, connected with pausing, which consists in conveying the impression to the hearer that what is said is the immediate prompting of the mind. The sudden thought dashing on the mind is indeed expressed by the point known as the 'dash, at which there is a momentary pause, and a suddenness in coming on the succeding word; but when the ideas flow continuously and in order, the same pause and sudden seizing on the word which expresses the idea which is labouring in the mind, are equally applicable. The pause indicates that the mind is employed in conceiving, and the sudden seizing of the word shows that the orator is afraid of its escaping him. This artifice—for it is only as an artifice that it can be regarded in Elocution—is rendered more imposing if there is a triumphant seizing of the word; for thus the speaker, who seems, as it were, gratified that he has hit on what he wanted, will appear more in the light of one really interested. Besides, this appearance of extemporaneous expression given the hearer an idea of the power of the speaker's mind, and disposes him to listen with the greater respect. This artifice gives reality to the language of passion in the actor, and lends an interest to the orator. It is not meant that an orator should consist of broken words; it is at times only, when the mind seems oppressed with a labouring thought, or entangled in difficulty, that this artifice can be resorted to with safety. At the same time, in all public speaking, in order to give it this extemporaneous effect, there should be a deliberate timing; without this, the hearer is apt to imagine that the rapidity arises from the fear of the speaker's losing the connection. This connection, too, in cases of servile reliance on the memory, is frequently dependent not merely on the intimacy of thought, but on verbal associations, as is often seen in the case of school-boys, who pronounce with extreme rapidity those tasks which they do not understand. This deliberative speaking does not interfere with the rapidity of extreme earnestness; when the mind is excited, the ideas will come rapidly, and the language will be ready; but there must be a visible excitement to account for the rapidity; as,

What ! my lord ! the aristocracy set themselves in a mass against the people!—they who sprang from the people—are inseparably connected with the people—are supported by the people—are the natural chiefs of the people?

On the Second Reading of the Reform Bill—**Brougham**.

Gesture regulates the looks, movements, and attitudes which are natural in certain passions and emotions. In strong excitement, there is a similarity of gesture among all nations; but the extent and variety of its employment in common conversation, and in formal addresses to the public, are greatly regulated by the temper, taste, and intellectual improvement of each individual nation. The gesture of the actor is more violent and profuse than that of the orator, who is supposed to be more under the influence of reason, and to address himself to the understanding of his audience. In civilised and polished countries a profusion of gesture is to be avoided in public discourse: it should be neither minute nor violent. The first is inconsistent with that absorption of thought which is necesssary in an intellecutal address; the second is an outrage on the taste and feelings of the audience, and is apt to raise indignation and aversion. Many modern speakers offend by the vehemence and impropriete of their gesticulation; indeed, the instruction which is given on gesture should often be occupied in reducing wihin the limis of grace extravagent positions and movements. The ancients were more chaste in their gesture than is commonly imagined. Although, in seasons of great excitement, they adopted at times a bold and striking gesture, they were generally more restrained in their movements than many modern speakers. Gesture regulates the position and movement of the body, the eye, the limbs, and, indeed, the whole deportment. In oratory, the regulation of the hand is of peculiar importance, not only as it serves to express passion, but to mark the dependence of clause, and to express the emphasis. In the suspension of a sentence, for instance, the hand may take an upward slide; while at the completion, the hand may sink in a line with the breast. In the stroke of emphasis, the hand rests in the same position, but comes down with a combined jerk of the elbow and wrist. The arm in its movements must not be much curved, but come freely from the shoulder.

❐